Communications in Computer and Information Science 523

More information about this series at http://www.springer.com/series/7899

Robin Doss · Selwyn Piramuthu
Wei Zhou (Eds.)

Future Network Systems and Security

First International Conference, FNSS 2015
Paris, France, June 11–13, 2015
Proceedings

 Springer

Editors
Robin Doss
Deakin University
Burwood, VIC
Australia

Wei Zhou
ESCP Europe
Paris
France

Selwyn Piramuthu
Department of Information Systems
   and Operations Management
University of Florida
Gainesville, FL
USA

ISSN 1865-0929   ISSN 1865-0937 (electronic)
Communications in Computer and Information Science
ISBN 978-3-319-19209-3   ISBN 978-3-319-19210-9 (eBook)
DOI 10.1007/978-3-319-19210-9

Library of Congress Control Number: 2015939428

Springer Cham Heidelberg New York Dordrecht London

Springer International Publishing AG Switzerland is part of Springer Science+Business Media
(www.springer.com)

Preface

Welcome to the proceedings of the Future Network Systems and Security Conference 2015 held in Paris, France!

The network of the future is envisioned as an effective, intelligent, adaptive, active, and high-performance Internet that can enable applications ranging from smart cities to tsunami monitoring. The network of the future will be a network of billions or trillions of entities (devices, machines, things, vehicles) communicating seamlessly with one another and is rapidly gaining global attention from academia, industry, and government. The main aim of the FNSS conference series is to provide a forum that brings together researchers from academia, practitioners from industry, standardization bodies, and government to meet and exchange ideas on recent research and future directions for the evolution of the future Internet. The technical discussions were focused on the technology, communications, systems and security aspects of relevance to the network of the future.

We received paper submissions by researchers from around the world including Australia, China, France, Germany, India, Japan, Sweden, UK, USA, UAE among others. After a rigourous review process 13 full papers were accepted covering a wide range of topics. The overall acceptance rate for the conference was 35% ensuring that the accepted papers were of a very high quality. We thank the Technical Program Committee for their hard work in ensuring such an outcome.

June 2015

Robin Doss
Selwyn Piramuthu
Wei Zhou

Organization

FNSS 2015 was held at ESCP Europe, Paris Campus during June 11–13, 2015

Conference Chairs

Robin Doss   Deakin University, Australia
Selwyn Piramuthu   University of Florida, USA
Wei Zhou   ESCP Europe, France

Technical Program Committee

Adil Al-Yasiri   University of Salford, UK
Elizabeth Basha   University of the Pacific, USA
Lejla Batina   Radboud University Nijmegen, The Netherlands
Aniruddha Bhattacharjya   Narasaraopeta Engineering College, India
David Boyle   Imperial College London, UK
Sammy Chan   City University of Hong Kong,
                              People's Republic of China
Roberto Di Pietro   Bell Labs, France
Ángel García-Fernández   Curtin University, Australia
Rama Garimella   IIIT Hyderabad, India
I-Hong Hou   Texas A&M University, USA
Shweta Jain   York College, City University of New York, USA
Jiong Jin   Swinburne University of Technology, Australia
Gul Khan   Ryerson University, Canada
Sachin Agarwal Kumar   Delhi Technological University, India
Lambros Lambrinos   Cyprus University of Technology, Cyprus
Yee Wei Law   University of South Australia, Australia
Albert Levi   Sabanci University, Turkey
Li Liu   National University of Singapore, Singapore
Cicero Martelli   Federal University of Technology, Brazil
Sjouke Mauw   University of Luxembourg, Luxembourg
Rakesh Nagaraj   Amrita School of Engineering, India
Yang Peng   Iowa State University, USA
Pedro Peris-Lopez   Carlos III University of Madrid, Spain
William Plymale   Virginia Tech, USA
Rajib Rana   CSIRO, Australia
Damith Ranasinghe   University of Adelaide, Australia
Rui Santos Cruz   Universidade de Lisboa, Portugal
Zhefu Shi   University of Missouri–Kansas City, USA

Houbing Song	West Virginia University, USA
David Sundaram	University of Auckland, New Zealand
Sameer Tilak	University of California at San Diego, USA
Neelanarayanan Venkataraman	VIT University, India
Hui Wu	University of New South Wales, Australia

Contents

Elimination of DoS UDP Reflection Amplification Bandwidth Attacks,
Protecting TCP Services.   1
   Todd G. Booth and Karl Andersson

Evaluation of Cryptographic Capabilities for the Android Platform 16
   David González, Oscar Esparza, Jose L. Muñoz,
   Juanjo Alins, and Jorge Mata

Specification-Based Intrusion Detection Using Sequence Alignment
and Data Clustering. 31
   Djibrilla Amadou Kountché and Sylvain Gombault

Novel Approach for Information Discovery in Autonomous Wireless
Sensor Networks. 47
   Menik Tissera, Robin Doss, Gang Li, and Lynn M. Batten

A Review of Security Protocols in mHealth Wireless Body
Area Networks (WBAN) 61
   James Kang and Sasan Adibi

An Efficient Detection Mechanism Against Packet Faking Attack
in Opportunistic Networks 84
   Majeed Alajeely, Asma'a Ahmad, Robin Doss, and Vicky Mak-Hau

An Integrated Access Control Service Enabler for Cloud Applications 101
   Tran Quang Thanh, Stefan Covaci, Benjamin Ertl, and Paolo Zampognano

Authentication Scheme for REST 113
   Luigi Lo Iacono and Hoai Viet Nguyen

Transmission Channel Switching Based on Channel Utilization
in ROD-SAN 129
   Takeo Hidaka, Daiki Nobayashi, Yutaka Fukuda, Kazuya Tsukamoto,
   and Takeshi Ikenaga

Malware Biodiversity Using Static Analysis 139
   Jeremy D. Seideman, Bilal Khan, and Antonio Cesar Vargas

IoT and Supply Chain Traceability 156
   Wei Zhou and Selwyn Piramuthu

Secure and Reliable Power Consumption Monitoring in Untrustworthy
Micro-grids   166
    Pacome L. Ambassa, Anne V.D.M. Kayem, Stephen D. Wolthusen,
    and Christoph Meinel

cl-CIDPS: A Cloud Computing Based Cooperative Intrusion Detection
and Prevention System Framework   181
    Zahraa Al-Mousa and Qassim Nasir

Author Index   195

Elimination of DoS UDP Reflection Amplification Bandwidth Attacks, Protecting TCP Services

Todd G. Booth[1] and Karl Andersson[2]([⊠])

[1] Luleå University of Technology, Information Systems, Skellefteå, Sweden
Todd.Booth@ltu.se
http://OrcID.org/0000-0003-0593-1253,
http://www.ResearcherID.com/rid/C-3576-2015
[2] Luleå University of Technology, Mobile and Pervasive Computing,
Skellefteå, Sweden
Karl.Andersson@ltu.se
http://OrcID.org/0000-0003-0244-3561,
http://www.ResearcherID.com/rid/E-3611-2010

Abstract. In this paper, we propose a solution to eliminate a popular type of Denial of Service (DoS) attack, which is a DoS amplification attack. Note that a DoS is a subset of DDoS. Our solution protects servers running any number of TCP services. This paper is focused on the most popular type of DoS amplification attack, which uses the UDP protocol. Via DoS UDP amplification attacks, an attacker can send a 1 Gbps traffic stream to reflectors. The reflectors will then send up 556 times that amount (amplified traffic) to the victim's server. So just ten PCs, each sending 10 Mbps, can send 55 Gbps indirectly, via reflectors, to a victim's server. Very few ISP customers have 55 Gpbs provisioned. Expensive and complex solutions exist. However our elimination techniques can be implemented very quickly, easily and at an extremely low cost.

Keywords: DoS · DDoS · Reflection · Amplification · Bandwidth · UDP · Cyber-attacks · Critical Infrastructure Protection · Design Science Research

1 Introduction

The terms and definitions used in this paper are found below in the Table 1. In computing, a DoS attack is an attempt to make a machine or network resource unavailable to its intended users. A DoS attack generally consists of efforts to temporarily or indefinitely interrupt or suspend services of a host connected to the Internet. As clarification, DDoS attacks are sent by two or more hosts and DoS attacks are sent by only one host. Our solution protects against both DoS amplification attacks and DDoS amplification attacks, so we'll use the term DoS.

To understand our paper, we will show how DDoS bandwidth attacks work. Previous to the attack, many computers become infected (zombies) with the

© Springer International Publishing Switzerland 2015
R. Doss et al. (Eds.): FNSS 2015, CCIS 523, pp. 1–15, 2015.
DOI: 10.1007/978-3-319-19210-9_1

Table 1. Term Definitions

Term	Definition
BotNet	Group of Zombie computers, controlled by Bad Guys
DoS	Denial of Service
DDoS	Distributed Denial of Service
DRDoS	Distributed Reflection Denial of Service
DSR	Design Science Research
IP	Internet Protocol (in this paper, IPv4)
NIC	Network Interface Card
Nmap	Utility for network discovery and security auditing
TCP	IP Transmission Control Protocol
SSH	Secure Shell
UDP	IP User Datagram Protocol
Zombie	Infected computers in a BotNet

bad guy's malware. This malware allows the attacker to control thousands or millions of innocent computers. Some of these DDoS attacks use reflection and others don't. In a DDoS attack without reflection, the attacker's controlling computer instructs their masters to order the zombies to send a massive amount of traffic directly to the victim's computer. The following DDoS bandwidth attack (without reflection) is shown in Fig. 1.

We will now present a DDoS bandwidth attack, which uses both reflection and amplification. Note that in Fig. 2, we have introduced several reflectors.

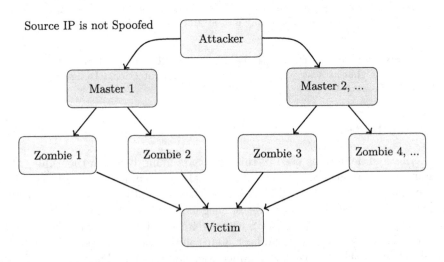

Fig. 1. DDoS bandwidth attack, without reflection

Source IP is Spoofed

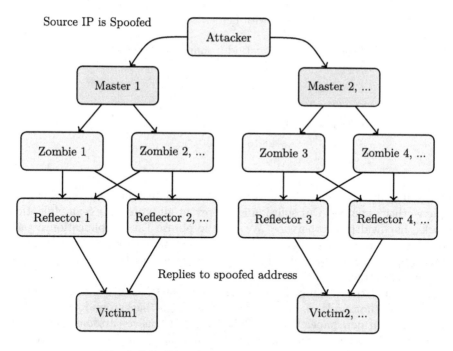

Fig. 2. DDoS bandwidth attack, with reflection

Again, without reflectors, traffic was send directly from the zombies to the victim. So if a particular zombie sent 1 Gbps of traffic, the victim would receive exactly 1 Gbps of traffic. However, in this DoS amplification attack, the zombie sends a massive amount of traffic indirectly, via the reflectors, to the victim's computer. How this works, now follows. The zombies spoof their source IP address. They change their source IP address, to be that of the victim. They send the spoofed datagrams to the reflectors. When the reflectors reply to the given source address, they are actually replying to the victim's IP address (not the zombie's source address).

The reason that the DoS amplification attack is sent, indirectly, via the reflectors, is so that the attack bandwidth can be amplified. Amplification works as follows: We will use network time protocol (NTP) as our example. It is possible for a client, to send a request to an NTP server, whereby a very large amount of information is returned to the client. The amount of information returned to the client can be 556 times larger (more) than the amount of request. For example, if the zombies send an aggregate total of 1 Gbps to the reflectors, the reflectors may send up to 556 Gbps of traffic, to the victim computer. There are several UDP protocols, other than NTP, which also have large amplification effects. The top 5 are as shown in Table 2 [13].

Since the zombies spoof their source IP address is it is much harder locate the zombies and remove the malware. These DoS amplification attacks are often successful bandwidth attacks. However, even if the amplification attack is not

Table 2. UDP Protocols with Large DoS Amplification Effects

Protocol	Bandwidth Amplification Factor
NTP	556
CharGen	358
QOTD	140
Quake Network	63
DNS	28 to 54

successful against the victim's bandwidth, the attack may be a successful DoS to deplete other resources. Our solution is to prevent all types of DoS amplification attacks, bandwidth or otherwise. We use the phrase DoS amplification attack but again, our paper is focused on UDP amplification attacks. An amplification attack implies a reflection attack, but a reflection attack does not imply an amplification attack.

As our case study example, we discuss the recent DDoS cyber-attacks, which were against thousands of French web servers. The background follows. The French satirical newspaper Charlie Hebdo issues offensive cartoons concerning the Roman Catholic Church, Judaism, Islam, secular targets, and politicians. On January 7th, 2015, Charlie Hebdo published a cartoon, which was concerning the Islam's Prophet Muhammad. Eleven people were then slaughtered, by two brothers, which was concerning this cartoon. This happened soon after Charlie Hebdo published the cartoon, and happened inside the newspaper's office in Paris. The brothers have links to the global militant Islamist organization, Al-Qaeda (hereinafter, "Islamist Organization"). The Islamist Organization has claimed responsibility for these murders.

After these murders, the French Defense Ministry and security bodies have reported that thousands of French websites have been targeted by an unprecedented wave of DDoS attacks. Any DDoS attack is a violation of the Internet Architecture Board's Internet proper use policy and a violation of most ISP's acceptable use policies.

Related to these murders, the Anonymous group then performed DDoS attacks against militant Islamists [1]. What is interesting and relevant is that in the beginning, there was a physical attack. Very quickly thereafter, instead of physical attacks, there were cyber-attacks, where the source was both the Islamic Organization and the Anonymous group. In the past the British Government has initiated cyber-attacks against Anonymous [3]. In this paper, as an example, we will show how DoS amplification attacks against both the Islamic Organization's web servers and the French web servers can be easily eliminated (defended against), in a very simple way and for a very low cost.

DoS amplification attacks require IP source address spoofing, which requires administrative privilege. There are millions of zombie hosts. However, not all zombie hosts have malware with administrative privileges. Even if a zombie can spoof the source IP address, many ISPs will filter spoofed traffic. Therefore, there are only tens or hundreds of thousands of zombie hosts which can be used for these DoS amplification attacks. However, not many zombies are needed, in order to perform a successful DoS amplification attack.

Even if you have 100 % protection against DoS protocol attacks and application layer attacks, if the DoS bandwidth attack is greater than your ISP connection bandwidth and if you only defend it from the customer side, the attack would be successful. The most efficient way to perform a DoS bandwidth attack, is via a DoS amplification attack. Our solution is to protect servers which are running any number of TCP services (such as Web, Email, Database servers).

In this paper the Design Science methodology is used. The artifact we have designed and studied is a set of methods, techniques, and network configuration guidelines used to eliminate DoS amplification attacks, in order to protect TCP services.

The initial context for our artifact is the following. Organizations who wish to protect their servers, which are connected to the Internet and running IPv4 TCP services. The organizations which can benefit and wish to benefit from our artifact will be referred to as the stakeholders. We can then say that the elimination of DoS amplification attacks is a specific goal, of the stakeholders.

We are using this design science methodology for problem solving, where the contextual problem is the DoS amplification attacks. Note that an amplification attack implies another contextual constraint, which is that the attack traffic originates from hosts which are spoofing their source IP address, in order to achieve reflection.

In the design cycle we develop and describe the artifact, which is based on firewall technology. Then in the empirical cycle, we analyze and explain how the artifact will operate in the context of our stakeholders. There is an interaction between the artifact and context, as shown in Fig. 3.

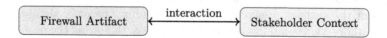

Fig. 3. Firewall artifact interacting with the stakeholder context

Our problem solving activities are fallible. Therefore we perform a validation to determine if the artifact in context has met the stakeholders' goals.

Our design science used in this paper is case-based research as opposed to sample-based research. We therefore study one case scenario, at a time, and draw conclusions after each scenario is analyzed.

The DSR process used in this paper is shown in Fig. 4.

The rest of this paper is organized as follows. Section 2 presents the related academic work. Section 3 details our scientific research. Section 4 shows our experiment. Section 5 contains our conclusion and recommended future work.

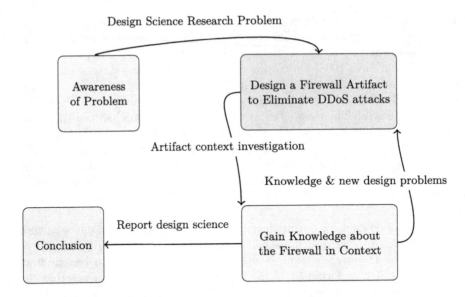

Design Science Research Problem

Awareness
of Problem

Design a Firewall Artifact
to Eliminate DDoS attacks

Artifact context investigation

Knowledge & new design problems

Conclusion

Report design science

Gain Knowledge about
the Firewall in Context

Fig. 4. Firewall artifact interacting with the stakeholder context

2   Related Academic Work

We have been unable to find any related academic work, which has proposed our
specific solution, to very easily, efficiently and for a very low cost, to eliminate
DoS UDP amplification attacks against any server running TCP services (web
server, email server, etc.). Our innovative solution is extremely low cost and
simple to implement.

Here are the more relevant academic papers which we have reviewed. We
first present the authors' viewpoints. Then, regarding the more significant and
relevant authors' viewpoints, we present our analysis, (following the phrase "**Our
comments:**").

Bhuyan et al. [2] empirically evaluate several major information metrics,
namely, Hartley entropy, Shannon entropy, Renyi's entropy, generalized entropy,
Kullback-Leibler divergence and generalized information distance measure in
their ability to detect both low-rate and high-rate DDoS attacks. They claim
that there are four places to implement the defense: source-end, victim-end,
intermediate inline network and distributed. **Our comments:** Our novel solution has found a new defense location, a cloud provider.

Geva et al. [4] provides a review of the bandwidth DDoS attacks, stating
that in the future they may be significantly more effective and harmful. They
discuss that cloud based overlay networks can be used to absorb and scrub traffic.
However, they then mention that overlay networks may require new protocols
and updated host software.

Kavisankar et al. [5] proposes a scheme, Efficient Spoofed Flooding Defense (ESFD) which provides two level checks which, consists of probing and

non-repudiation, before allocating a service to the servers. **Our comments:** Their solution will eliminate DoS amplification attacks. However that will also cause significant latency to all valid UDP traffic. The whole purpose of UDP is to maintain very low latency. Further, their solution provides a new attack vector. Spoofed traffic could be sent to these anti-DoS servers, which could then be used as reflector, to attack an innocent victim.

Lin et al. [6] propose a Double Check Priority Queue structure that, based on traffic of received packets and the interval of arrival time, they can determine if a given user's traffic is normal or malicious.

Lu et al. [7] make the first effort on studying the filtering location to maximize the protected network bandwidth while not permitting any attack flow to reach the victim. They formulate this problem to an integer linear programming problem and design an efficient heuristic filtering location algorithm.

Nam et al. [8] propose a new scheme, concerning DDoS bandwidth attacks, to estimate the available bandwidth ratio of a remote link or remote path segments, a group of consecutive links, without deploying tools at the remote nodes. The scheme would be helpful in accurately pinpointing anomalous links.

Panja et al. [9] state that one of the largest security obstacles is how to defend against a Denial-of-Service (DoS) or Distributed Denial-of-Service (DDoS) attacks from taking down a cloud server. They have stated that no cloud servers have been able to completely prevent DoS attacks. They state that the search continues for an effective solution to keep data available to legitimate users who need it when the cloud network that stores that data is the target of a DoS attack. Their proposed method (DOSBAD) explains how to effectively detect the band-width limit of a cloud network and the bandwidth currently in use to know when a DoS is beginning. **Our comments:** This is the problem that we have partially solved (solved for UDP), for customers who are running TCP services and who are being attacked, via a DoS UDP amplification attack.

Peng et al. [10] provide a comprehensive survey, concerning many DDoS attacks, including DoS amplification attacks. They state that it is not easy to detect spoofed traffic. **Our comments:** Our novel approach takes into consideration that spoofed traffic which uses amplification most often uses the UDP protocol, so we just have the cloud filter all UDP traffic before reaching servers, which are only running TCP services.

Preetha et al. [11] develops an autonomous agent based DDoS defense in real time without human intervention. A mathematical model based on Lanchester law has been designed to examine the strength of DDoS attack and defense group. Once attack strength is formulated efficient defense mechanism is deployed at the victim to block malicious flows. They claim that their defense mechanism paves way to apply to Critical Information Infrastructure Protection.

Shanmugam et al. [12] present an analysis and study on attacks and its impact on distributed networks is focused moreover, particularly on DDoS attack.

Varalakshmi et al. [14] propose a five-fold DDoS Defense Mechanism using an Information Divergence scheme that detects the attacker and discards the adversary's packets for a fixed amount of time in an organized manner. The trust value is adjusted based on the attack intensity to ensure a trustworthy system. The mitigation is carried out by limiting the bandwidth of the attacking IP source address, instead of completely blocking all of the attackers traffic.

Wei et al. [15] propose a Rank Correlation based Detection (RCD) algorithm. The preliminary simulations indicate that RCD can differentiate reflection flows from legitimate ones efficiently and effectively, thus can be used as a useable indicator for DRDoS. **Our comments:** While our solution, from the customer side, simple drops all DoS amplification attack (which is UDP), in order to protect servers running just TCP services.

3   Design Science Research Process

3.1   Scenario 1

A French web server is located on the ISP customer's own premises. Under normal conditions, (when there is not a DoS UDP amplification attack), their Internet download throughput requirement is well below 1 Gbps. They have purchased 1 Gbps bandwidth, from their ISP.

Problem: During a DoS amplification attack, assume that the attackers are sending, for example, 2 Gbps towards the customer's on premises web server.

Since they only have purchased 1 Gbps throughput, the DoS bandwidth attack has saturated the ISP link. At least 50 % of the malicious DoS traffic will be dropped. However, perhaps 50 % of the customer's valid traffic will also be dropped. We need to defend against this problem scenario. We will now explore some possible suggestions and then evaluate those suggestions.

Suggestion 1. One suggestion is to simply increase the provisioned bandwidth to some value, which will protect the customer from a great percentage of DoS amplification attacks. Let's assume that 95 % of the DoS amplification attacks, against web servers, generate 2 Gpbs or lower traffic.

Evaluation: There are two ways, as to how the customer can order ISP bandwidth to defeat an attack. They can either order the bandwidth before the DoS amplification attack or they can order the bandwidth after the attack.

Let's assume that the customer increases their ISP provisioned bandwidth to 2 Gpbs, before any attack. One issue is that it may be very expensive for customers in many locations to order more than 1 Gbps bandwidth. Let's assume that this is not a problem.

Another issue is that they are paying for 2 Gbps bandwidth, when they only need 1 Gbps. The extra 1 Gps is simply to protect them from most DoS amplification attacks. Even if they are only attacked for one hour, during each year, they are paying for the extra bandwidth every day of the year. So the utilization of the extra bandwidth is very low.

Another issue is that even if 95 % of the DoS amplification attacks generate less than 2 Gbps, we may have the following situation. Assume that the attacker has specifically targeted this customer and the attacker is monitoring the attack. If the 2 Gbps attack does not saturate the link, the attacker may just increase the attack bandwidth, in increments of 1 Gpbs, until the attack is successful. The customer would then need to order more bandwidth from the ISP, to overcome the attack. However, this may take the ISP several days. Assume the attack was increased to a maximum of 8 Gbps.

The customer could order 10 Gbps, to cover the attack and their normal traffic. Even if the customer ordered 10 Gpbs, and this protected from the attacks, the customer would be paying for this bandwidth every day of the year, even if there was only a one hour attack per year. The customer would also need to have anti-DoS equipment and expertise, on site. So the cost per actual attack would be very high.

Knowledge Contribution: We recommend searching for a model, where the cost per actual attack is much less. To do this, we wish to find a model, in which any defense, has a much higher utilization.

Suggestion 2. Another suggestion is for the customer to order the bandwidth dynamically after the DDoS attack. Let's assume that have a 10 Gbps link but that they have only purchased 2 Gbps of download throughput. When there is an attack, they can dynamically increase their bandwidth to try and mitigate the attack. In this model, the customer is only paying for the extra bandwidth, during an actual attack. So this model is a better solution.

Evaluation: However, if the 2 Gbps attack does not saturate the link, the attacker may just increase the attack bandwidth, in increments of 1 Gpbs, until the attack is successful. The attacker may simply increase the attack bandwidth over the 10 Gpb link speed. Even if the customer had two 10 Gbps links, the attacker may just decide to send 30 Gpbs. Also, most ISPs do not support speeds greater than 10 Gpbs. So this better model fails, when the attacker sends more traffic than the ISP to customer links support.

Knowledge Contribution: Even with dynamically provisioned ISP bandwidth, it is simply not possible to defend against aggressive DoS bandwidth attacks, by only using a customer premises solution.

Suggestion 3. In order to overcome the previous issues, a suggestion is to have the customer order an anti-DoS amplification service, from their own ISP.

Evaluation: Most ISP's do not offer an anti-DoS service, for their customers.

An alternative is for the customer to install their own anti-DoS attack equipment, in the ISP's location. However most ISP's do not allow customers to install their own anti-DoS equipment, at their ISP's premises. Even if they did, we are back to the problem where the customer might be paying for their own ISP located equipment for the whole year, even if there was only a one hour attack per year.

Knowledge Contribution: It is not a general and efficient solution, for most customers to try and defeat the DoS amplification attack, at the ISP's location.

3.2   Scenario 2

Assume the customer puts their web server into a cloud provider's network, in order to overcome the above on premises bandwidth issue. We will use the Microsoft Azure cloud as our example. So the customer would run their web server as a virtual machine guest (vm guest) in the Azure cloud. The DoS UDP amplification attack would now be against the vm guest web server. Assume the customer is also running some UDP services on the same web server. Let's assume that the customer starts the web server with a virtual Ethernet 10 Gbps NIC.

Problem: The new problem is that the DoS amplification attack may saturate the cloud based web server's bandwidth. The attack would just need to send more than 10 Gpbs.

Suggestion 1. To overcome the cloud bandwidth issue, the customer could add more virtual Ethernet 10 Gpbs NICs. The Azure cloud allows you to have a maximum of eight 10 Gbps NICs, which could provide a maximum of 80 Gbps.

Evaluation: For this evaluation, it is assumed that the same server is running both TCP and UDP services. Let's assume that the web server receives all traffic which is sent, to the server's IP address. DoS bandwidth attacks can be larger than 80 Gbps, so this does not provide a general solution. Even if attacks were only 70 Gbps, the virtual machine guest would not be able to keep up with this bandwidth, due to a CPU processing power limitation. As a practical note, the Azure cloud does not charge customers for incoming traffic.

Knowledge Contribution: We have found a partial solution which has overcome bandwidth limitation issues, as long as the malicious traffic is less than or equal to 80 Gpbs. The cost of this solution is extremely low, as compared to having the customer provision 80 Gpbs from their ISP. However, we have run into a new bottleneck, which is the processor speed on the vm guest. So even with this cloud based solution, it is not possible to, with a single server alone, to defend against DoS amplification attacks, which are against servers running both TCP and UDP services.

Suggestion 2. Previously we considered the case of just one Azure cloud based virtual web server. We will start with that case and make the following change. The Azure cloud has a load balancing feature. This feature allows customers to scale up, by automatically starting up hundreds or thousands of virtual servers, as needed. Let's now consider that the customer wishes to take advantage of this specific feature, in order to mitigate the DoS amplification attacks.

Evaluation: We no longer need eight 10 Gbps NICs in the web server. Traffic coming into a given public IP address, can be distributed among multiple virtual servers. Each of these servers can have a single 10 Gbps NIC, which will keep the CPU processor load much lower than our eight NIC solution. As these servers become busy (due to a DoS amplification attack), more virtual servers can be very quickly and automatically started, as shown in Fig. 5. Assuming that the Azure load distribution does not become overloaded, we could easily and automatically start up enough virtual web servers, to handle several hundred Gpbs of incoming DoS amplification traffic. The customer's engineer can design the specific CPU load % which will cause more virtual web servers to automatically start sharing the load. So only during an attack, the customer would need to pay for the dynamic servers which are started up.

Knowledge Contribution: We have now found a solution, which is much more efficient, than any previous solution. Further, we have eliminated any possible bandwidth limitation. Only during an actual attack does a customer pay for the extra dynamically started vm guests. So we have met our model goal, where the customer is only paying extra, during an actual attack. Let's assume that if a vm guest receives more than 5 Gbps of traffic, another vm guest is automatically started.

Let's assume that there is an attack of 50 Gbps. Again, assume we just have about 1 Gpbs of customer traffic. Then with just 11 vm guests (each handling 5 Gpbs), we can defeat the 50 Gbps attack and have 5 Gbps available for normal customer traffic. Even if the attack is 500 Gbps, we can easily defeat this, with just 101 vm guests and still have good performance.

So this contribution is a solution, which can be implemented easily, at a very low cost. We will now search for another solution, but which is more optimal.

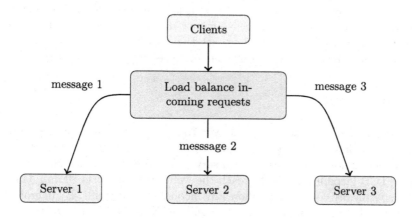

Fig. 5. Cloud based load balancing

3.3   Scenario 3

The customer is paying higher costs, during the DoS bandwidth attack. We would like to lower the costs (from our previous knowledge contribution) which the customers pay, when their virutal web servers are being attacked, in a DoS bandwidth attack.

Suggestion. Our suggestion is to try and use the Azure controlled firewall.

Evaluation: The most popular DoS amplification attacks are using the protocol UDP. Again, we assumed that the customer is running some UDP services. Our very simple to understand and implement firewall strategy is the following. The customer can move any UDP services, from the virtual web server, to some other virtual server. Then the customer could leave the Azure firewall in the default configuration, which will filter out all UDP traffic.

Now, when the incoming DoS amplification attack traffic comes in, it will be filtered by the Azure firewall. This UDP traffic will not be processed by the customer's virtual web server. So the customer no longer needs to spin up 101 vm guests to defeat a 500 Gbps DoS UDP amplification attack. During the 500 Gbps attack, the customer would only need a single virtual web server.

Knowledge Contribution: Via our novel design, we have found a solution whereby the cloud provider will completely eliminate any and all DoS UDP amplification attacks and whereby Azure cloud does not charge the customer any addition money for this service (over the very low per year cost of 110 Euro/year for the virtual server) [6].

Our solution is a solution for running any number of TCP services (web server, email server, etc.). Now let's compare our 110 Euro/year solution to a competing solution. To purchase a full anti-DDoS service (including DDoS bandwidth, protocol attacks and web application attacks) from a major provider, such as CloudFlare, can cost 52,800 Euro/year [3].

One might think that the massive DoS amplification attack will always need to be processed by Azure. However the attackers should soon realize that they will not be successful in DoS attacks against the web servers hosted in Azure. Then, via game theory, we would expect the attackers to stop attacking any Azure located web servers, which use our proposed Azure firewall solution.

4   Experiment

We created a virtual web server, in the Amazon cloud. Here were our steps. Image used: Ubuntu Server 14.10 (from Azure), Size: Standard A2 (2 cores, 3.5 GB). Via SSH we installed the Apache web server. We configured the Azure firewall to allow TCP incoming traffic to reach the web server on ports 80 and 443. We did not specifically configure to allow any incoming UDP traffic. By default, the Azure firewall is not configured to allow any incoming initiated UDP traffic.

We ran tcpdump on the server, to monitor all traffic which was received by the server. Then we used Nmap to generate UDP traffic, which was sent to the server, using a very large number of UDP ports. We verified, via tcpdump, that absolutely none of the UDP traffic reached the server.

An interesting question then becomes, what if the server needs to send out, a UDP request? We then tested this scenario. We verified that UDP outgoing requests from the server were send out and answered. So we know that the Azure firewall is UDP stateful. So at the same time as there is an incoming DoS amplification attack, the web server can send outgoing UDP requests, which will be answered.

Based on the above, our initial (but not yet verified) conclusion is that, since no UDP traffic reached the server, that even if there was a DoS UDP amplification attack, none of that traffic would reach the server. There is perhaps a limit, as to the exact volume of traffic that the Azure cloud will filter.

So the obvious experiment that should be performed next, is to launch a an actual DoS amplification attack, against the virtual web server, which is hosted in the Azure cloud. The attack should start with 1 Gbps and, for example, increase by 1 Gbps, until the attack reaches a high value, for example 500 Gbps. Due to the Azure license agreement, we were not allowed to run this test.

So we would like to run the tests in our labs, using the same anti-DoS equipment that Microsoft uses in their cloud. We have tried but were unable to find out exactly what type of anti-DoS equipment Microsoft uses. Perhaps Microsoft wishes to keep it a well kept secret, in order to make it harder for the bad guys, to find a vulnerability.

So we are unable to perform the required verification experiment, on our own. We therefore plan the following. We will contact companies who are frequently the victims, of DoS amplification attacks. We will then help them implement our solution and measure the success. Also, perhaps some researcher will gather data, which will help us understand the exact Gbps limit, which the Azure cloud will filter, for no additional cost.

5 Conclusion

There are many successful DoS UDP amplification attacks and the attack bandwidth is steadily increasing. We reviewed the currently suggested mitigations. In summary, it is very expensive for all customers to build their own customer based anti-DoS amplification solution. Even if they build their own solution, they may only need their anti-DoS amplification solution for a few hours per year. So the customer cost per attack is very high.

So we searched for some other theoretical model, in order to lower the costs to defend against these attacks. We then came up with a novel solution, in which we could completely prevent these attacks, at an extremely low cost and which is extremely easy to set up. Via our Azure cloud based anti-DoS amplification solution, it is the Azure cloud that will defend against these DoS attacks every day. The utilization of the cloud based anti-DoS amplification is much higher, which greatly lowers the cost per DoS attack, however Microsoft will take these costs. The cost per attack must be extremely low, since the Azure cloud does not charge any additional money for our anti-DoS amplification attack solution.

Our paper has shown one anti-DDoS service, which costs 52,800 Euro/year. Our paper has suggested a way, to completely eliminate DoS attacks, for servers which are only running TCP services. We proposed using the Azure cloud firewall and filtering out all UDP traffic. It would be the Azure cloud firewall which is responsible to processing the entire DoS amplification attack bandwidth. The Azure cloud offers this firewall service to completely eliminate these anti-DoS attacks, for absolutely no extra charge.

Our solution should be considered by any and all Critical Infrastructure Protection (CIP) servers, which need to run public TCP services. Our recommended future work, which we have started, is to provide a solution similar to the one presented in this paper, but which will also mitigate DoS TCP amplification attacks.

References

1. Anonymous Takes Down ISIS Websites, Confirms Leaked Government Documents Were Real/Softmates Inc. http://www.softmates.org/2015/01/22/anonymous-takes-down-isis-websites-confirms-leaked-government-documents-were-real/. Accessed on 29 January 2015
2. Bhuyan, M.H., Bhattacharyya, D.K., Kalita, J.K.: An empirical evaluation of information metrics for low-rate and high-rate DDoS attack detection. Pattern Recogn. Lett. **51**, 1–7 (2014)
3. British Spies Hit Anonymous With DDoS Attacks, vol. 2015. http://www.darkreading.com/attacks-and-breaches/british-spieshit-anonymous-with-ddos-attacks/d/d-id/1113719
4. Geva, M., Herzberg, A., Gev, Y.: Bandwidth distributed denial of service: attacks and defenses. IEEE Secur. Priv. **12**(1), 54–61 (2014). doi:10.1109/MSP.2013.55
5. Kavisankar, L., et al.: A pioneer scheme in the detection and defense of DrDoS attack involving spoofed flooding packets. KSII Trans. Internet Inform. Syst. **8**(5), 1726–1743 (2014)
6. Lin, C.-H., et al.: Preserving quality of service for normal users against DDoS attacks by using Double Check Priority Queues. J. Ambient Intell. Humaniz. Comput. **4**(2), 275–282 (2013)
7. Lu, N., et al.: Filtering location optimization for the reactive packet filtering. Secur. Commun. Netw. **7**(7), 1150–1164 (2014)
8. Nam, S.Y., et al.: Estimation of the available bandwidth ratio of a remote link or path segments. Comput. Netw. **57**(1), 61–77 (2013)
9. Panja, B., et al.: Monitoring and managing cloud computing security using denial of service bandwidth allowance. Recent Pat. Comput. Sci. **6**(1), 73–81 (2013)
10. Peng, T., Leckie, C., Ramamohanarao, K.: Survey of network-based defense mechanisms countering the DoS and DDoS problems. ACM Comput. Surv. **39**(1), 3-es (2007). doi:10.1145/1216370.1216373. ISSN: 03600300. Accessed on 21 March 2015
11. Preetha, G., Devi, B.S.K., Shalinie, S.M.: Autonomous agent for DDoS attack detection and defense in an experimental testbed. Int. J. Fuzzy Syst. **16**(4), 520–528 (2014)
12. Shanmugam, M., Saleem Basha, M.S.: DDos attack traceback and chaosin a distributed network a survey. Int. J. Appl. Eng. Res. **8**(10), 1159–1169 (2013)

13. UDP-based Amplification Attacks — US-CERT. USA Homeland Security, US-CERT, UDP Attackss. https://www.us-cert.gov/ncas/alerts/TA14-017A. Accessed on 25 March 2015
14. Varalakshmi, P., Selvi, S.T.: Thwarting DDoS attacks in grid using information divergence. Future Gener. Comput. Syst. **29**(1), 429–441 (2013)
15. Wei, W., et al.: A rank correlation based detection against distributed reflection DoS attacks. IEEE Commun. Lett. **17**(1), 173–175 (2013). Cited By: 8

Evaluation of Cryptographic Capabilities for the Android Platform

David González, Oscar Esparza[✉], Jose L. Muñoz, Juanjo Alins,
and Jorge Mata

Network Engineering Department, Universitat Politècnica de Catalunya,
Jordi Girona 1-3, Campus Nord UPC, 08034 Barcelona, Spain
oscar.esparza@entel.upc.edu

Abstract. Future networks will be formed by millions of devices, many of them mobile, sharing information and running applications. Android is currently the most widely used operating system in smartphones, and it is becoming more and more popular in other devices. Providing security to these mobile devices and applications is a must for the proper deployment of future networks. For this reason, this paper studies the cryptographic structure and built-in tools in Android, and shows that the operating system has been specially designed for plugging-in external cryptographic modules. We conclude that the best option for providing cryptographic capabilities is using these external modules. We show the existent options and compare some features, like licensing, source code availability and price. We define some requirements, evaluate each module, and provide guidelines for developers who want to use properly security primitives.

1 Introduction

The use of mobile devices has increased intensely over the last years, and it is becoming ubiquitous. A recent report, developed by the American research company eMarketer, states that mobile users are picking up smartphones instead of traditional mobile devices as they become more affordable [7]. So, trends carry us to a future where mobile applications will be involved in a lot of aspects of our daily life.

People use their mobile devices for more than the built-in functionalities, which has introduced a radical change in the concept of mobile device. Today, mobile devices are based on the idea that operating systems must support users installing embedded applications on their devices. This transformation has created a tempting marketplace for programmers and software companies. Thus, both smartphone manufacturers and developers of mobile operating systems have created centralized application market places. Well-known examples are Google Play, which hosts 950,000 applications and produces a daily revenue of about 12$ million for the top 200 applications [13], and App Store, which hosts 1 million applications and produces a daily revenue of 18$ million for the top 200 applications [13].

© Springer International Publishing Switzerland 2015
R. Doss et al. (Eds.): FNSS 2015, CCIS 523, pp. 16–30, 2015.
DOI: 10.1007/978-3-319-19210-9_2

From both development and research points of view, Android is the perfect target platform. On one hand, as market analysis show, Android is the most widespread mobile operating system [12]. Android is used by a wide range of devices of several manufacturers, e.g. Samsung, Sony and Huawei. It has a large number of applications available, and many software companies use one or more of its official marketplaces as a primary source for distribution. Android is free and open source. All development tools are available at no cost and run over all main operating systems [26]. Anyone can inspect the Android source code, and modify and recompile it to extend functionalities. The security of Android devices is becoming a hot research topic as mobile applications are managing more and more sensitive data every day.

The study carried out by William Enck et al. [8] clearly shows the need to improve security of Android applications. The authors analyzed 1,100 popular free Android applications and discovered several security flaws. The authors found that many developers fail to take the necessary security precautions and sensitive information was occasionally broadcast without being previously protected by means of encryption. This is even more important, since available information about how to develop secure applications for Android is quite reduced, especially regarding how cryptography works in Android and which are the available tools.

This paper is focused on analyzing the cryptographic features of Android, explaining the available tools to perform common cryptographic operations, and evaluating their performance using a testing methodology. Our assumption is that, given a set of security features, developers are going to map them to a set of strong cryptographic primitives. In our opinion, this study produces relevant results and could be of interest for both researchers and developers. This paper states that it is possible to provide security at a high level in Android applications today, but further efforts should be done to improve compatibility in previous, present and future operating system versions, as Android will probably be the leading operating system in future networks devices.

This paper is organized as follows: Sect. 1 introduces the problem of security in Android devices and applications; Sect. 2 summarizes some previous papers that studied performance of cryptographic tools on mobile devices, Java and Android; Sect. 3 briefly describes how cryptography works in Android; Sect. 4 introduces our testing application and methodology; Sect. 5 includes some of the most relevant performance results obtained with the testing application; and finally, in Sect. 6 we can find the conclusions of the paper.

2   State of the Art

Some authors decided to analyze the level of security that mobile operating systems offer, as well as their weak points. For example, a pair of comprehensive Android security assessments has been published by William Enck et al. [9] and Asaf Shabtai et al. [29]. Joseph Packy Laverty et al. took a slightly different approach and developed a detailed comparative analysis of security models among Android, iOS, Black Berry and Windows Mobile [14].

A very similar work is the proposal of Michael A. Walker [33], which proposes a standard method to evaluate the cryptographic capabilities and efficiency of Android devices. The author developed an Android testing application and determined a list of built-in available algorithms using a HTC G1 device with Android 1.6. As stated by the author, this initial project was meant as a starting point for future research. The study is very elaborate and presents, as of today, the unique available results about performance of cryptographic operations over Android. However, the scope of the study is limited.

Jeremy S. Nightingale studied six Java cryptographic providers and developed a comparative analysis for public key cryptography [15]. Nevertheless, this study is for the Java Platform Standard Edition (J2SE) [5], not for Android. Other similar studies [3, 4] are rich in information and contain a detailed outline of the tools and methodologies used, but they target a different hardware.

3   Cryptography in Android

Android applications are written in a Java-based programming language, also called Android, which is not fully compatible with Java SE standards or applications. While Java core libraries are used, Android provides additional APIs to integrate with the operating system, the platform resources and the security model. It is also possible to use native code in C/C++ by means of the Java Native Interface (JNI) framework, or even writing a whole application in C/C++ [26], but this is discouraged because it makes the code non-portable.

Several versions of the operating system have been released (e.g. Froyo (2.2), Gingerbread (2.3), Ice Cream Sandwich (4.0), etc.), and version upgrade process has been difficult since its origins. Difficulties are mainly due to the lack of direct control of the operating system developers over the firmware, as well as the large range of device manufacturers. Although such fact is improving lately, statistics show how older versions are still running on older devices in greater or lesser extent, i.e. Gingerbread (17.8 %), Ice Cream Sandwich (14.3 %), Froyo (1.1 %), Honeycomb (0.1 %) [24].

Like in traditional Java, the overall design of the cryptography classes in Android is governed by the Java Cryptography Architecture (JCA), which was inherited from Apache Harmony. However, there are some significant differences, mainly originated by the limitations of mobile devices. The main difference is the non inclusion of an independent version of the SunJCE provider in Android. This means that Android does not include, by default, the same algorithms than Java. However, no list of discrepancies between the Android built-in cryptography and the traditional SunJCE is available at this moment.

Android source code is publicly available in a repository [1]. As usual, the source code follows a tree structure and is divided in branches. We are going to center in branches shown in Table 1. The core branch is libcore, which shows that Apache Harmony ships its own cryptographic provider, Crypto [19]. Additionally, Apache Harmony includes a Java Secure Socket Extension provider called HarmonyJSSE [21], which is based on the specifications of TLS v1 and

Table 1. Built-in provider/library by branch

Provider/Library	Branch
Crypto	platform/libcore [19]
HarmonyJSSE	platform/external/conscrypt [21]
Bouncy Castle	platform/external/bouncycastle [2]
OpenSSL	platform/external/openssl [23]
AndroidOpenSSL	platform/external/conscrypt [22]

SSL v3 protocols. However, the number of algorithms provided by Crypto is very limited, so Android engineers needed an alternative provider to cover all the security requirements that applications may need. Instead of programming their own provider from scratch, Android developers modified an existent Java provider, Bouncy Castle [16], and set it as the default provider. The original source code of Bouncy Castle is different from the modified version included in Android. In particular, some algorithms have been removed and some classes have been changed to improve both speed and memory consumption. The problem is that these changes vary depending on the Android version. In addition, some algorithms within Bouncy Castle have been combined with a well-known cryptographic library written in C, OpenSSL [32].

Our source code inspection revealed that the reduced set of capabilities provided by the providers Crypto, DRLCertFactory and HarmonyJSSE remains constant, while security services provided by Bouncy Castle vary from version to version. However, the support of SSL and TLS protocols is guaranteed since API level 1 [20]. Therefore, all versions of the platform provide built-in tools for establishing a secure communication between an Android device and a server machine. For implementing both SSL and TLS, Android uses code from both Bouncy Castle and OpenSSL. A list of all built-in providers, with the minimum version from which are included, is detailed in Table 2.

Even though Android ships with a set of built-in tools which cover most usual cryptographic algorithms and standards, we cannot be sure that such built-in libraries are updated with the last patches for all versions of the operating system. Moreover, there are discrepancies between versions, and older versions,

Table 2. Built-in cryptographic service providers

Provider	From version
Crypto	1.5 or previous
HarmonyJSSE	1.5 or previous
DRLCertFactory	1.5 or previous
Bouncy Castle	1.5 or previous
AndroidOpenSSL	3.0

which still have an important market share, lack some popular algorithms, e.g. Gingerbread (2.3) lacks SHA224 and ECDSA. For this reason we recommend developers to use in their applications the last version of a third-party cryptographic service provider, as this will allow them to control critical updates.

4   Testing Application

We recommend developers to include external cryptographic service providers in their applications. For this reason, we have developed a simple application to test these providers and rank their performance.

Cryptographic providers targeting the Android platform (or stating being compatible with it) do not seem to abound. We only found these two options:

- IAIK-JCE, which can be downloaded from [10].
- SpongyCastle: as previously mentioned, Android ships with a cut-down version of Bouncy Castle. But installing the classic Bouncy Castle library is impossible due to classloader conflicts, as the names for most packages and classes are the same. SpongyCastle [31] is a repackage of the classic Bouncy Castle library provided by Roberto Tyley, an independent developer. In our tests, we are going to use a repackage of the classic Bouncy Castle library, which was performed by following the guidelines of Roberto Tyley. In fact, we do not recommend developers to use SpongyCastle directly in applications, but as a guide for repackaging the classic Bouncy Castle. The main reason is that this project maintenance relies on this only developer.

We are also interested in traditional cryptographic providers for Java that may be compatible with Android. Four non-commercial cryptographic Java libraries were found:

- Logi Crypto [28], which was discarded because it was not designed to be compatible with the JCA/JCE structure, and hence cannot be easily integrated into Android.
- GNU Crypto [11], which was not well documented, and its interaction with the JCA/JCE structure was messy. After integrating the provider and making some quick encryption/decryption tests, we realized that GNU Crypto was slow and difficult to integrate into Android, so it was discarded too.
- Cryptix [27], which was inspected and tested and no compatibility problems were found.
- FlexiProvider [17], which was also tested with no problems.

The summary of the available providers compatible with Android is detailed in Table 3.

4.1   Cryptographic Requirements

Choosing an appropriate cryptographic algorithm is essential in any system with security requirements. A large number of cryptographic algorithms exist, but the

Table 3. External cryptographic service providers

Provider	Last version
Bouncy Castle	1.50
Cryptix	1.3
FlexiProvider	1.7.7
IAIK-JCE	5.2

devices used for communications sometimes have limited processing capacity and reduced storage capacity. So, it is important to have available algorithms that work correctly in devices with scarce resources, while maintaining a high level of security. Moreover, algorithms should be widely tested through time, and security holes should be solved with the help of the cryptographic community.

Thus, we prepared a list of requirements that cryptographic providers must accomplish in order to provide enough tools for implementing common security features. For completeness of the study, our proposal not only addresses common cryptographic algorithms, but other related features. The coverage of these features takes into account additional capabilities that are usually required in application security, e.g. opening and creating digital envelopes, securely distributing key pairs, establishing secure communications, etc. The complete list of requirements is specified in Table 4.

The proposal of algorithms and standards to evaluate is mostly based on the recommendations of the NIST [30]. We focused on the Federal Information Processing Standards (FIPS), a compilation of standards and guidelines issued by NIST for government use. Nevertheless, we have taken into account recommendations of other institutions (as detailed in Table 4), e.g. ITU, IETF, RSA Security Labs. Although Triple-DES and SSL are no longer recommended by NIST, we consider them for compatibility reasons since they still are widely used. Table 5 complements Table 4 by specifying recommended parameters.

4.2   Coverage of Requirements

By inspecting the official documentation of the selected providers, the classes in charge of registering the different algorithms, and the source code, we prepared Tables 6 and 7. These tables detail the coverage of algorithms and standards according to requirements introduced in Subsect. 4.1. Support of SSL and TLS is guaranteed since API level 1 [20], and covered by the operating system. Table 8 details the supported protocol versions for the built-in Android JSSE Provider.

4.3   Testing Framework

We developed a testing application to carry out performance tests in an easy and efficient way. We also established a testing methodology to set up a fitting benchmarking environment. The testing application has been designed so that

Table 4. Requirements for development of secure applications

Requirement	Type	Standard
SHA-1	Hash Function	FIPS 180
SHA-256	Hash Function	FIPS 180
HMAC	Message Authentication Code	FIPS 198
PBKDF2	Key Derivation Function	PKCS#5 v2.0
AES	Symmetric Cipher	FIPS 197
3DES	Symmetric Cipher	ANSI X9.52
RSA	Asymmetric Cipher	PKCS#1 v1.5, PKCS#1 v2.1
RSA	Signature Algorithm	PKCS#1 v1.5, PKCS#1 v2.1
DSA	Signature Algorithm	FIPS 186
X509	Digital Certificate	RFC 5280
PKCS #7	Digital Envelope	PKCS#7
PKCS #12	Information Exchange Syntax	PKCS#12
SSL	Secure Transport Protocol	RFC 6101
TLS	Secure Transport Protocol	RFC 2246
		RFC 4346
		RFC 5246

Table 5. Required algorithms with parameters

Algorithm	Key length (bits)	Operation mode	Padding
SHA-1	N/A	N/A	N/A
SHA-256	N/A	N/A	N/A
HMAC	Variable	N/A	N/A
PBKDF2	Variable	N/A	N/A
AES	128, 192, 256	CBC, OFB, CFB, CTR	PKCS#5 or PKCS#7
3DES	192	CBC, OFB, CFB, CTR	PKCS#5 or PKCS#7
RSA	2048	ECB	PKCS#1, OAEP
RSA	2048	N/A	PKCS#1, PSS
DSA	224(key)	N/A	PKCS#1
	2048(group)		

a user can select a subset of the algorithms, depending on the variants of the algorithms to be tested, as well as the parameters to use, e.g. length of the input, key size, number of samples, etc. Once the user finishes the set up, the application runs the tests, and it stores all the performance data on the memory of the device for later processing.

Table 6. Coverage of algorithms

Requirement	BC	Cryptix	Flexi	IAIK
SHA1	X	X	X	X
SHA256	X	X	X	X
HMAC/SHA1	X		X	X
HMAC/SHA256	X		X	X
PBKDF2/HMAC/SHA1	X		X[1]	X
PBKDF2/HMAC/SHA256	X			X
AES/CBC/PKCS5	X		X	X
AES/CFB/PKCS5	X		X	X
AES/OFB/PKCS5	X		X	X
AES/CTR/PKCS5	X		X	X
3DES/CBC/PKCS5	X	X	X	X
3DES/CFB/PKCS5	X	X	X	X
3DES/OFB/PKCS5	X	X	X	X
3DES/CTR/PKCS5	X		X	X
RSA/ECB/PKCS1	X	X	X	X
RSA/ECB/OAEP	X	X	X	X
RSA/SHA1/PKCS1	X	X	X	X
RSA/SHA256/PKCS1	X	X	X	X
RSA/SHA1/PSS	X	X	X	X
RSA/SHA256/PSS	X	X		X
DSA/SHA1/PKCS1	X	X	X	X
DSA/SHA256/PKCS1	X		X	X

Table 7. Coverage of cryptographic standards

Requirement	BC	Cryptix	Flexi	IAIK
X509	X		X	X
PKCS7	X			X
PKCS12	X		X	X

Table 8. Built-in secure communication protocols

Requirement	HarmonyJSSE
SSL	v2, v3
TLS	v1

We use the built-in function nanoTime to determine the amount of time consumed by a given cryptographic operation. According to the official documentation, nanoTime returns the value of the most precise system timer available with nanosecond precision. The clock accessed is guaranteed to be monotonic and suitable for interval timing when the interval does not span device sleep.

The key generation process required by public key cryptography is more complex than the one required for secret key cryptography, since it involves more costly mathematical operations which tend to be long in time. Nevertheless, background execution and memory management are very important in Android, because they are tightly related with power consumption and memory efficiency [25]. For this reason, we decided to generate the secret keys in the mobile devices, while the tests using public key algorithms took pre-generated keys. These pre-generated keys were stored using personal identity information standards and included beforehand on the testing application.

Another problem we found in Android was the presence of outlier measures. Since the operating system has been devised as an application ecosystem, all applications are kept alive as long as possible, and the scheduler considers them all when dispensing execution time. As a consequence, we found that, even shutting down all unnecessary applications, tests contained outlier measures, and these deteriorated both mean and standard deviation values. This effect was also noticed in the study lead by Michael A. Walker [33].

We analyzed the samples and noticed that the generation of outliers was not periodic. Then, we redesigned the testing methodology, so that the test application could be able to mitigate the effect of the outlier measures by itself. For each atomic cryptographic operation to benchmark, the application performs a previous round of measures and computes an initial estimation of the measure. Then, uses such estimation to fix a threshold value, i.e. by multiplying the estimation value by a threshold factor defined by the user. This outlier threshold will be used later to check if the measures are out of the range of expected values. Then, the application proceeds and gathers a second round of samples. Now the application knows the range of expected values, so it is capable of disscarding the outlier measures using the threshold. Once included the new methodology in our Android testing application, we found that with a small number of discarded measures (less than a 5 %) the standard deviation is considerably reduced, around 10 and 50 times smaller depending on the parameters of the test.

5 Measures

5.1 Tuning

In Android, the CPU frequency may change depending on the power consumption, affecting the device performance [6] and the reliability of the results. We carried out some test trials using CPU Spy, confirming that the frequency kept stable, without fluctuations, while executing the tests. For reducing the effects of possible sources of interference, we forced quit all, non-critical, running applications and services in the device. In addition, we disconnected both Wi-Fi and Bluetooth services in order to avoid external interferences that could have affected the behavior of the device during the tests.

Table 9. Testing Hardware

Device	Hardware	Operating System
Nexus S	ARM Cortex-A8 single-core 1GHz 512 MB RAM	Android 2.3 upgraded to Android 4.1.2

Tests were carried out in a Samsung Nexus S, upgraded to Android 4.1.2. Detailed characteristics of the testing hardware are summarized in Table 9. All tests were conducted by gathering 10.000 samples by operation. This number of samples does not include the additional 1.000 samples used for estimating the value beforehand and discarding outlier measures. These numbers were chosen after a short period of trial and error, in which we confirmed how fixing these parameters the standard deviation of the measures decreased considerably.

5.2 Performance Evaluation

From the collected data we generated more than 20 graphics for different operations and algorithms, varying parameters, key sizes and lengths of inputted data. Tables 10, 11 and 12 and Figs. 1, 2, 3 and 4 show a representative sample for the most common algorithms, i.e. SHA-2, AES, RSA and DSA. Even from these samples, one can discern several interesting trends.

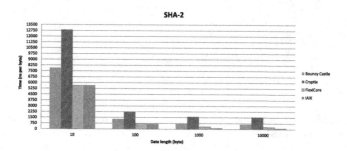

Fig. 1. Mean micro-second time per byte when hashing using SHA-2 for varying data lengths (10,000 samples, less 1 % of outliers)

For secret key cryptography, FlexiCore and IAIK-JCE are faster than Bouncy Castle and Cryptix. FlexiCore performed better for SHA-1 while IAIK-JCE performed better for SHA-2. For example, according to Table 10, FlexiCore is

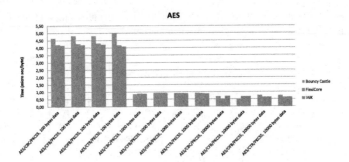

Fig. 2. Mean micro-second time per byte when encrypting using AES with a 128-bit key for varying data lengths and operation modes (10,000 samples, less 2 % of outliers)

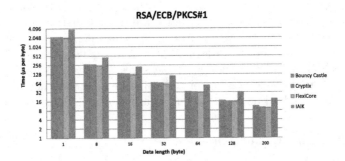

Fig. 3. Mean micro-second time per byte for encrypting using RSA with PKCS#1 padding (10.000 samples, less 1 % of outliers)

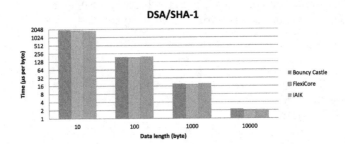

Fig. 4. Mean micro-second time per byte for signing using DSA/SHA-1 (10.000 samples, less 0.1 % of outliers)

Table 10. Average time for hashing a 100-bytes input data with SHA-1 & SHA-2 (ns/byte)

Algorithm	BC	Cryptix	Flexi	IAIK
SHA-1	724	715	572	603
SHA-2	1309	2270	731	671

Table 11. Average time for encrypting a 100-bytes input data with AES & 3DES (µs/byte)

Algorithm	BC	Cryptix	Flexi	IAIK
AES/CBC/PKCS#5, 128-bits key	4.65	N/A	4.19	4.14
3DES/CBC/PKCS#5, 192-bits key	8.73	5.66	6.42	7.33

Table 12. Average time for encrypting a 128-bytes input data with RSA & for signing a 100-bytes input data with DSA (µs/byte)

Algorithm	BC	Cryptix	Flexi	IAIK
RSA/PKCS#1, 2048-bits key	16.88	15.87	15.08	32.96
DSA/SHA-1, 224-bits key	190.73	N/A	179.96	196.02

35 ns/byte faster than IAIK-JCE when hashing 100 bytes using SHA-1, and both FlexiCore and IAIK-JCE are more than 100 ns/byte faster when compared with Bouncy Castle and Cryptix. By the contrary, when hashing 100 bytes using SHA-2 the differences increase: IAIK-JCE is 60 ns/byte faster than FlexiCore, and both FlexiCore and IAIK-JCE are about 600 ns/byte faster than Bouncy Castle. Figure 1 shows how such differences remain similar for smaller and longer lengths of the input data. Although it is not included in this data sample, our study showed that Bouncy Castle is the fastest option when generating HMACs.

When encrypting, IAIK-JCE performed better for AES and Cryptix for 3DES. Table 11 shows how, when encrypting a 100-bytes datablock using CBC mode and PKCS#5 padding, IAIK-JCE performed 0.05 µs/byte better for AES than FlexiCore, the second best, and Cryptix performed 0.76 µs/byte better for 3DES, being FlexiCore the second best too. Just remark the small differences of speed between IAIK-JCE and FlexiCore, as shown in Figs. 1 and 2. From Figs. 1 and 2 one can deduce that Cryptix is the slowest provider. Meanwhile, Bouncy Castle keeps decent differences with IAIK-JCE and FlexiCore.

For public key cryptography, FlexiCore is the fastest provider for encrypting and signing with RSA, and for signing with DSA. However, differences were small. For example, according to Table 12, when encrypting a datablock of 128 bytes with RSA and a 2048-bits key, there was a difference of 0.79 µs/byte with Cryptix and of 1.8 µs/byte with Bouncy Castle. Another example, are the differences of 10.77 µs/byte, between FlexiCore and Bouncy Castle, and of 16.06 µs/byte, between FlexiCore and IAIK-JCE, when signing a datablock of 100 bytes with DSA and a 224-bits key.

An important trend we observed in Fig. 3, is that IAIK-JCE is the slowest provider when encrypting and verifying signatures with RSA. Nevertheless, without being able to inspect the source code, we cannot come up with a logic explanation for this issue. IAIK-JCE performed as well as FlexiCore and Bouncy Castle when signing and verifying with DSA as indicates Fig. 4.

These small differences regarding performance when using public key algorithms (see Figs. 3 and 4) were expected. In public key algorithms, the modular product, exponentiation and inversion operations are more expensive in terms of time than other operations, e.g. hashing. Therefore, the speed of these modular operations is what ultimately defines the speed of the implementations. Speeds were so close because all four cryptographic providers use the Android native implementation of the class BigInteger [18]. One can corroborate this by inspecting the source code of Bouncy Castle, Cryptix and FlexiCore.

If we consider both performance results and coverage of requirements, as well as source code availability and license, FlexiCore and Bouncy Castle are, individually, very good choices. Both providers have permissive licenses, give access to the source code and offer a good coverage of usual cryptographic requirements: Bouncy Castle covers them all, while FlexiCore covers a large number. FlexiCore provides a very fast implementation, and Bouncy Castle is slower, but remains close in performance. Nevertheless, it is not clear how the inclusion of the ASN.1 CoDec package affects in the use of FlexiCore, since it is GPL licensed.

IAIK-JCE is also recommended in case developers already purchased a commercial license. IAIK-JCE covers all requirements, it shows a good performance and it is specially intended for Android, unlike the previous providers. Moreover, IAIK-JCE provides the fastest implementations for the common algorithms SHA-2 and AES. Despite differences are small, in general FlexiCore and IAIK showed better performance.

6   Conclusions

Providing security to Android devices and applications is, for sure, one of the main objectives to achieve prior to the proper deployment of future networks. Android has inherited the cryptographic design of Java. Cryptographic services are provided by a series of modules, some of them are built-in, e.g. Bouncy Castle, Crypto, HarmonyJSSE, etc. Nevertheless, we cannot guarantee that these built-in modules are updated with the last patches. Moreover, old versions of Android, some still with an important market share, are limited in functionality and lack some common algorithms. For this reason, our recommendation is using a third-party provider to provide security to applications.

All the evaluated providers have both positive and negative aspects. Bouncy Castle covers all usual cryptographic requirements, provides access to the source code and is free. So, Bouncy Castle would be a good option if we are interested on covering a wide range of algorithms and standards at no cost. FlexiCore provides access to the source code and it is free too, but covers a slightly smaller range of requirements. However, FlexiCore has proved its superiority in speed, being the fastest provider for a lot of common algorithms, e.g. SHA-1, RSA, DSA. So, FlexiCore is the best option if we are interested on speed at no cost. IAIK-JCE covers all usual cryptographic requirements and has proved to be very fast. Nevertheless, it requires purchasing a commercial license when it is used in commercial products. So, IAIK-JCE is the best option for those developers who are interested on both speed and coverage of algorithms, and are willing to pay. We do not recommend using Cryptix, since covers a very limited range of requirements, and it is deprecated, meaning that its maintenance has been discontinued long time ago.

Acknowledgments. This work was supported partially by the Spanish Research Council with Project SERVET TEC2011-26452, and by Generalitat de Catalunya with Grant 2014-SGR-1504 and 2014-SGR-375 to consolidated research groups.

References

1. Android Git repositories. https://android.googlesource.com/
2. Bouncy Castle repository. Android Git repositories. https://android.googlesource.com/platform/external/bouncycastle/
3. Abusharekh, A.: Comparative Analysis of Multi-Precision Arithmetic Libraries for Public Key Cryptography. Ph.D. thesis, George Mason University, Washington, DC (2004)
4. Bingmann, T.: Speedtest and comparsion of open-source cryptography libraries and compiler flags. https://panthema.net/2008/0714-cryptography-speedtest-comparison/
5. Campione, M., Walrath, K., Huml, A.: The Java Tutorial: A Short Course on the Basics, 3rd edn. Addison-Wesley Longman Publishing Co., Inc., Boston (2000)
6. Carroll, A., Heiser, G.: An analysis of power consumption in a smartphone. In: Proceedings of the 2010 USENIX Conference on USENIX Annual Technical Conference, USENIXATC 2010, pp. 21–21. USENIX Association, Berkeley (2010)
7. eMarketer Inc.: 2 billion consumers worldwide to get smartphones by 2016 (2014). http://www.emarketer.com/Article/2-Billion-Consumers-Worldwide-Smartphones-by-2016/1011694
8. Enck, W., Octeau, D., McDaniel, P., Chaudhuri, S.: A study of android application security. In: Proceedings of the 20th USENIX Conference on Security, SEC 2011, pp. 21–21. USENIX Association, Berkeley (2011)
9. Enck, W., Ongtang, M., McDaniel, P.: Understanding android security. IEEE Secur. Priv. **7**(1), 50–57 (2009)
10. Institute for Applied Information Processing and Communication. Gratz University of Technology. Core Crypto Toolkits. https://jce.iaik.tugraz.at/sic/Products/Core-Crypto-Toolkits
11. Free Software Foundation. The GNU Crypto project. http://www.gnu.org/software/gnu-crypto/
12. Goasduff, L., Rivera, J.: Gartner says smartphone sales surpassed one billion units in 2014 (2015). http://www.gartner.com/newsroom/id/2623415
13. Jones, C.: Google Play catching up to Apple's App Store (2013). http://www.forbes.com/sites/chuckjones/2013/12/19/google-play-catching-up-to-apples-app-store/
14. Laverty, J.P., Wood, D.F., Kohun, F.G., Turchek, J.: Comparative analysis of mobile application development and security models. Issues Inf. Syst. **12**(1), 301–312 (2011)
15. Nightingale, J.S.: Comparative analysis of Java cryptographic libraries for public key cryptography (2006). http://teal.gmu.edu/courses/ECE746/project/reports_2006/JAVA_MULTIPRECISION_report.pdf

16. The Legion of Bouncy Castle. Boncy Castle. http://www.bouncycastle.org/java. html
17. Research Group of Prof. Dr. Johannes Buchmann. FlexiProvider. http://www. flexiprovider.de/
18. Android Open Source Project. BigInteger class, Android API. http://developer. android.com/reference/java/math/BigInteger.html
19. Android Open Source Project. Crypto Provider, Android platform 'libcore' repository. Android Git repositories. https://android.googlesource.com/platform/ libcore/+/master/luni/src/main/java/org/apache/harmony/security/provider/ crypto/CryptoProvider.java
20. Android Open Source Project. javax.net.ssl package, Android API. http:// developer.android.com/reference/javax/net/ssl/package-summary.html
21. Android Open Source Project. JSSE Provider, Android platform 'conscrypt' repository. Android Git repositories. https://android.googlesource.com/platform/ external/conscrypt/+/master/src/main/java/org/conscrypt/JSSEProvider.java
22. Android Open Source Project. OpenSSL Provider, Android platform 'conscrypt' repository. Android Git repositories. https://android.googlesource.com/platform/ external/conscrypt/+/master/src/main/java/org/conscrypt/OpenSSLProvider. java
23. Android Open Source Project. OpenSSL repository. Android Git repositories. https://android.googlesource.com/platform/external/openssl/+/master
24. Android Open Source Project. Platform versions. http://developer.android.com/ about/dashboards/index.html?utm_source=ausdroid.net#Platform
25. Android Open Source Project. Processes and threads. http://developer.android. com/guide/components/processes-and-threads.html
26. Android Open Source Project. Android Developers (2014). http://developer. android.com/index.html
27. The Cryptix Project. Cryptix. http://www.cryptix.org/
28. Ragnarsson, L.: The logi.crypto Java package. http://www.logi.org/logi.crypto/ devel/
29. Shabtai, A., Fledel, Y., Kanonov, U., Elovici, Y., Dolev, S., Glezer, C.: Google android: a comprehensive security assessment. IEEE Secur. Priv. 8(2), 35–44 (2010)
30. National Institute Standards and Technology. Cryptographic Toolkit. http://csrc. nist.gov/groups/ST/toolkit/index.html
31. Roberto Tyley. SpongyCastle. http://rtyley.github.io/spongycastle/
32. Viega, J., Chandra, P., Messier, M.: Network Security with Openssl, 1st edn. O'Reilly & Associates Inc., Sebastopol (2002)
33. Walker, M.A.: Standard method of evaluating cryptographic capabilities and efficiency for devices with the Android platform (2010). https://www.truststc.org/ education/reu/10/Papers/WalkerM_paper.pdf

Specification-Based Intrusion Detection Using Sequence Alignment and Data Clustering

Djibrilla Amadou Kountché[(⊠)] and Sylvain Gombault

Institut Mines-Télécom; Télécom Bretagne; IRISA/D2/OCIF RSM,
Université Européenne de Bretagne, Rennes, France
{djibrilla.amadoukountche,sylvain.gombault}@telecom-bretagne.eu

Abstract. In this paper, we present our work on specification-based
intrusion detection. Our goal is to build a web application firewall which
is able to learn the normal behaviour of an application (and/or the user)
from the traffic between a client and a server. The model learnt is used to
validate future traffic. We will discuss later in this paper, the interactions
between the learning phase and the exploitation phase of the generated
model expressed as a set of regular expressions. These regular expressions
are generated after a process of sequence alignment combined to BRELA
(Basic Regular Expression Learning Algorithm) or directly by the later.
We also present our multiple sequence alignment algorithm called AMAA
(Another multiple Alignment Algorithm) and the usage of data clustering
to improve the generated regular expressions. The detection phase is
simulated in this paper by generating data which represent a traffic and
using a pattern matcher to validate them.

Keywords: Positive security · Sequence alignment · Data clustering ·
Web application firewall · Specification-based ids

1 Introduction

An *intrusion detection is the process of monitoring the events that occur in
a computer system or network and analysing them for signs of possible incidents* [16]. Two major paradigms of intrusion detection methods can be defined
based on the way the system determines that an attack took place or is being
carried [5]: knowledge-based and behaviour-based. However, another classification of intrusion detection paradigms is given in [7,8,19]: misuse, anomaly and
specification. Knowledge-based systems are the most common in computer security and correspond to misuse-based. These systems achieve high performance
in term of false positive rate when known attacks are being carried on. But,
they require frequent updates of the knowledge base and have difficulties to
determine the variant of the same attack. Mostly, the algorithms used by these
systems are based on string matching like Aho-Corasick. Many works have been
done for automatic learning of the signature based as well on data mining [1]
as on sequence alignment [11,13]. Behaviour-based intrusion detection systems

© Springer International Publishing Switzerland 2015
R. Doss et al. (Eds.): FNSS 2015, CCIS 523, pp. 31–46, 2015.
DOI: 10.1007/978-3-319-19210-9_3

design the normal and/or the abnormal behaviour of the user and the system. Therefore, an attack is defined as an abnormal use of a given application or a deviation from the normal behaviour. However, not all deviations from the model are attacks, thus, this raises the rate of false positive. Behavioural intrusion detection made possible the detection of unknown attacks but has the following drawbacks [5]: (i) a high level of false positive due to difficulty to cover the whole behaviour of the target (system or user) at the learning phase; (ii) when the behaviour changed, an update of the model is required and (iii) some attacks can be introduced in the reference model and considered as normal. Behaviour-based systems are getting more popular in commercial intrusion detection and protection systems (IDPS) because of the potential of positive security. Specification and anomaly-based intrusion detection are part of behaviour paradigm and specification-based is defined in deep in Sect. 2.

These two approaches (knowledge and behaviour) can be combined to perform better results [15]. Indeed, depending on the modelling of the problem, most of the machine learning algorithms can be used for both purposes. In this project, we plan to use the mixed approach and the user of our WAF will be given the possibility to combine many algorithms at the learning and the exploitation phase.

This paper is organized as follow: the next section describes some related works and Sect. 3 develops sequence alignment. The Sect. 4 presents our contributions which are evaluated in the Sect. 5. Finally, the last section concludes this paper and gives the perspectives on our work.

2   Related Works

Specification-based intrusion detection made the hypothesis that an intrusion can be detected by observing the deviation from the normal or accepted behaviour[1] of the system or the user. The model can be expressed as: (i) dictionaries; (ii) finite automata or regular expressions; (iii) statistics, ontologies, etc. Uppuluri and Sekar [19] defined a domain specific language called BMSL (Behaviour modelling specification language) in which a specification can be defined as:

$$pat \rightarrow action \tag{1}$$

where *pat* is a set of regular expression representing the *history* of normal behaviour observed and *action* corresponds to the services accessed after this normal behaviour. Other DSL have been defined for negative security [20].

A specification-based IDPS comprises two main steps:

1. the learning phase: determination of the model from the data gathered (incomplete and noisy);
2. and the exploitation phase: comparison of the observed behaviour to the model.

---

[1] In the rest of the paper, the term behaviour and specification are considered the same.

The step before the learning phase has a great importance. Indeed, the quality of the data from which the specification will be drawn conditioned the results of the learning phase. In web applications, many factors made the collection of data and their accuracy difficult to guarantee. For example, the rapid evolution of frameworks, the coexistence of different version of protocols, applications and the fact that input validation is not always done. However, we consider functional tests as important data source for the learning phase [12]. Also, the specification can be done by "hand" by security experts. The next section reviews some algorithms used for the learning and exploitation phases and presents in depth the regular expression learning problem.

2.1 Algorithms Used in Intrusion Detection

Statistical methods are the most intuitive for characterizing the behaviour which is describe by variables:

$$B = x_i, i \in [1, .., n] \tag{2}$$

where x_i is a characteristic of the system. The variables may represent a mean or any other central tendency measure or a complex probability distribution like Gaussian Mixture Model. Therefore, methods like statistical tests or expectation maximisation can be used to estimate the parameters of the model [9,21]. Expert systems and Finite state machines have also been used to model the behaviour of the target [5]. In this project, we focus on using data mining algorithms at all the levels from the data preprocessing to the exploitation phase. Many algorithms are described in [1] for using data analysis methods for computer security. Also, we distinguish detection algorithms used for validation and algorithms used for generation of the model. This model can be deeply tied to the algorithms as in the statistical case but for regular expressions, two different algorithms can be used. In the next section, the problem of regular expression learning is presented followed by a study of sequence alignment.

2.2 Automatic Learning of Regular Expressions

We consider learning a regular expression form positive data. This problem consists of learning a regular expression which corresponds the most to the given dataset and permit to generalize to data expressed in different forms. However, there is an infinite number of regular expression corresponding to the learning dataset. C. De La Higuera gives a detailed description of other related problems [4].

H. Fernau [6] proposed some algorithms for generating a regular expression based on suffix tree and finite automata. These algorithms first build the suffix tree and determine a corresponding regular expression from the automata.

ReLIE was proposed by Yunyao et al. [10] for automatic generation of regular expressions from text documents in the goal of information retrieval. ReLIE took as input a regular expression R_0 and a document D. It transforms iteratively R_0 in a set of regular expressions and choose the one which maximise the objective function (the *F-Measure*).

A. Bartoli et *al.* [2] proposed a genetic algorithm which took as input a couple (s, t) where: s is a string and t the substring for which to construct the regular expression. The initial population is a set of individual corresponding to valid regular expressions. Every individual is represented as a tree and the fitness function is the sum of Leveinstein distances between the string and other strings which correspond to it toward the regular expression and the length of the regular expression.

Y. Tang et *al.* proposed methods based sequence alignment for polymorphic worms signature generation. They proposed: (i) a pair alignment algorithm (Contiguous Substring Reward (CSR)) based on Needleman-Wunsch by modifying the score function to favour the alignment of contiguous sequences; (ii) and a simplified regular expression (SRE) generation method based on a lookup Table [17]. They also proposed the usage of multiple sequence alignment [18] in order to improve the SREs.

In the following, we proposed two algorithms for generating positive rules as basic regular expression which are more strict than the SRE. Also, our algorithm AMAA can take CSR as parameter.

3 Sequence Alignment

Sequence alignment determines between many strings if invariant characters are present at the same position in all the strings by insertion of a gap character. It is originated from bioinformatics [3] where it is used for:

- observing patterns of conservation (or variability) between sequences (modelled as a string);
- finding commons patterns in the sequences;
- determining if the two sequences have not evolve from the same sequence.

Definition 1. *Given:*

- $s = s_1 \ldots s_n$ *and* $t = t_1 \ldots t_m$ *two strings defined on an alphabet* Σ
- β *the gap character,* $\beta \ni \Sigma$
- $\Sigma' = \Sigma \cup \beta$
- $h : (\Sigma')^* \implies \Sigma^*$ *an homomorphism defined by* $h(\alpha) = \alpha, \bigvee \alpha \in \Sigma$ *and* $h(\beta) = \lambda$. λ *is the empty character.*

An alignment of s *and* t *is a pair* (s', t') *of strings of length* $l \geq \max |s|, |t|$ *define on* Σ' *such that the following conditions hold:*

1. $|s'| = |t'|$
2. $h(|s'|) = s$ *and* $h(|t'|) = t$
3. *there can not be at the same position in* s' *and* t' *only gap characters.*

The second condition means that by deleting all the gap, we find back the strings s and t. An example is given by the Table 1 for the strings "Telecom-Bretagne" and "Kereval" where, the '+' character is used for the gap (Fig. 1).

Telecom-Bretagne
Kere+++++++val++

Fig. 1. Example of an alignment of Kereval and Telecom-Bretagne.

For an alignment of a pair of sequences, there exist four cases:

- insertion: the gap characters is inserted in the first string;
- deletion: the gap character is inserted in the second string;
- match or correspondence: the 2 characters are identical in the same column;
- mismatch: the two characters are different from each other and different from the gap character.

Definitions. The score of an alignment (s', t') of length l is defined as follow:

$$\delta(s', t') = \sum_{i=1}^{l} d(s'_i, t'_i) \qquad (3)$$

$$d(s'_i, t'_i) = \begin{cases} \text{match} & \text{if} s'_i, t'_i \in \Sigma \quad \text{and} \quad s'_i = t'_j \\ \text{mismatch} & \text{if} s'_i, t'_i \in \Sigma \quad \text{and} \quad s'_i \neq t'_j \\ \text{penalty} & \text{if} s'_i \text{or} t'_j \quad \text{equals} \quad \beta \end{cases} \qquad (4)$$

where $d(.,.)$ is a function defined on Σ and determine the similarity or the distance of the two characters. The value of *match*, *mismatch* and *penalty* are chosen in accordance to the application domain. Based on this score function, the alignment problem can be seen as an optimisation problem where the goal is to maximize the score function [3].

The score matrix indicates the score between the two sub-strings of s and t at a certain time of the progression of the alignment. This is the basis of the approach of dynamic programming of sequence alignment: determination of partial optimal solutions for the problem. The score matrix of the pair (s, t) having length n and m is a $(n+1) \times (m+1)$ matrix where:

- the first column and the first row are filled with $(j \times penalty)$ and $(i \times penalty)$
- Any other cell is filled with:

$$M(i, j) = \max \begin{cases} M(i-1, j) + penalty & \text{(i)} \\ M(i, j-1) + penalty & \text{(d)} \\ M(i-1, j-1) + d(s_i, t_j) & \text{(m)} \end{cases} \qquad (5)$$

The tracing of this matrix gives the results of the alignment (s', t'). Depending on the way the matrix is initialized and backward traced, one can distinguish:

- **Global alignment**: the initialization is as described earlier and the tracing starts at the $(n+1, m+1)$ cell;
- **Local alignment**: the function used to fill the cells became:

$$M(i, j) = \max(\max(i, d, m), 0) \qquad (6)$$

And the tracing starts at the cell having the maximum value in the whole matrix.

- the **Semi global alignment** case is describe in detail in [3].

The gap penalty is the parameter which favour the insertion or the deletion. A high value of the gap tends to prevent the gap character to be inserted in both of the sequences. This parameters is mostly chosen in bio-informatics based on an affine function.

3.1   Multiple Sequence Alignment

Definition 2. *Given* n *sequences* $s_1, \ldots, s_n$ *defined on an alphabet* Σ *having different lengths.* β *is the gap character and* $h(\alpha) = \alpha$ *an homomorphism.*

A multiple alignment of $s_1, \ldots, s_n$ *is an* $n - uplet(s'_1, \ldots, s'_n)$ *of length* $l \geq |s_i|, i \in [1 \ldots n]$ *on the alphabet* Σ' *where the following conditions hold:*

1. $|s_i| = |s_j|, \bigvee i, j \in [1 \ldots n]$
2. $h(s'_i) = s_i, \bigvee, i \in [1 \ldots n]$
3. *there is no row in the* $(n \times l)$*-matrix where there is only gap characters.*

Multiple sequence alignment problem is NP-Complete, therefore many algorithms have been proposed ranging from exact computation of the best alignment, determination of the consensual alignment to a combination with a pair alignment method [3]. Most of the algorithms were proposed for the purpose of bioinformatics and implementations are available online as servers. In this project, we started an adaptation of T-Coffee [14] for our purpose.

4   The Proposed Approach

The Fig. 2 shows the approach used for the learning process. The preprocessing phase consists of cleaning the redundant and noisy data and clustering them before the learning phase. Also, the user can visualise them in order to choose the partitioning appropriate for the learning phase. After the preprocessing phase, when the data are of the same size, BRELA can be directly applied on them or applied after a multiple sequence alignment by AMAA. Then, the results are evaluated. Also, it can be possible, after the evaluation to include certain data in the learning dataset and redo the process. AMAA and BRELA are described in the next section.

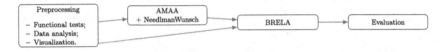

Fig. 2. Description of the learning and evaluation process.

4.1   AMAA: Another Multiple Alignment Algorithm

To illustrate how AMAA works, the GARFIELD dataset [14], described in
Table 1, is used. The parameters of AMAA are the alignment algorithm and
it's parameters. The configuration used is: '+' as gap character, $match = 1.0$,
$mismatch = 0.0$ and the $penalty = -1.0$.

Table 1. The GARFIELD dataset.

GARFIELD THE LAST FAT CAT
GARFIELD THE FAST CAT
GARFIELD THE VERY FAST CAT
THE FAST CAT

1. AMAA searches the best alignment among all the sequences which is shown
   in the first column of Table 2.
2. the set $Q = \{$''GARFIELD THE LAST FAT CAT'', ''GARFIELD THE VERY FAST
   CAT''$\}$ is suppressed form the input which now contains (GARFIELD THE
   FAST CAT, THE FAST CAT).
3. The content of the input set is aligned to the result of 1. The best alignments
   for these sequences are given in the second and the third columns of Table 2.
4. In this example, AMAA did nod pad the sequences, as they are very similar.

The final result is displayed in Table 3.

Table 2. Description of the steps of AMAA.

$i = 0$	$i = 1$	$i = 2$
GARFIELD THE LAST FA+T CAT	GARFIELD THE+++++ FAST CAT	+++++++++THE+++++ FAST CAT
GARFIELD THE VERY FAST CAT	GARFIELD THE LAST FA+T CAT	GARFIELD THE VERY FAST CAT

4.2   BRELA: Basic Regular Expression Learning Algorithm

BRELA will consider an array $n \times m$ like the result of AMAA in Table 3. It determines the character frequencies for each column generate the regular expression
given in the last line of Table 3 as follow: in the first column, the character 'G'
and '+' are encountered, so G can be considered as a fixed field. The same holds
until the character 'D'. So the sequence of characters [GARFIELD] is inserted
in the regular expression followed by an interval indicating that this word was
observed as is 0 time or once. The process is continued until the last column.
The words 'THE' and 'CAT', for example, have been identified as invariant fields
(Table 4).

Algorithm 1. AMAA: Another Multiple Alignment Algorithm

1: Input: $S = \{s_i, i = 1, \ldots, n\}$ set of sequences to be aligned.
2: $S' = \emptyset$
3: And a pair alignment algorithm (Needleman-Wunsch [3])
4: Output: $S' = \{a(s_i), i = 1, \ldots, n\}$ the aligned sequences (with the same length). Where $a(s_i)$ is the alignment of s_i produce by the algorithm.
5: Initialization:
6: Determine $n \times (n-1)$ alignments of all sequences and choose the best alignment:
7: $A^* = (s'_k, s'_p)$ such that $score(s'_k, s'_p) > score(s'_i, s'_j)$
8: Insert the best pair (A^*) of sequences in S' and delete (s_k, s_p) form S
9: **while** S is not empty **do**
10:     $s \leftarrow pop(S)$
11:     Align s with all the sequences in S' and choose the best sequences
12:     **for** All the sequences $s' \in S'$ **do**
13:        **if** s' has been modified by the alignment **then**
14:           Replace s' in S' by the new sequences s''
15:        **else if** the length of the a sequence changed **then**
16:           Insert padding in the position where an insertion or a deletion took place
17:        **end if**
18:     **end for**
19:     Add the new best alignment for the sequence s in S'
20: **end while**

Table 3. The final result of AMAA on the GARFIELD dataset.

	Result of AMAA
	GARFIELD THE VERY FAST CAT
	++++++++++THE+++++ FAST CAT
	GARFIELD THE+++++ FAST CAT
	GARFIELD THE LAST FA+T CAT
Result of BRELA	[GARFIELD]{0,1}THE[LAST]{0,1} FA[S]{0,1}T CAT

Table 4. Examples of datasets used for the evaluation.

Data sets					
	Date	Phone	Curr	Password	GUID
Samples	15/12/2024	01 97 74 34 19	$8,803	e?DEm8Wo	6E6BA93F-5960-BA96-4572
	23/12/2016	05 27 24 82 61	$6,794	.ZyE-FKv	BF54713E-E402-7515-763D
	13/11/2003	04 96 03 64 98	$9,067	@'@H"z'[	20E2E738-0AF1-F7B7-3EF1
	01/09/2230	05 99 44 53 73	$7,030	<2iEo3dN	47016986-1837-55F6-C019
Size	89	100	100	89	100

5   Experimentations

The flow of evaluations is describe as follows:

1. we generate data from generatedata.com;

Algorithm 2. Basic Regular Expression Learning Algorithm

1: Input: a set $I = \{s_i, i = 1, \ldots, n\}$ with $len(s_i) = len(s_j) = m, i \neq j, 1 <= i, j <= n$
2: Output: The corresponding regular expression RE
3: **for** every column $c_k, 0 <= k < m$ **do**
4:     Determine the characters distribution for c_k
5:     **if** c_k contains only one type of character α **then**
6:         α is an invariant character and append α in RE
7:     **else**
8:         **while** c_k is not a fixed character **do**
9:             Create a set (V) and insert the characters of c_k in it
10:            Determine the min and max length (stop at the next fixed character)
11:            $k \leftarrow k + 1$
12:        **end while**
13:        Sort the characters of V and append the character to RE as $[ordered(V)]\{min, max\}$
14:    **end if**
15: **end for**

---

2. BRELA is applied on data with the same size then is combined with AMAA;
3. in this scenario, the result of AMAA/BRELA are evaluated using the: true positive rate, false positive rate, the accuracy and the F-Measure[2].
4. for this case, the datasets are mixed and data clustering is used to discriminate them and a regular expression is generated for each cluster.

5.1 Comparison of BRELA and AMAA/BRELA

For this case, the experimentations are conducted as follow:

1. for every dataset, a regular expression is generated with BRELA;
2. first, the parameters of AMAA had constant values: ($match = 1.0, mismatch = 0.0, penalty = -1.0$)
3. then, uniform distributions are applied to generate values for the parameters.

The algorithms are implemented in Java and the experimentations where run on a Intel $core^{TM} i5$ computer with $4GB$ of RAM. The colt[3] implementation of the MersenneTwister was exploited for the uniform distributions. The experimentations where run 100 times for each dataset.

The random seed generator provided in colt was used for each parameters. The configuration of the generators is described in the Table 6.

Discussions. The results in Table 5 show that BRELA and AMAA/BRELA produce the same regular expression. These regular expressions preserved the invariant fields (which are identifiable without alignment). But in the case of the password dataset, any invariant field is present. Therefore, BRELA produced a *pattern* which is an ordering of the characters followed by the total length of the strings. In the third scenario, the results are illustrated in Table 7. The regular

---

[2] These criteria are explained on http://en.wikipedia.org/wiki/F1_score.
[3] https://dst.lbl.gov/ACSSoftware/colt/.

Table 5. Results obtained for both BRELA and the combination of AMAA and BRELA. In the second case, the parameters are $match = 1.0, mismatch = 0.0, penalty = -1.0$

Data set	Regex
Dates	`[0-9]{2}/[0-9]{2}/2[0-9]{3}`
Phone	`0[1-9]{1} [0-9]{2} [0-9]{2} [0-9]{2} [0-9]{2}`
Currency	`$[56789]{1},[0123456789]{3}`
Password	`[!"#$% &'()* +,-./[0-9] :;<=>? @[A-Z][]^-'[a-z]{|}~] {8}`
GUID	`[0-9A-F]{8}-[0-9A-F]{4}-[0-9A-F]{4} -[0-9A-F]{4}`

Table 6. The configuration of the uniform random generation.

Parameter	Interval	Seed
$match$	$[1.0, 100.0]$	9876
$mismatch$	$[-1.0, 0.0]$	1299961164
$penalty$	$[-100.0, -1.0]$	669708517

expression generated depends on the parameters of the alignment algorithm. While a high value of match allows the alignment of the same characters in the same column, a high value of mismatch will change the natural alignment of the characters. When the data are similar and the invariant are distinguishable (even if they are different), BRELA is faster for determining the regular expression. Aligning the sequences before applying BRELA can produce the same result or will help to identify some field which are hidden in the dataset. We will study this case in the next section with datasets composed by different string of different lengths.

Table 7. This table summarised the results obtained for 100 runs. Up to two kinds of regular expressions are generated.

Regex	Parameters (match, mismatch, penalty)
Date	
`[/0-9]{10}`	9.65,-0.15,-92.46
Currency	
`\$[5-9]{1},[0-9]{3}`	66.21,0.0,-87.29
`[$,0-9]{6}`	2.06,-0.0015,-73.60
GUID	
`[-0-9A-F]{24}`	52.80,-0.008,-98.55
`[0-9A-F]{8}-[0-9A-F]{4}-[0-9A-F]{4}-[0-9A-F]{4}`	28.51,0.0,-90.87
Phone	
`[0-9]{14}`	83.54,-0.31,-12.71
`0[1-9]{1}\[0-9]{2}\[0-9]{2}\[0-9]{2}[0-9]{2}`	79.79,0.0,-92.36
Password	
`[!"#$%&'()*+,-./0-9:;\<=\>\?@A-Z[\]^_'a-z{|}~]{8}`	21.60,-0.35,-39.41

5.2   Detection Performances Analysis

The process of this experimentation is describe by the Fig. 3.

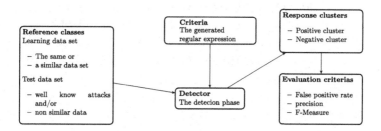

Fig. 3. The evaluation process.

The dataset represents a *specification* of the system captured at a certain time. These data are employed to generate a regular expression which in turn is use to evaluate a mixed dataset containing the same and/or similar data and know XSS and SQL injections. After the evaluation, two classes are generated: the positive cluster which contains the data considered as normal and the negative cluster contains the data considered as not conform to the specification.

Case 1: The negative test dataset for password, date, phone and currency. contains only XSS or SQL injections while the positive contains corresponding data. The results are summarized in the Table 9.

Discussion. When the positive and negative datasets are significantly different, all the data in the negative class will be considered as attacks. Even for the passwords dataset, which contains characters used for XSS and SQL injections. In this case, the length of the strings are inferior to the length of an XSS or SQL injections attacks (Table 8).

Case 2: The Test Dataset Contains Confusing Data. The lengths, certain fields of the data are varied so that the negative dataset will contain data which are close to learning dataset but must be classified as attacks. Other criteria for the evaluation will be used: the accuracy, the true positive rate, the false negative rate.

Discussion. In Table 10, the currency dataset has the best values for all the criteria. The regular expression discriminates well-formed currencies expressed as prefixed Dollar, Euro and Pounds and others from others numeric values. However, in the case of the password, some XSS and SQL attacks were considered as normal. As stated before, this is due to the presence of some ambiguous

Table 8. Examples of datasets used for the evaluation.

Regular expression learning datasets				
	Date	Phone	Currency	Password
samples	29/11/2104	01 97 74 34 19	$8,803	= o9_(om
	06.30.22	(+33)0408017767	£12.63	}x5"C
	10-14-55	0298623840	107,774€	@'@H"z'[
	10/22/43	+332 40 77 54 65	€ 0,266	%|Y} : A&5eAb
Total size	103	99	57	74

Table 9. Results where the negative test dataset is composed only of XSS or SQL attacks.

Results for the first case				
	Date	Phone	Currency	Password
F-Measure	1.0 (0.0)	1.0 (0.0)	1.0 (0.0)	1.0 (0.0)

characters. Also the specification is defined strictly so that the date is considered different than password. But, in real use cases, some users consider a date or phone numbers as a password. For the date dataset, the format use for the generation was *day* : *sep* : *month* : *sep* : *year*. Where : *sep* : is a separator. Therefore, the validator has to reject other date format until the user decides to use them in future. However, permutations of the field like year and day, are accepted. In the case of the phone dataset, some plain number are also accepted as normal phone number. However, for all these datasets, the validator continues to consider the injections dataset as abnormal.

5.3   The Data Clustering

Clustering is used for the cases where, at the learning phase, different types are present. Thus, we believed that determining the appropriate partitioning of the data and generate the corresponding regular expression can improve the

Table 10. Results where the test dataset is contains confusing data and XSS or SQL injections.

Results for the second case				
	Date	Phone	Currency	Password
TPR	0.63	0.77	1.0	0.52
FPR	0.36	0.23	0.0	0.47
Accurary	0.58	0.79	1.0	0.53
F-Measure	0.62	0.81	1.0	0.67

performances. At the exploitation phase, the validator will also cluster the data or use a hierarchy of the regular expressions to determine for a data which regular expression is most appropriate for validating it. However, in this paper, only the clustering at the learning phase is studied. The data from each of the four datasets are mixed and each corresponds to 25 %. The total length of the clustering dataset is 200. We use the LingPipe Java Library[4].

Case 1: One Regular Expression the Dataset. We generate one regular expression without clustering. The result is given in the Fig. 4.

`[ !"#$%&'()*+,-./0-9:;<=>?@A-Z[\]^_'a-z{|}~£€]{5,103}`

Fig. 4. Regular expression generated with default values for the alignment algorithm.

This regular expression will consider validate any sequence of characters having a length between 5 and 103. Therefore, it is not accurate to discriminate inappropriate inputs. In the Table 11, we show the result for the evaluation criteria by considering only a dataset where the positive data are the mixed from the four datasets and the negative dataset consists of XSS and SQL attacks.

Table 11. Results where the test dataset is composed only of XSS or SQL attacks.

One regular expression	
TPR	0.86
FPR	0.14
Accurary	0.86
F-Measure	0.92

In this case, the accuracy, F-measure and true positive rate are higher and corresponds to the analysis on the regular expression.

Case 2: Determining the Appropriate Number of Regulars Expressions. In this experimentation, we present result with hierarchical clustering with Jaro and Winkler distance although we tried K-Means. We also tried edit distance, but in our case, it tends to produce a higher number of sparse clusters than Jaro Winkler distance. In order to evaluate the clustering:

1. we choose a partitioning of 16 clusters;
2. for each clusters we generate a regular expression using AMAA/BRELA;
3. then we determine the values of the criteria for the 4 datasets used to build the clustering dataset. Therefore, we consider the three others as negative.

---

[4] http://alias-i.com/lingpipe/index.html.

Table 12. A cut of the dendrogram to have a number of clusters $N = 16$. FM (F-Measure), AC (Accuracy), TP (True positive rate), FP(false positive rate).

N	Phone				Password				Date				Curr.			
	FM	AC	TP	FP	FM	AC	TP	FP	FM	AC	TP	FP	FM	AC	TP	FP
	0.66	0.52	0.60	0.40	0.65	0.52	0.60	0.40	0.70	0.58	0.64	0.36	0.76	0.67	0.69	0.31
	0.66	0.61	0.74	0.26	0.57	0.51	0.64	0.36	0.64	0.60	0.72	0.28	0.56	0.50	0.62	0.38
	0.76	*0.61*	*0.63*	*0.37*	*0.78*	*0.65*	*0.64*	*0.36*	*0.75*	*0.61*	*0.62*	*0.38*	*0.75*	*0.60*	*0.62*	*0.38*
	0.76	0.62	0.63	0.37	0.77	0.64	0.63	0.37	0.76	0.62	0.62	0.38	0.76	0.61	0.62	0.38
	0.60	0.50	0.61	0.39	0.61	0.51	0.61	0.39	0.86	0.82	0.86	0.14	0.60	0.50	0.60	0.40
	0.76	0.62	0.63	0.37	0.77	0.64	0.64	0.36	0.76	0.61	0.62	0.38	0.75	0.61	0.62	0.38
	0.59	0.50	0.61	0.39	0.59	0.50	0.60	0.40	**0.95**	**0.94**	**0.97**	**0.03**	0.59	0.50	0.60	0.40
	0.75	0.60	0.62	0.38	0.77	0.64	0.64	0.36	0.75	0.62	0.63	0.37	0.74	0.59	0.61	0.39
16	**0.85**	**0.82**	**0.91**	**0.09**	0.59	0.52	0.63	0.37	0.59	0.52	0.63	0.37	0.59	0.52	0.63	0.37
	0.75	0.61	0.62	0.38	0.78	0.65	0.65	0.35	0.75	0.60	0.62	0.38	0.74	0.60	0.61	0.39
	0.70	0.56	0.62	0.38	0.70	0.55	0.61	0.39	0.70	0.56	0.61	0.39	0.79	0.69	0.68	0.32
	0.69	0.55	0.61	0.39	0.69	0.55	0.60	0.40	0.69	0.55	0.60	0.40	**0.82**	**0.74**	**0.72**	**0.28**
	0.69	0.56	0.62	0.38	0.67	0.53	0.60	0.40	0.80	0.72	0.72	0.28	0.67	0.53	0.60	0.40
	0.75	0.60	0.62	0.38	0.78	0.66	0.65	0.35	0.74	0.60	0.62	0.38	0.74	0.59	0.61	0.39
	0.59	0.50	0.61	0.39	0.59	0.50	0.60	0.40	**0.95**	**0.94**	**0.97**	**0.03**	0.59	0.50	0.60	0.40

Discussion. For each of the dataset, the combination of the clustering and regular expression learning is able to association a cluster. The bold results in the Table 12 show which cluster can be associated to the dataset. These clusters have for example the highest F-measure and the lowest false positive rate. However, some clusters can also correspond to all the datasets at the same time (Bold and italic results). One particular case is the password dataset which summarises the case where it is difficult to determine an appropriate cluster. We show that the clustering phase can allow the user to determine which data to gather together as similar and generate a regular expression. Therefore, when he goes through the dendrogram, he can choose the number of partitions or decide to merge some of them. An important remark is regarding the number of clusters. We choose 16 to illustrate the potentialities of the clustering but there are many other possible partitioning in the dendrogram. Therefore, we will applied statistical criteria to determine the number of clusters and visualisation.

6   Conclusion

Specification-based intrusion detection is a promising model. In this paper, we presented our algorithms AMAA and BRELA for automatic learning of the specification and we combine them to data clustering. When the data are of the same length, BRELA can be directly use but it will not be able to determine hidden invariant fields. AMAA can determine these fields before the generation of the regular expression. In the case of web forms for example, many data types can be mixed. Thus, the clustering will help the user of our WAF to organise the data in clusters corresponding to the needs. Also, we are working to integrate other string clustering metrics and data clustering algorithms. Also a tree levels of comparison is under the way: (i) AMAA with other sequence alignment algorithm; (ii) comparison of AMAA/BRELA with other regular expression learning algorithms and (iii) an evaluation of the clustering using statistical tests and partition evaluation criteria.

Acknowledgements. This work is a part of the RoCaWeb project carried at Kereval and Telecom-Bretagne and financed as a RAPID project by the DGA-MI. We would like to thank Alain Ribault, Constant Chartier, Fr?d?ric Majorczyk and Yacine Tamoudi.

References

1. Adams, N., Heard, N.: Data Analysis for Network Cyber-Security. World Scientific, Singapore (2014)
2. Bartoli, A., Davanzo, G., De Lorenzo, A., Mauri, M., Medvet, E., Sorio, E.: Automatic generation of regular expressions from examples with genetic programming. In: Proceedings of the 14th Annual Conference Companion on Genetic and Evolutionary Computation, pp. 1477–1478. ACM (2012)
3. Böckenhauer, H.J., Bongartz, D.: Algorithmic Aspects of Bioinformatics. Natural Computing Series. Springer, Heidelberg (2007)
4. De La Higuera, C.: A bibliographical study of grammatical inference. Pattern Recognit. **38**(9), 1332–1348 (2005)
5. Debar, H., Dacier, M., Wespi, A.: Towards a taxonomy of intrusion-detection systems. Comput. Netw. **31**(8), 805–822 (1999)
6. Fernau, H.: Algorithms for learning regular expressions from positive data. Inf. Comput. **207**(4), 521–541 (2009)
7. Garcia-Teodoro, P.: Anomaly-based network intrusion detection: Techniques, systems and challenges. Comput. Secur. **28**(1), 18–28 (2009)
8. Jokar, P., Nicanfar, H., Leung, V.C.M.: Specification-based intrusion detection for home area networks in smart grids. In: 2011 IEEE International Conference on Smart Grid Communications (SmartGridComm), pp. 208–213. IEEE (2011)
9. Kruegel, C., Vigna, G., Robertson, W.: A multi-model approach to the detection of web-based attacks. Comput. Netw. **48**(5), 717–738 (2005)
10. Li, Y., Krishnamurthy, R., Raghavan, S., Vaithyanathan, S., Jagadish, H.V.: Regular expression learning for information extraction. In: Proceedings of the Conference on Empirical Methods in Natural Language Processing, pp. 21–30. Association for Computational Linguistics (2008)
11. Li, Z., Sanghi, M., Chen, Y., Kao, M.-Y., Chavez, B.: Hamsa: Fast signature generation for zero-day polymorphic worms with provable attack resilience. In: 2006 IEEE Symposium on Security and Privacy, 15 p. IEEE (2006)
12. Mouelhi, T.: Testing and Modeling Security Mechanisms in Web Applications. Theses, Institut National des Télécommunications (2010)
13. Newsome, J., Karp, B., Song, D.: Polygraph: automatically generating signatures for polymorphic worms. In: 2005 IEEE Symposium on Security and Privacy, pp. 226–241. IEEE (2005)
14. Notredame, C., Higgins, D.G., Heringa, J.: T-coffee: a novel method for fast and accurate multiple sequence alignment. J. Mol. Biol. **302**(1), 205–217 (2000)
15. Saltzer, J.H., Schroeder, M.D.: The protection of information in computer systems. Proc. IEEE **63**(9), 1278–1308 (1975)

16. Scarfone, K., Mell, P.: Guide to intrusion detection and prevention systems (idps). NIST Spec. Publ. **800**(2007), 94 (2007)
17. Tang, Y., Lu, X., Xiao, B.: Generating simplified regular expression signatures for polymorphic worms. In: Xiao, B., Yang, L.T., Ma, J., Muller-Schloer, C., Hua, Y. (eds.) ATC 2007. LNCS, vol. 4610, pp. 478–488. Springer, Heidelberg (2007)
18. Tang, Y., Xiao, B., Xicheng, L.: Using a bioinformatics approach to generate accurate exploit-based signatures for polymorphic worms. Comput. Secur. **28**(8), 827–842 (2009)
19. Uppuluri, P., Sekar, R.: Experiences with specification-based intrusion detection. In: Lee, W., Mé, L., Wespi, A. (eds.) RAID 2001. LNCS, vol. 2212, p. 172. Springer, Heidelberg (2001)
20. Vigna, G., Valeur, F., Kemmerer, R.A.: Designing and implementing a family of intrusion detection systems. In: ACM SIGSOFT Software Engineering Notes, vol. 28, pp. 88–97. ACM (2003)
21. Ye, N., Li, X., Chen, Q., Emran, S.M., Xu, M.: Probabilistic techniques for intrusion detection based on computer audit data. IEEE Trans. Syst. Man Cybern. Part A Syst. Hum. **31**(4), 266–274 (2001)

Novel Approach for Information Discovery in Autonomous Wireless Sensor Networks

Menik Tissera[✉], Robin Doss, Gang Li, and Lynn M. Batten

School of Information Technology, Deakin University,
Burwood, VIC 3125, Australia
{wmrt,robin.doss,gang.li,lynn.batten}@deakin.edu.au
http://www.deakin.edu.au

Abstract. Autonomous Wireless sensor networks(WSNs) have sensors that are usually deployed randomly to monitor one or more phenomena. They are attractive for information discovery in large-scale data rich environments and can add value to mission–critical applications such as battlefield surveillance and emergency response systems. However, in order to fully exploit these networks for such applications, energy-efficient, load balanced and scalable solutions for information discovery are essential. Multi-dimensional autonomous WSNs are deployed in complex environments to sense and collect data relating to multiple attributes (multi-dimensional data). Such networks present unique challenges to data dissemination, data storage of in-network information discovery. In this paper, we propose a novel method for information discovery for multi-dimensional autonomous WSNs which sensors are deployed randomly that can significantly increase network lifetime and minimize query processing latency, resulting in quality of service (QoS) improvements that are of immense benefit to mission–critical applications. We present simulation results to show that the proposed approach to information discovery offers significant improvements on query resolution latency compared with current approaches.

Keywords: Wireless sensor networks · Data Centric Storage · Distributed Index for Multi-dimensional data

1   Introduction

Autonomous Wireless sensor network (WSN) is composed of a densely scattered group of autonomous sensors that are intended to work without a main control centre (such as sink). These wireless sensors collect data from the environment to detect or measure one or more physical phenomena. The data gathering capabilities of WSNs are particularly attractive for mission–critical operations that can be deployed in unattended and hostile environments such as battlefield surveillance [1–3] military reconnaissance and emergency response [4,5] so intelligence can be gathered without the risk of human casualties. Traditional approaches for information discovery in WSNs have assumed the communication pattern as

© Springer International Publishing Switzerland 2015
R. Doss et al. (Eds.): FNSS 2015, CCIS 523, pp. 47–60, 2015.
DOI: 10.1007/978-3-319-19210-9_4

many-to-one where sensors gather information and then push to a central data repository called the "sink". However, mission–critical applications on WSNs are intended to work without a main control centre (such as sink), but they do demand life and/or time critical information and support for unique traffic patterns that maximize the network lifetime. Further, the nature of such mission–critical applications require high quality of service (QoS) requirements for the information discovery process. These requirements make information discovery a challenging task because the complexity and energy constraints of wireless sensors make this an important problem and is the main motivation for this work.

Early approaches to information discovery, such as flooding and gossiping with push-pull strategies use the simplest communication pattern of broadcast. The broadcast of packets will result in problems such as unnecessary retransmission of packets that could lead to high energy consumption and bottlenecks in the network. Traditional approaches and strategies for information discovery can be proactive or reactive [6]. Suppose, the sensors are deployed randomly in a battlefield. Sensors that detect an event can "push" this information out to every sensor in the network (e.g., sensors detect tanks and enemies and can periodically "push" that information to the other sensors on the network) or they can wait and allow a sensor to "pull" this information through querying (e.g., soldier sends a query such as "Where are the tanks or enemies?"). The efficiency of the above mentioned "push" or "pull" methods varies and depends on the demand for information. However, since the frequency of events and queries are not taken into consideration, pure pull-based or push-based methods are inefficient in real deployments. This is further motivation for our work.

Recent approaches for routing, such as comb needle [7], double ruling [8] and cross roads [6], aim to successfully balance push and pull approaches to improve the QoS in terms of efficiency and lifetime of the WSN. The above mentioned approaches mainly considered storing a single attribute. Distributed Index for Multi-dimensional data (DIM) and Time-Parameterized Data Centric Storage (TPDCS) [9] are examples of later attempts [10] that have accommodated multiple attributes in the WSN. However, these approaches have severely suffered with the hotspot problem. Furthermore, such approaches have not considered incorporating multi-resolution [11] to the solution in an effort to reduce the hotspot problem. According to [11], having multi-resolution data storage has several advantages, including reduction of the energy consumption by decreasing the overhead of redundant packets traveling throughout the network to an ultimate detailed aggregate point. Less overhead of redundant packets will avoid unnecessary storage and processing. Further, multi-resolutional data helps to balance the overall network traffic by mitigating the congestion effects and hotspots in the network and reduces the query response time. However, most of the previous solutions on multi-resolution are not in-network and need a base station. In addition, these solutions are hierarchical or cluster based and very complex in nature and also designed for a single attribute.

In this paper, we formulate the information discovery problem as a load balancing problem for multiple attributes and an optimal routing structure problem based on the frequency of event. The combined aim is to increase network lifetime and reduce query processing latency by introducing multi-resolution and identifying an optimal routing structure that exploits the advantages of push and pull strategies, plus adapting to event and querying frequencies. Our work differs from other recent developments, such as [9,12], in that we do not employ greedy mechanisms for data dissemination, depending on topological constraints or required knowledge of information location. Further, the aggregated data is stored at multiple levels of resolutions to enable fast query resolution without the need for always accessing a detailed level of information. Multi-resolution reduces overall network traffic, mitigates congestion effects and hotspots in the network and reduces the query resolution latency.

Our main contributions in this paper are:

- a decentralized storage architecture and self-organization method that enables distributed data collection of multi-dimensional data,
- a method for energy efficient routing for energy efficient data dissemination and query resolution in WSNs,
- a strategy for fast query resolution with multi-resolution that aims to decrease the latency associated with query resolution and increase the lifetime of the network.

The remaining sections of the paper are organized as follows. Section 2 discusses related work. Section 3 describes our proposed approach. The simulation results are discussed in the Sects. 4 and 5 concludes the paper.

2   Related Work

Initially, information discovery was diffusion based. Flooding and gossiping [13] were the most classical diffusion based approaches for disseminating data within the WSN.

Sarkar *et al.* [8] proposed the double rulings scheme for information brokerage as an extension of GHTs hashing. They choose a rendezvous node (i.e. producer) along a continuous curve with the data of the same type being hashed to the same location. The consumer travels along another curve guaranteed to intersect the curve where the producer resides or data exists if replication is performed on all the nodes along the curve. The double ruling scheme has improved query locality in terms of proximity to the producer and improves on GHT which allows for distance sensitive query resolution. However, the choice of nodes in the replication and retrieval curves are not energy sensitive and hence both schemes suffer from energy inefficiencies.

As a solution for storage hotspots and the issues raised by the DIM, the k-D tree based Data-Centric Storage (KDDCS) [14] was proposed. It uses the same strategy as DIM to split the nodes into zones. However, the division ensures equal numbers of sensors on each side of the split line and makes sure each data zone is individually assigned to a sensor. The split lines are automatically adjusted in order to avoid data hotspots and the split lines are automatically adjusted according to the amount of data. Readjusting the splitting lines will add an overhead to the zones even though it avoids hotspots. For the query hotspot problem which was not solved efficiently by the DIM or KDDS [14], Park has proposed another DCS based technique namely Time-Parameterized Data Centric Storage (TPDCS) [9]. A query is forwarded to the relevant sensor based on the time dimension and it avoids selecting the sensor of the same data region repeatedly. This helps to avoid query hotspots, unbalanced energy consumption and data losses due to storage hotspots. However, if the time period T is too long then in a manner similar to DIM, TPDCS would suffer from storage and query hotspots. If T was small then sensors would consume more storage space in the network. Therefore, TPDCS should be further improved for storage utilization and efficient management of energy in a sensor network.

Together, data storage, data dissemination and query resolution make the information discovery process a challenge. Therefore, in this paper, we have proposed the Multi-Dimensional and Multi-Resolution Architecture Random (MDMRA random) for multiple attribute storage and also for information reduction on WSNs. The proposed architecture is further discussed in the following sections.

3   The Proposed Approach

An efficient information discovery process will significantly enhance the quality of service of such a network. The proposed scheme that incorporates network self-organization and energy-sensitive dissemination of data for aggregation on inner-path and information retrieval. For this approach, it is assumed the network is fully connected and that each sensor is aware of its own location and the relative coordinates of the deployment area including the origin. The specifics are presented in the following subsections.

3.1   Network Self-Organization

Consider a random network as in Fig. 1. In the middle of the network, a set of nodes on a path, has closer x-coordinate as the origin's x-coordinate act as data collection points. This path is called the inner-path and nodes on the inner-path store the most detailed levels of data in the WSN. The inner-path holds n_a different attributes and two different replicas of each attribute in different halves of the network. Consequently, the width of the inner-path is dependant on the number of attributes that will be stored and observed by the network. As shown in Fig. 1, to the both sides of the inner-path and towards the boundary, the level-paths are defined. The level-paths aggregate different resolution levels of the information stored. The number of resolution levels or level-paths β is dependent on the application and can be defined by the user. Since sensor networks are deployed through random scattering, our first goal is to organize the network so we can identify clearly the perimeter of the network, the inner-path and level-path nodes, and n_a number of data storage points. For this purpose, a simple

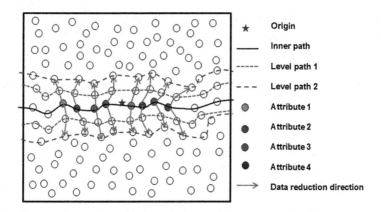

Fig. 1. The organization of the inner-path and the level-paths with their respective attributes

decentralized algorithm was proposed. Since each sensor node is location aware, all nodes within a certain distance d from the origin of the deployment area self-elect themselves to be boundary nodes on the network.

Similarly, the nodes with the closest y coordinate to the origin y coordinate will be selected as the nodes on the inner-path nodes. However, with the random scattering of nodes, the inner-path is limited to a single chain (line) of nodes going into the middle of the sensor network. The closest next level of nodes to the inner-path will be selected as the first level-path and continue further towards the boundary until the number of levels defined by the user is achieved.

From the set of these inner-path nodes, a group of nodes are selected to be data storage points as shown in Fig. 1. The purpose of the data storage nodes is to serve as data storage centers and the number of data storage nodes n_a is defined based on the attributes the application is required to store. The level-paths are marked from origin to the boundary in an increasing order. The inner-path is usually marked as level 0. Once the inner-path, level-paths and the storage nodes are identified, the nodes start the network self-organization process. The nodes on the inner-path are called *iNodes* and the nodes on the level-paths are called as *lNodes*. Each sensor node sends out a short hello packet to its neighbouring nodes within the transmission range R and helps to identify the closest nodes to the origin by every sensor node. Forwarding of the hello packet stops after learning all the neighbours within a sensor node's transmission area R.

3.2   Strategy for Energy Efficient Sensor Node Selection

A major consideration of this metric is the number of packets sent and received from a neighbour sensor node. The sensor node with the lowest packet count will be included in the data dissemination or query resolution tree. The motivation behind this is to use those nodes with higher residual sensor node energy. The overall aim of this is to increase the network lifetime. To achieve this, every sensor node i maintains, two vectors, one to store the number of packets sent to each neighbour and another to store the number of packets received from the neighbours, Λ_i and Γ_i respectively.

The problem can be formulated as follows. Let N be the total number of nodes in the network. If sensor node $node_i$ and $node_j$ are neighbours and if $node_i$ and $node_j$ has n number of neighbours, then the vector for the number of packets sent to each neighbour by N_i could be written as,

$$\Lambda_i = \begin{pmatrix} P_{s1} \\ P_{s2} \\ \vdots \\ Pn \end{pmatrix}$$

Further, the vector for the received number of packets on N_i from the neighbours Γ_i could be written as follows:

$$\Gamma_i = \begin{pmatrix} P_{r1} \\ P_{r2} \\ \vdots \\ P_n \end{pmatrix}$$

When forwarding data or a query, following assumptions were made in relation to the packets received and sent by neighbours. If the energy consumption of N_i and N_j is ϵ_{ci} and ϵ_{cj} respectively, the energy consumption for N_i and N_j can be written as $\epsilon_{ci} \propto \Lambda_i + \Gamma_i$ and $\epsilon_{cj} \propto \Lambda_j + \Gamma_j$

As a result, the sensor node N_i will select the sensor node with lowest summation of Λ_n and Γ_n among its neighbours.

3.3 Data Dissemination Tree Construction

The data and query trees are constructed using the two vectors mentioned in Sect. 3.2. A producer will forward the data to one of the neighbours with a lowest $\Lambda_n + \Gamma_n$ and every sensor node will continue the same process by generating an energy efficient tree to the inner-path as shown in Fig. 2. In the next step the data will be synchronized on nodes along the inner-path and to the nodes on the level-paths as shown in Fig. 2. As a result, the data will be available with the nodes on the inner-path and the level-paths will have different resolution levels. This process of data dissemination makes it easier fo r data consumers to access data with lesser latency and consumption of energy.

3.4 Increase Data Spread Through Opportunistic Dissemination

Information can be opportunistically stored at multiple locations within the transmission range for the same dissemination cost. The data spread in the network can be achieved by exploiting the broadcast nature of the wireless medium. This can provide a further improvement in the QoS offered to query resolution. When the data dissemination tree is constructed from the producer sensor node,

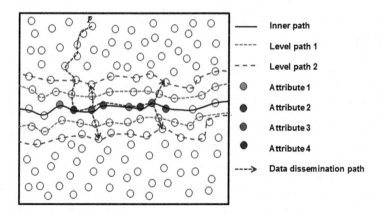

Fig. 2. Sensor node p detects a value for attribute-4 and disseminate it on the inner-path to the level-paths

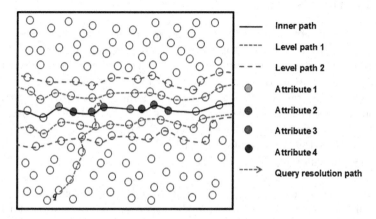

Fig. 3. Sensor node q needs detailed information of attribute-4 and querying from the inner-path

nodes that are adjacent to the dissemination tree will overhear the transmissions. The opportunistic storage of these transmissions increase the number of locations at which information relating to a particular event is available. This approach can significantly decrease the query resolution time for ANY-type queries as the number of locations at which an ANY-type query can be resolved is increased. As a result, the query resolution cost is reduced as the required number of transmissions is decreased and this achieves network-wide energy savings which results in an increase of the network lifetime.

3.5   Query Resolution

For the process of query resolution, the consumer sensor node will indicate both the desired level of information and the attribute in the data packet. For example, if the query needs very detailed information for an attribute on the inner-path then the level of the information will be marked as 0 in the packet with the required attribute.

The query dissemination tree is built towards the origin, by considering the lowest value for the summation of Λ_n and Γ_n. However, if the packet reaches the level mentioned by the consumer, the packet will then stop moving towards the origin.

Instead, the *lNode*, which received the packet and is on the required level, will forward the packet along the level-path (*i.e.,* inner-path or a level-path) towards the origin's x-coordinate, as shown in Fig. 3. If the packet has not met the storage node which stores the search attribute then, the packet further traverses to the same direction towards the boundary until it meets the search attribute. Following this, the query uses the shortest path to the consumer from the data storage sensor node.

4   Simulation Results

Performance evaluation of the MDMRA was carried out using network simulator 2 (NS–2). Initially, the network topology was a deployment of 9×9 nodes distributed randomly over a deployment area of $800\,\mathrm{m}^2$. Every node in the network was capable of generating data and queries with each simulation run.

For each simulation run one node was randomly chosen to be the query generation. The *inner-path* and *level-path* nodes were marked with the attributes and the levels they were responsible for storing. The consumer node generated queries following a Poisson distribution with a *mean inter-arrival rate* (λ) of 2 s.

To study the scalability of the approach on network performance, the number of nodes in the network was varied from 81 to 1681.

The choice of consumer nodes were restricted to the core nodes (i.e., the nodes that were not on the *inner-path*) within the network. We compare performance with comb needle, double ruling and TPDCS approaches.

In our implementation of the comb needle approach, the size of the needle l was set to 5 with an inter-comb spacing, s, of 1. We also implemented the double rulings approach. Data replication was performed along the greater path formed between the producer and the aggregator (which was chosen at random from within the core nodes). We considered the case where there is only a single data type and hence, all data was aggregated to the single aggregator. Each consumer node selected a retrieval curve along which it traveled in a random direction until it intersected with the replication curve. We considered replication distances of 1 in our simulations. We further implemented TPDCS approach. In TPDCS, the data regions are assigned by a time dimension as well as data dimensions. Two attribute dimensions were considered during time dimension t_0 to t_4. The data generation nodes, time dimensions t_n, data querying nodes and data used for queries were chosen randomly, in each simulation run. The routing process is carried out using the Greed Perimeter Stateless Routing(GPSR) method [15].

In our simulation, initial spacing between two nodes was set to 100m. At this width, we found a connected path to the network edge was achieved. The communication range of each sensor node was approximately 100m. We used 802.11 as the MAC protocol [16]. All results are averaged over 30 simulation runs (with random seeds) with each run of 180 s duration. The energy model deployed was the NS–2 energy model and every simulation run started with the initial energy of 1000 J in every node for residual energy calculations and to generate the energy maps.

In the first instance, the main focus of the simulation was to study the QoS improvements of the proposed approach. We identified four main performance metrics that were studied to measure the QoS improvements and the lifetime improvements of the network. These are:

- Average data availability latency: the average time taken to make the attribute available on the data storage nodes.
- Average query resolution latency: the average time taken to resolve a particular query.
- Average information discovery latency: summation of the average time taken to make the attribute available on the storage node and the average time taken to resolve a query.
- Average consumed energy: the average energy consumed for data dissemination and query resolution by individual nodes.

The first three metrics provide information on the effectiveness and completeness of the proposed approach in improving QoS. The fourth metric provides information on the energy-efficiency and the usage of the different approaches.

In Fig. 4, the fastest data availability is recorded by comb needle model and slowest data availability is with double rulings approach. The data dissemination path for comb needle is the shortest and hence the data would be quickly available on the data storage sensor nodes. Double rulings scheme is the slowest in make data available on a replication curve, because we have considered $R = 1$ and the replication is done at all nodes along the replication curve. Therefore,

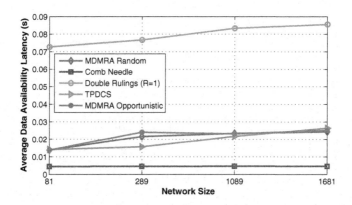

Fig. 4. The average data availability latency Vs network size

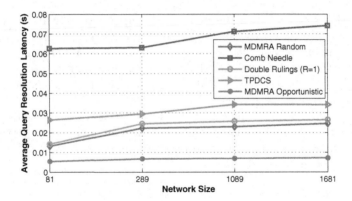

Fig. 5. The average query resolution latency for data querying Vs network size

data dissemination cost with double rulings scheme is high (in terms of construction of the replication curve).

Figure 5 presents the average query resolution times with varying number of sensor nodes for eight different approaches. From Fig. 5, it can be observed the average query resolution latency are lowest for MDMRA opportunistic scheme. MDMRA opportunistic scheme has advantaged by the opportunistic storage of the data. Further, the resolution levels and local availability of the data have helped to acquire a low average query resolution for MDMRA random and MDMRA opportunistic. Further, as shown in Fig. 5, we observe that the average query resolution latency is the highest for the comb needle in comparison to the other approaches. Traveling along the network vertically and horizontally over the network to resolve a query contributes to the higher average query resolution latency for comb needle approach.

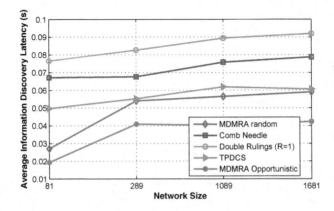

Fig. 6. Average information discovery latency Vs number of nodes in the network

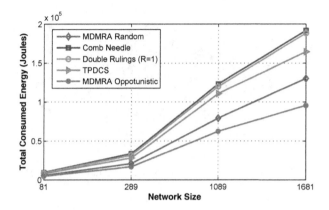

Fig. 7. Total consumed energy Vs number of nodes in the network

In Fig. 6 we present the results of the five different approaches with respect to average information discovery latency. We observe that the MDMRA opportunistic has the minimum average information discovery latency compared to the comb needle, double ruling, TPDCS and MDMRA random approaches.

In Fig. 7 we present the results of the total consumed energy for the different approaches.

We observe the energy consumption is the highest comb needle and double ruling approaches in comparison to the other three approaches. For MDMRA random consumes more energy due to synchronization of the attributes in the *inner-path* and the *level-paths* in different quadrants. The highest energy consumption by the comb needle approach can be attributed to the fact that in the comb needle scheme the pushing cost is very low while the query resolution cost is high. Consequently, the energy consumption will be high. In comparison, with the double ruling approach, the pushing cost is high (in terms of construction of the replication curve). The query resolution cost will be greater than the data dissemination cost (*i.e.,* the cost in terms of traveling along the retrieval

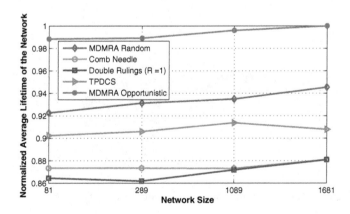

Fig. 8. Total consumed energy Vs number of nodes in the network

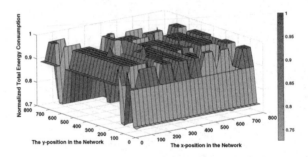

Fig. 9. The energy map for comb needle for network size 1089

curve and then to the storage point along the replication curve). TPDCS decentralizes the skewed data and queries by assigning data regions using a time dimension and data dimension. This reduces the query and storage hotspots across the network and hence, reduces total energy consumption. In Fig. 8, the results for the normalized lifetimes for the different approaches are presented. With the MDMRA random and MDMRA opportunistic approaches, the data dissemination cost varies based on the size of the inner-path and number of levels. However, with MDMRA random, the query resolution cost is low due to multi-resolution. Further, the opportunistic storage of data reduces the query resolution cost for ANY-type queries with the MDMRA opportunistic approach. Hence, the MDMRA opportunistic energy consumption tends to be quite low and has the highest residual energy compared to the other four approaches. As a result, MDMRA opportunistic has the highest lifetime compared with the other five approaches as shown in Fig. 8. Figures 9, 10, 11, 12 and 13 show the energy maps for normalized consumed energy for different algorithms. As shown in Figs. 9 and 13, the normalized consumed energy is equally distributed with MDMRA random and MDMRA opportunistic, with fewer hotspots. Further, the comb needle approach seems to consume more energy compared to other approaches.

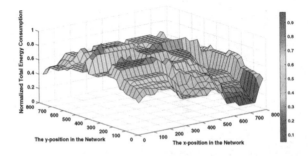

Fig. 10. The energy map for double rulings for network size 1089

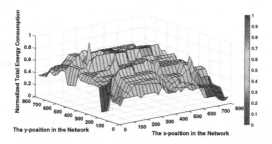

Fig. 11. The energy map for MDMRA random for network size 1089

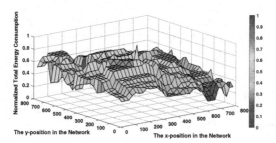

Fig. 12. The energy map for MDMRA opportunistic network size 1089

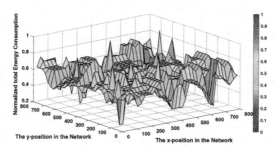

Fig. 13. The energy map for TPDCS network size 1089

5   Conclusion

In this paper, we have presented a novel approach which supports the storing of
multiple attributes with multi-resolution in a mission–critical autonomous multi-
dimensional WSNs. Multi-resolution with different information levels enables
fast query resolution and is important for information discovery in mission–
critical WSNs. The combined aim of MDMRA random is to increase network
lifetime and decrease query processing delay resulting in QoS improvements. Our
proposed information storage and distribution mechanism takes into account
the residual energy levels in individual sensors and proposed an energy efficient
routing mechanism. Further, the proposed MDMRA random enables fast query
response and energy efficient information discovery process.

References

1. Lamont, L., Mathieu, D., Patterson, G.: Tiered wireless sensor network architecture for military surveillance applications. In: The Fifth International Conference on Sensor Technologies and Applications, SENSORCOMM 2011, France, pp. 288–294 (2011)
2. Pannetier, B., Dezert, J., Sella, G.: Multiple target tracking with wireless sensor network for ground battlefield surveillance. In: 17th International Conference on Information Fusion (FUSION), pp. 1–8, July 2014
3. Mittal, P., Mitthal, A.: Target tracking in wireless sensor networks. Int. J. Comput. Sci. Manage. Stud. **14**(06), 98–104 (2014)
4. Sitanayah, L., Sreenan, C.J., Brown, K.N.: A hybrid MAC protocol for emergency response wireless sensor networks. Ad Hoc Netw. **20**, 77–95 (2014)
5. Yuan, W., Guan, D., Huh, E.-N., Lee, S.: Harness human sensor networks for situational awareness in disaster reliefs: a survey. IETE Tech. Rev. **30**(3), 240–247 (2013)
6. Doss, R., Li, G., Mak, V., Tissera, M.: Information discovery in mission-critical wireless sensor networks. Comput. Netw. **54**(14), 2383–2399 (2010)
7. Liu, C., Lee, C., Wang, L.: Distributed clustering algorithms for data-gathering in wireless mobile sensor networks. J. Parallel Distrib. Comput. **67**(11), 1187–1200 (2007)
8. Sarkar, R., Zhu, X., Gao, J.: Double rulings for information brokerage in sensor networks. In: Proceedings of the 12th Annual International Conference on Mobile Computing and Networking - MobiCom 2006, p. 286 (2006)
9. Park, Y., Seo, D., Yun, J., Ryu, C.T., Kim, J., Yoo, J.: An efficient data-centric storage method using time parameter for sensor networks. Inf. Sci. **180**(24), 4806–4817 (2010)
10. Liu, Y., Liu, K., Tao, W., Xu, Y.: A distributed index based multi-resolution data storage architecture in wireless sensor networks. In: First International Conference on Intelligent Networks and Intelligent Systems, pp. 174–177, November 2008
11. Palazzo, S., Cuomo, F., Galluccio, L.: Data aggregation in wireless sensor networks: a multifaceted perspective. In: Ferrari, G. (ed.) Sensor Networks. Signals and Communication Technology, pp. 103–143. Springer, Heidelberg (2009)
12. Andreou, P., Zeinalipour-Yazti, D., Pamboris, A.: Optimized query routing trees for wireless sensor networks. Inf. Syst. **36**(2), 267–291 (2011)
13. Akkaya, K., Younis, M.: A survey on routing protocols for wireless sensor networks. Ad Hoc Netw. **3**(3), 325–349 (2005)
14. Aly, M., Pruhs, K., Chrysanthis, P.K.: KDDCS : a load-balanced in-network data-centric storage scheme for sensor networks. In: CIKM 2006, Proceedings of the 15th ACM International Conference on Information and Knowledge Management, pp. 317–326. ACM (2006)
15. Seok, K.K., Saxena, N.: Analysis of a novel advanced greedy perimeter stateless routing algorithm. In: 2013 International Conference on ICT Convergence (ICTC), pp. 831–834, October 2013
16. Sanandaji, A., Jabbehdari, S., Balador, A., Kanellopoulos, D.: Mac layer misbehavior in manets. IETE Tech. Rev. **30**(4), 324–335 (2013)

A Review of Security Protocols in mHealth Wireless Body Area Networks (WBAN)

James Kang(⊠) and Sasan Adibi

School of Information Technology, Deakin University,
Burwood, Victoria, Australia
{jkang, sasan.adibi}@deakin.edu.au

Abstract. The popularity of smartphones has led to an increasing demand for health apps. As a result, the healthcare industry is embracing mobile technology and the security of mHealth is essential in protecting patient's user data and WBAN in a clinical setting. Breaches of security can potentially be life-threatening as someone with malicious intentions could misuse mHealth devices and user information. In this article, threats to security for mHealth networks are discussed in a layered approach addressing gaps in this emerging field of research. Suite B and Suite E, which are utilized in many security systems, including in mHealth applications, are also discussed. In this paper, the support for mHealth security will follow two approaches; protecting patient-centric systems and associated link technologies. Therefore this article is focused on the security provisioning of the communication path between the patient terminal (PT; e.g., sensors) and the monitoring devices (e.g., smartphone, data-collector).

1 Introduction

Security is considered a top priority in monitoring centre (MC) networks for health data processing and medical monitoring systems. WBAN, which is used for mHealth applications, also require proper security mechanisms in order to protect the individual's data and WBAN devices from malicious attackers. At the McAfee conference in 2011, Barnaby Jack demonstrated the hacking of an insulin pump [1] by overriding its default controls and injecting a deadly dose of insulin to the pumps. This occurred without any detailed knowledge of the device and highlighted the need for effective security measures for personal mHealth devices. Jack also demonstrated at the Melbourne Breakpoint security conference in 2012 [2] that a pacemaker transmitter could be reverse engineered and hacked to deliver a deadly electric shock with a maximum voltage of 830 volts, resulting in a simulated cardiac arrest as well as continuous shocks. While these examples illustrate attacks on devices on the human body, there are also large-scale risks such as attacks on MC networks or caregiver terminal (CT) databases, which have the potential capabilities to cause major damage to a large number of people. Security attacks can be approached from a Network (horizontal) and Protocol (vertical) perspective. The vertical approach looks at the threats and protocols from the OSI 7 layers whereas the horizontal approach looks at the mHealth network consisting of five sub networks including Wireless Sensor Network (WSN), WBAN, PT, MC and CT. Data traffic flows from the sensor devices in the

© Springer International Publishing Switzerland 2015
R. Doss et al. (Eds.): FNSS 2015, CCIS 523, pp. 61–83, 2015.
DOI: 10.1007/978-3-319-19210-9_5

WSN to the CT across the WBAN/PT and the MC. These areas are explained in the next subsections and also summarized in Fig. 1.

1.1   WSN

A WSN is normally consisted of sensors, monitoring devices and a sensor aggregation node [3]. Monitoring devices include sensors that are implanted inside or attached on the body such as neurostimulators, insulin pumps, electrocardiography (ECG), electroencephalography (EEG) and electromyography (EMG) sensors, cochlear implants, gastric stimulators and cardiac defibrillators [4]. Sensor aggregation node is a cluster of various sensors which connects with a PT to send and receive messages on a point to point, point to multipoint or routing protocol. Due to the limited resources of the sensor nodes such as less computing power and low source of battery power, typical security mechanisms cannot be used in WSNs. For this reason, the security mechanism of WSN should be designed with consideration to the constraints of the resources available. Apple iOS and Android devices occupy 94% of mobile devices used in the healthcare industry [5]. Some intelligent sensors are now being introduced in the market included in wearable devices such as Apple Watch and Samsung Gear. Wrist devices allow checking blood pressure, blood oxygen saturation, body temperature and heart rhythm to be checked. Samsung S5 smartphones allow heart rate tracking over time by simply scanning the finger [6]. Some smartphones and associated devices include embedded sensors such as accelerometers, magnetometers and gyroscopes and devices with these features are estimated to reach a total of 515 million units by 2017 [7]. For example, a tiny electrode sensor can be inserted under the skin to measure tissue fluid glucose levels and transmits it via a wireless radio frequency to a monitoring device. The communication can be done by Bluetooth Low Energy (BT-LE) [8].

1.2   WBAN

IEEE 802.15.6 specifies communication standards for low power wireless sensor devices worn on or implanted inside the human body that will communicate with health information collection devices [3]. WBAN consists of the WSN and PTs (smartphone and monitoring devices) with signaling protocol stacks and application. It accommodates approved frequency bands of national medical authorities as well as industrial scientific medical bands with data rates up to 10 Mbps supporting quality of service (QoS) [32]. The security of WBAN is discussed in detail in the security mechanisms section.

1.3   PT

The PT is equipped with mHealth application and database collection and storage functions with the ability for mobile communication as well as monitoring devices such as oximeters heart pulse monitors and blood pressure monitors which collect information from sensors. As some PTs such as smartphones allow for greater computing power and capacity of applications, it is possible to implement stronger and more resilient security mechanisms in PTs. Sensors are more focused on simplified functions which result in less security functions being implemented in WSN. In this article, PT mainly refers to processing units such as smartphones rather than monitoring devices which have less computational capacity.

1.4   MC

The MC health data processing and storage centre can be located on a Cloud network. A physician can access it to obtain the patient's data. Typical security network designs such as hardware and software firewalls, DMZ (Demilitarized Zone: subnet for external network facing) and checkpoints for MCs can be implemented. In order to secure the collected and processed data in the server, it requires additional security measures such as separating patients' personal information and health data (isolation), hardening, network separation, air-gapping and physical security which restrict access to the server and limits to trusted staffs [9].

1.5   CT

The CT has the database of a physician and can connect to the MC for patient's data. The physician's system decides on how to store the patient's data.. One possible security option is to switch the caregiver network offline during periods of no data transaction between the MC and the CT, or partially online during business hours, and turned offline after hours and so on. A general rule of online and Internet security may be applied to workers in the physician's office environment such as the mandatory installation of firewall software on every computer with regular updates. Education and training staff would also be an effective defense against attacks at the caregiver's network. Health information should be separated from the CT network after it has been used to avoid threats.

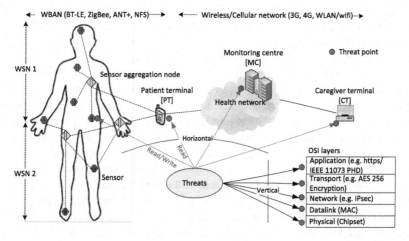

Fig. 1. mHealth network security threat points

2 Threats and Attacks

The motives of threats and attacks can be for personal reasons, financial gain, corporate espionage or terrorism. For mHealth threats, the motives can change based on the threat points as shown in Fig. 1. While attacks on WBAN can be more to do with personal reasons, attacks on the MC or CT can be targeted for financial or terrorism at a larger scale.

Methods of attacks are constantly evolving, however, they fall into two categories of passive and active attacks [10]. Passive attacks are intended to obtain health information via techniques such as eavesdropping and/or monitoring data being transmitted across mHealth networks. Active attacks attempt to modify the data stream and re-inject it into the network without changing the nature of communication, which makes the detection of these attacks difficult. Attacks can be done by initially accessing the network from within the WBAN, or externally by targeting the MC database or the CT network. The question is why the attacker targets an individual and with what motivation. Is it really important and worthwhile to implement strong security mechanisms on a personal WBAN network with constraints and limited physical access such as a 5 to 30 m diameter from the target? Some users may not require or want high security levels as it may compromise processing power. Therefore, users should be able to choose the level of security they want in their WBAN. For example, Federal Information Processing Standard (FIPS) Publication 140-2 is a US government security standard which defines four levels of security for cryptographic modules [11].

Threats on sensor nodes can be on two areas: sensors and monitoring devices. Sensors in general have very simple functions on layers 1 and 2 collecting data and sending it through to monitoring devices which have higher layer functions and are able to communicate with smartphones (smart sensors are discussed later in the article). Some monitoring devices are intelligent and able to interact with PT (smartphone) where threats can occur at various layers including the physical, data link, network, transport and application layers across the monitoring devices and the smartphone. There can be two activities in the attacks including monitoring and capturing of message content and traffic analysis which can be mitigated by masking the information using encryption. The other attack is to modify the data and inject it into the mHealth network so that the attacker can achieve what they intended to provide in the modified content. These are shown as 'read' and 'read/write' in Fig. 1.

Open source sniffing devices can easily capture Bluetooth and Bluetooth Low Energy (BT-LE) signals and data between sensors and PTs. This sniffing device can be purchased online or constructed at home according to an open source manual from affordable parts with software that is provided [12]. It can also be purchased off the shelf in many countries. This allows potential attackers to develop a hacking device without investing large amounts of money for equipment being used by labs and vendors in the industry. If a security mechanism has been implemented in this case, it will make it difficult to hack the security code and obtain the data whilst traffic analysis is still able to be done by the sniffing device. Michael Ossman built and presented Ubertooth One at Shmoocon conference in 2011 [13]. This device allows for Bluetooth Basic Rate injection, BT-LE monitoring and injection, 802.11 FHSS monitoring and injection, and basic spectrum monitoring [12]. This kind of device can be used by attackers to intercept health information of mHealth users posing privacy concerns. There is also the threat of the ability to modify information which could be used to directly manipulate monitoring devices to perform a malicious task such as delivering a lethal dose of insulin. It is only a matter of time for this simple device to evolve and be capable of attacking all layers such as DoS (denial of service) from the physical layer up to the application layer.

As mHealth protocols are based on an OSI 7 layer model, various threats may occur at each of these specific vertical layers. Therefore, the threats will be discussed from a layered approach as security mechanisms can also be approached at each layer. For example, the National Security Agency (NSA) Suite B can be deployed at the Application, Transportation and Network layers [14]. In the case of dumb sensors which is only responsible for collecting data and delivering it to the data collector such as monitoring devices or PT without providing any additional services, physical and media access control (MAC) layers may be the only layers applicable (MAC layer is a sub layer of the data link layer). The following shows some of the types of attacks at each layer, and they always evolve along with technologies.

2.1   Layer 1 (Physical Layer)

The physical layer sometimes termed PHY provides the means of transmitting raw bits (bit stream) via frequency and modulation in the form of electronic signals. Attacks can be made by transmitting the same frequency bandwidth to the target area so that the receiving device may have additional noise and changed phased of signal.

Jamming: Jamming involves interfering with a network's radiofrequency signals in an attempt to disrupt communication between nodes. Defenses against jamming include spread-spectrum communication techniques such as frequency hopping and code spreading.

Tampering: If an attacker is able to physically gain access to a node, they can be altered or replaced with a node controlled by the attacker. They may also obtain sensitive information such as encryption keys and other data available on the node. Defenses include protecting the physical package to prevent the incidence of tampering.

2.2   Layer 2 (Data Link Layer)

In a broadcasting domain, there can be a collision when transmitting logical bits (frames) to adjacent nodes within the same local area network. The data link protocol prevents this by specifying how devices detect and recover errors. MAC flooding is a common attack in this layer.

Collision: When two nodes attempt to simultaneously transmit data on the same frequency. A typical defense against collisions is the use of error-correcting codes [15].

Exhaustion: An attacker can cause resource depletion by making many repetitive collisions. A defense is to prevent the energy drain by limiting rates to the MAC admission control allowing the network to ignore excessive requests.

Unfairness: An attacker can cause other nodes to miss their transmission deadline and undermine the communication channel capacity.

2.3   Layer 3 (Network Layer)

Across WSNs in between or to WBAN, a routing is required to transmit data through the network layer which will be carried over lower layers as a payload including origination and destination information. Routing attacks and distributed denial of service (DDoS) are common in this layer making resources unavailable by using multiple compromised systems to target a single device or system.

Selective Forwarding: A compromised node blocks packets in the network by rejecting to forward or block messages that pass through them. They also redirect the message to a different path to create false routing information. A defense includes using multiple paths to send data as well as attempting to detect the malicious node.

Sinkhole Attack: A compromised node advertises false routing information to attract all network traffic in a certain area to pass through that node [16].

Sybil Attacks: A single node in a network claims multiple identities and thus presents itself in more than one location. The attack aims at fault tolerant schemes such as distributed storage, multipath routing and topology maintenance. This can be defended against by authentication and encryption techniques.

Wormholes Attacks: An attacker gets packets at a point in the network and tunnels them to another point and replays them into the network from that point.

HELLO Flood Attacks: An attacker floods HELLO requests to legitimate nodes using a high-powered transmitter to override the security of WSNs. Cryptography is currently the main solution to this type of attack, but it suffers from limitations of computational complexity [17].

2.4   Layer 4 (Transport Layer)

The transport layer provides end to end communication system with intelligent functionality such as flow control and multiplexing.

Flooding: Where an attacker floods a network with large amounts of traffic so its resources are unable to handle the connection requests. As a result no further genuine connections can be made as the server has reached a maximum limit. A security mechanism against this is to require each client to solve a puzzle.

De-synchronization: Repeatedly sending messages to disrupt the established connection between two nodes.

2.5   Layer 5, 6 and 7 (Application Layer)

As the top layer of protocols, it communicates with end users in the form of application software such as smartphone apps. Since its usage and scopes are broad, there are many types of attacks such as DDoS which can consume the bandwidth with volumetric SYN floods followed by HTTP floods for instance. The attacks also disrupt transactions and access to database so that service can be denied with lack of resources which were taken by the attack.

3 Security Services

Security services mitigate threats and attacks and are provided by a protocol layer of communicating open systems to ensure adequate security of a system or of data transfers [18]. Security categories are divided into three major areas which include Confidentiality (information disclosure), Integrity (information modification) and Availability (information denial) also known as the C.I.A Triad [19]. mHealth networks including WSN, WBAN/PT, MC and CT require stringent and scalable security measures at all levels (layers) from application and transport layers up to physical layer [15].

3.1 Confidentiality

A patient's identity is authenticated by providing evidence that it holds the specified identity. These include digital certificates and signatures, tokens and passwords between WSN devices in addition to being registered in WBAN, which connects to a MC in a similar manner. This function is one of the most important roles of security before transferring any data. However it is also the most vulnerable when attacked [15, 20].

3.2 Data Integrity

Data collected and stored in a device or system of mHealth should be protected so that it cannot be accessed or altered by an unauthorized party to ensure that the data received is exactly the same as sent by an authorized entity [18, 21]. A patient's personal and health data can be separated with further security mechanisms so that attackers cannot identify the patient of the health data. This could be achieved if the health data stored in the MC or the CT does not store personal information such as names and health data in the same place but uses a randomly generated identification number. A patient's health data should also be protected from being extracted and re-injected into the same database to prevent manipulation of the data.

3.3 Availability

When a patient's monitoring device such as an insulin pump or pacemaker malfunctions, it is critical for a caregiver to communicate with the monitoring device as well as the patient as it may result in a loss of life. Switching to another node in the network from the attacked node can be an option and the network and system design should allow this redundancy even though it won't be necessary to have high availability such as full redundancy at all networks except the MC [15]. Health data should be available when needed and include a timestamp to avoid invalid treatment by caregivers. For example, the condition of the patient may change on an hourly basis and the caregiver may treat the patient with the most recent information which could be up to a few hours old due to the delay of data transmission from factors such as a network outage in a remote or rural region. Freshness of the data is important and the age of the data should be defined [20].

3.4 Privacy Policy

According to a study conducted in 2014, only 30.5% of the 600 most popular medical apps had a privacy policy including Android and Apple devices. Users of the apps are targeted for marketing and their personal and health information may be sold without their permission [22]. Privacy of mHealth is important as it includes collected information over a long term period of time as well as a broader range of personal information such as a patient's lifestyle and activities. Patients' health data is treated with confidentiality as is the case in offline hospitals and medical centers, and should not be distributed to other organizations or entities without the written consent from the owner of the health data. It is required by strict policies, laws and regulations as health information is sensitive material and can be detrimental to the owner if it is disclosed. Therefore, the privacy of patient's health data in a mHealth system should be securely protected and understood by personnel involved. Education and training via a certification program should also be considered [15]. The table below depicts extended security services further than the ITU-T X.800 and CIA Triad based on the mHealth network areas of threat points (Table 1).

Table 1. Security service categories within mHealth networks

Security category	WSN	WBAN	MC	CT
Confidentiality (C)	x	x	x	x
Data integrity (I)	x	x	x	x
Availability (A)	x	x	x	x
Privacy		x	x	x
Authentication	x	x	x	x
Authorization	x	x	x	x

4 Security Mechanisms

Security mechanisms refer to security protocols and security algorithms designed to prevent attacks from occurring. This section will cover two popular security protocols which are key management and route discovery protocols, and one security algorithm which is Suite B (and Suite E drafted by IETF) cryptography designed by the NSA. IEEE 802.15.6 provides a security protocol for WBAN. An algorithm is a procedure that is used to encrypt data for use in cryptography, whereas a security protocol describes how an algorithm should be used [23]. There are two cryptography algorithms; Symmetric and Asymmetric. Symmetric algorithm refers to using same keys for both encryption and decryption, and has the advantage of using less computational power. However, it is more vulnerable if the key is disclosed. Some well-known examples are Advanced Encryption Standard (AES), Data Encryption Standard (DES), 3DES, International Data Encryption Algorithm (IDEA), CAST5 (developed by Carlisle Adams and Stafford Tavares using 128 bits key size), Blowfish, Twofish, Revest Cypher 4 (RC4). Asymmetric algorithm requires two keys, one for encryption and another for decryption. The encryption key is used by all, and therefore it is called the public key, whereas the decryption key is kept secret and is called the private key which is not shared by all. For example, a smartphone may use private and public keys to communicate with monitoring devices which will use the public key given by the smartphone to encrypt and send data, which is then decrypted by the smartphone using the private key. There are RSA (Rivest Shamir Adleman), DSA (digital signature algorithm) and ElGamal for asymmetric algorithms. Asymmetric algorithm was first published by Diffie and Hellmann [24, 25]. Key management protocols are popular including many various public key infrastructures. Lightweight Public Key Infrastructure (L-PKI) is recommended for WSN and WBAN as it provides energy efficient security features suitable for the limitations of WSN devices [26]. Mohammed Faisal et al. recommended Secure and Energy-efficient Cluster based Multipath Routing (SECMRP) protocol for the route discovery protocol along with L-PKI within WSN as it prevents internal, passive and impersonation attacks. SECMRP provides a phased approach including route discovery, data transmission and route maintenance in a secured manner [27].

4.1 Authentication

In order to identify legitimate nodes between mHealth devices, there is a process required to identify whether the received data is coming from the authentic nodes. There is also a process to identify the user at the application level to access the smartphone using various methods such as user ID and password, fingerprint or retina scanning, voice recognition and so on. Security mechanisms can provide the authentication process before transmitting data. There are numerous types of technology used such as certificate, digital ID, bio-metric, two-factors and proximity [28]. If a patient loses their smartphone, there must be a way for them to securely regain connection with their sensor devices. Being able to authenticate the user when bringing in a new sensor device or a new processing device and securely integrating into the existing network must also be considered. For instance, certificates can be downloaded from the Certificate Authority (CA) onto the PT which will also require a preset password from the application software to be paired up with the replacing unit. The password should never be stored on the smartphone but stored with a hash function such as Secure Hash Algorithm 2 (SHA2) which can be encrypted and used by the smartphone to verify and authenticate the user.

4.2   Authorization

Whereas authentication is the process to identify legitimate nodes or users within WBAN, authorization is required to allow users such as patients or caregivers to access MC database to populate information required. For instance, physicians may have a different privilege level of access to health data than patients and health service providers. Within WBAN, sensors may have different rights to collect certain data and send them to certain destinations. For instance, cluster sensors may have a different authorization level to the other sensors.

4.3   IEEE 802.15.6 WBAN Security Protocol

IEEE 802.5 Wireless Personal Area Network (WPAN) task group 6 (TG6) Body Area Network (BAN/WBAN) developed a communication protocol for low power devices which also covers WBAN including security protocols. IEEE 802.15.6 standard security network topology has two entities, nodes and hubs. A node contains MAC and PHY layers, and a hub has a node's functionality and manages the medium access and power management of the nodes. All nodes and hubs have to select one of three security levels: unsecured communication, authentication but no encryption, and both authentication and encryption. There is a procedure of security association to identity a node and a hub with each other using a master key (MK) followed by generating a pairwise temporal key (PTK) which is used for unicast communication only once per session. For multicast communication, a group temporal key (GTP) is generated and shared with the corresponding group. Before the exchange of data, all nodes and hubs pass through various states at the MAC layer including Orphan, Associated, Secured and Connected for secured communication, while Orphan and Connected state are used for unsecured communication. Security association and disassociation procedure is done by typical three handshake phases (request, response, activate (or erase)). A 13 octet nonce is used for each instance of CCM (Counter with CBC-MAC, which refers to Cipher Block Chaining Message Authentication Code) frame authentication and encryption/decryption. Along with the MAC header, low-order security sequence number (LSSN) and high-order security sequence number are used to synchronize the frames [29]. There are four two-party key agreement protocols to generate a master key which can be used in IEEE 802.15.6: Unauthenticated, Hidden public key transfer authenticated, Password authenticated and Display authenticated key agreement protocols and procedures. All of them are based on elliptic curve public key cryptography. However Toorani argues that IEEE 802.5.16 is vulnerable to different attacks such as key-compromise impersonation (KCI), unknown key-share (UKS) and Denning-Sacco attacks [30, 31].

4.4   Key Management Protocols

Sarah Irum et al. [26] proposed using hybrid techniques for key generation. As opposed to the existing key management technique which pre-loads generated keys, this suggests generating keys using physiological values (PVs) of the human body, which are used for the sensor nodes to calculate keys. Key management systems have evolved into various sub areas to suit the purpose of various security requirements. A public key infrastructure (PKI) utilizes a CA in order to manage public keys. Many PKIs use asymmetric key algorithms such as Diffie-Hellman and RSA which consume a lot of resources and power [32]. High energy consumption in WSNs due to their limitation of resources is not ideal and there have been several proposed solutions to implementing PKI with this consideration in mind. While there are many proprietary key management systems such as TinyPK, μPKI and L-PKI, L-PKI can be considered for WSN/WBAN as it supports all of authentication, confidentiality, non-repudiation and scalability that is suitable for the resource-constrained platforms such as a wireless network of WSN and WBAN whereas other PKIs only provide a partial of these services [27]. L-PKI is based on Elliptic Curve Cryptography (ECC) to decrease its computational cost and consists of various components: Registration Authority (RA), CA, Digital certificates, Certificate Repository, Validation Authority (VA), Key generating server (KGS), End entities (smartphone) and Timestamp server. Compared to a traditional modular exponentiation (RSA) which is not suitable for the resource-constraint network such as WSN, L-PKI with an ECC based system requires significantly smaller keys which increase efficiency. For example, 160 bit keys in an ECC based system has the same level of security as those of a 1024 bit keys in an RSA based system [33]. The focus of key management systems are scalability and power efficiency as these are the deciding factors to what level of security mechanisms to implement in WSN and WBAN. For example, light weight data confidentiality and authentication algorithms might be implemented differently in WSN to WBAN as both networks have different hardware capacities [34].

While the number of keys generated in WSN is limited due to the constraint of power and computational capacity, it is possible to implement a full scale security mechanism in smartphones to store and transmit health data and patient information to MC. To generate a master key, a user login and password is required for key generation along with other information such as user random salt, fixed salt and iteration count, which will be used for encryption of health data, patient information, and account information before sending it to MC via a secured channel such as SSL/TLS and IPSec.

4.5   Route Discovery Protocols

In a simple sensor network, data exchange may occur by point to point between nodes without requiring a routing protocol, however a comprehensive network will require routing to provide path redundancy and efficient communication within the network. Route discovery protocols are used within the WSN to communicate with a PT (base station) where intelligent routing is required to find the shortest or better path within the WSN including cluster header. Secure and Energy Efficient Multipath (SEEM) Routing Protocol does not use the lowest energy route but rather finds multiple paths to the source of the data and selects one of them to use [35]. However, SEEM does not have cryptographic mechanisms and only provides security services for balancing. Intrusion-Tolerant Routing Protocol for Wireless Sensor Networks (INSENS) is also a multipath routing protocol designed to reduce the computational power and resources required. SECMRP uses secure route discovery, secure data transmission and route maintenance phases. It uses L-PKI and is a proposed route discovery protocol designed to be suitable for WSNs. It is able to provide security services for authentication, confidentiality, integrity, balancing and scalability whereas SEEM can only provide balancing and INSENS is unable to provide scalability.

4.6   NSA Suite B and E Algorithm

The approval and support for the use of the NSA Suite B cryptography in the public and private sectors is growing. The Australian Department of Defence officially approved the use of Suite B cryptography in 2012 to protect confidential information [36] while companies such as Cisco are now moving forward to accept Suite B cryptography to replace their previous proprietary security mechanisms. The NSA has also designed an IPSec Conformance Evaluator tool to allow the validation of vendor products and their compliance to NSA Suite B standards [37]. The NSA has promoted and made Suite B widely known in addition to the existing Suite A which is a set of algorithms [38]. The current evolution of cryptography from industry to NSA Suite B can be seen below [39] and it continues to evolve.

- Encryption: IPsec: 56-bit DES -> 168-bit Triple DES (3DES) -> 128-bit AES (Galois/Counter Mode [GCM] and Galois Message Authentication Code [GMAC]) -> 256-bit AES (GCM and GMAC)
- Digital Signature: Short RSA Keys -> 2048-bit RSA Keys -> Elliptic Curve Digital Signature Algorithm (ECDSA)
- Hashing: MD5 -> SHA-1 -> SHA-256 -> SHA-384 and SHA-512
- Key Exchange: Diffie-Hellman -> Elliptic Curve Diffie-Hellman (ECDH) (using P-256 and P-384 curves)

Since being accepted in industry by integrating Suite B, the military, government agencies, and both the public and private sectors can share information over the internet and non-trusted networks by increasing the security of sensitive content such as intellectual property and employee information [39]. It is now required to consider how Suite B should be implemented across mHealth networks as issues still remain on computational capacity with constraints of power limitations in WSN and WBAN. There was a need to develop a modified version of Suite B to suit handheld devices such as smartphones as Suite B is mainly used for larger systems. Suite E is lightweight and energy efficient which is suitable for smaller devices running WBAN that require low power consumption. Suite E components as shown in Table 2 are mainly designed to provide smaller certificate sizes, low computational complexity, bandwidth usage reduction and one way compression function. Suite E uses easily embeddable algorithms to reduce overall costs of running the system [14]. ECQV (elliptic curve Qu-Vanstone) implicit certificate scheme is used with a set of standard symmetric key and elliptic curve public key to provide 128-bit cryptographic security in Suite E, which also includes Elliptic Curve Menezes-Qu-Vanstone (ECMQV) key agreement protocol and Elliptic Curve Pinstov Vanstone Signature (ECPVS) signature scheme with message recovery for compact signed messages [40]. Detailed information of functionality of Suite E has been specified in IETF Draft document (2011) [41] along with other security standards being developed such as Standards being developed in the

Standards for Efficient Cryptography Group (SECG) and ANSI X9 [42]. Depending on the classification of security, different components are used such as AES with 128 bit keys, which is used up to the secret level and AES with 256 bit keys for the top secret level. The components of Suite B and E are shown below:

Table 2. Suite B and E algorithm [42]

Components of suite B	Suite E	Function
AES (128 or 256 bit key size)	AES-CCM/CGM	Encryption
ECDSA (256 or 384 bit prime moduli)	ECPVS/ECQV	Digital signatures/certificate
ECDH	ECMQV	Key agreement
SHA 2 (SHA-256 and SHA-384)	SHA2/AES-MMO	Message digest

4.7 Application Specific Security Mechanisms

Security mechanisms may be incorporated into the appropriate protocol layers in order to provide some of the OSI security services. They include: encipherment, digital signature, access control, data integrity, authentication exchange, traffic padding, routing protocol, notarization, trusted functionality, security label, even detection, security audit trail and security recovery [43].

5 Security of Application and Communication Protocols

While security mechanisms provide protocols and algorithms to securely transfer data, application and communication protocols are also required to transfer health information between sensors and a PT as shown in Fig. 1. This section looks at the security aspect of popular communication protocols including ANT+, ZigBee, Bluetooth/Bluetooth Low Energy (BT-LE), which were chosen as popular and emerging technologies with their market penetration (ANT+), Ultra low-power (BT-LE), low-power mesh networks with flexible routing (ZigBee). IEEE 11073 Personal Health Device (PHD) standard is also discussed in this section as an application protocol as it specifies how to exchange messages on top of the communications protocols as depicted in Fig. 4.

5.1 ANT/ANT+

ANT+ technology is preinstalled on many smartphones, particularly those by Samsung and Sony Ericsson [44]. ANT is a communication protocol whereas ANT+ is a managed network which allows interoperability between WBAN devices. For example, ANT+ enabled monitoring devices can work together to assemble and track performance metrics which provide a user with an overall view of their fitness. They provide ultra-low power wireless, high value at low costs, ease of development and interoperability as an open source for Android developers [45]. ANT communication protocol allows ANT+ installed devices to communicate with any product that uses this technology, universalizing its compatibility between all products with the ANT+ feature.

ANT+ also offers off the shelf packages including both the required sensor devices and the application. Similar to BT-LE, ANT can be configured in a low power sleep mode and wake up only when communication is required followed by returning to sleep mode afterwards. ANT channels are bi-directional supporting various messaging types [44]:

- Broadcast messaging: a one-way communication from point to point or point to multi-point. There is no need to acknowledge from the receiving node to the sender
- Acknowledged messaging: there is confirmation of the receipt of data packets whether it has been successful or failed, even though there is no re-sending of packets
- Burst messaging: a multi-transmission technique with the full bandwidth usage and acknowledges that it is sent with the re-sending feature for corrupted packets

5.2   ZigBee

ZigBee is a specification for communication protocols designed to be used in creating personal area networks. ZigBee is designed to provide simple and energy efficient connectivity between devices and is less complex than devices that use Bluetooth [46]. Due to its low power consumption and secure and easy management, ZigBee is used in many mHealth technologies. The ZigBee standard builds upon the IEEE 802.15.4 which provides Physical (PHY) and MAC layer, and provides security services for key exchange and authentication [47]. Security of ZigBee is based on a 128 bit AES algorithm in addition to the security model provided by IEEE 802.15.4. The trust centre provides authentication for devices requesting to join the network as well as maintaining and updating a new network key. ZigBee uses three types of keys including Master, Network and Link keys.

- Master key: Trust centre master keys and Application layer master keys
- Network keys: Provides ZigBee network layer security being shared by all network devices using the same key
- Link keys: Provides security between two devices at the application layer

ZigBee provides two security modes such as standard and high. High security mode provides network layer security (with a network key), application layer security (with a link key), centralized control of keys (with Trust centre), ability to switch from active to secondary keys, ability to derive link keys between devices and entity authentication and permissions table whereas the standard security mode does not provide the last two items of the high security mode.

5.3   Bluetooth/(BT-LE)

Bluetooth is a standard designed for the wireless transfer of data over short distances. While BT-LE reduced the number of channels to 40 with 2 MHz wide channels to minimize the energy consumption such as a tenth of the energy consumption of

Bluetooth [48], Bluetooth uses a frequency of 2.402 GHz to 2.480 GHz allowing communication on 79 channels with spread-spectrum frequency hopping which is called adaptive frequency hopping for robust and reliable transmission, and reduces the instances of interference between two or more devices [49]. While Bluetooth provides 2 mbps, BT-LE provides up to ~ 100 kbps payload throughput with much less energy consumed [50] by remaining in constant sleep mode until a connection is initiated [51]. Bluetooth packets show the LAP (lower address part) of a particular Bluetooth device address (BD_ADDR) which is a 48 bit MAC address. Lower 24 bit of the BD_ADDR is LAP (or device ID) which is transmitted with packets while upper 24 bit is a manufacturer's ID. In other words, a different LAP refers to a different Bluetooth device.

A simulation was conducted to investigate the effects of encryption and no encryption on packet size during data transfer over Bluetooth. For this simulation, Bluetooth packets were captured using Android 4.4 Bluetooth HCl snoop feature and decoded using the Wireshark protocol analyzer (v1.12) software. Figures 2 and 3 illustrates the message captured between two devices via Bluetooth during the simulation of data transfer between a sensor and a PT (smartphone) with no encryption and no compression. It shows the decoded captured message which is viewable including the source and destination device address using LAP (i.e. lower half of MAC address) as well as the content of the information (scan event report of the sensor) transmitted between the two Bluetooth devices. Figure 4 shows the data captured with the file compressed and encrypted with AES-256 with a private key which does not allow the content to be viewed. Sample message transferred:

object handle 1
nu-obvs-val-simp 60.7
2014-12-23 4:30:59

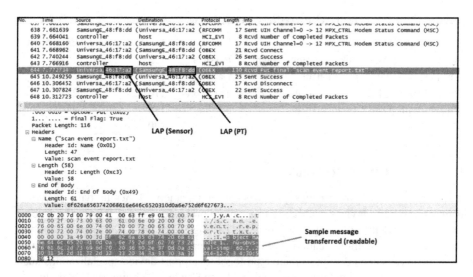

Fig. 2. Bluetooth packet capture (No compression or encryption)

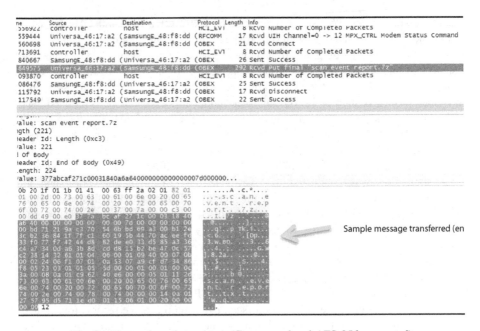

Fig. 3. Bluetooth packet capture (Compressed and AES 256 encrypted)

A comparison between the transmitted file with no compression and no encryption versus the file with compression and encryption is detailed in the table below. It shows that the latter includes 124 % more than the former, while the gap will be smaller for larger packet size. This implies that encryption will use more resources (Table 3).

Table 3. Packet size comparison with encryption

Bluetooth protocols	Layers	No encryption	Encryption
Bluetooth HCI ACL packet data total length	Physical	125	287
Bluetooth L2CAP protocol length	Data link	121	283
Payload length (RFCOMM protocol)	Transport	116	277
Packet length (OBEX protocol)	Session	116	277
Capture length		130 bytes	292 bytes

5.4 IEEE P11073 PHD Protocol

IEEE 11073 health informatics provides communication of health data exchange between mHealth devices such as sensors, monitoring device and PT at a high level (layer 5–7) as depicted in Fig. 4 whereas ANT+, ZigBee or BT-LE only provides low-level (layer 1–4) communication protocols in mHealth [52]. IEEE 11073-20601 provides the base standard with exchange protocol to support device specializations such as a pulse oximeter, blood pressure monitor, thermo-meter, weighing scale and glucose monitoring device. It covers the data exchange between the agent (sensors) and the manager (PT) on top of communication protocols such as Bluetooth and ZigBee, however, it does not specify what the manager does with the data transmitted from the agent. Interestingly, it treats the agents (sensors) as a 'server' and the manager as a 'client', which means that the sensors initiate communication with its manager rather than the manager initiating the communication with the sensors.

IEEE 11073 protocols do not address security in their PHD standard documents. PHD standard family mainly focuses on application-level data exchange and hardly provide a method to ensure security of data exchange rather than providing proper security mechanisms [53]. Instead, the area of security is up to the vendors, who may choose to independently build security mechanisms on top of the P11073 standard. This work group operates under the assumption that security measures are dealt with by lower layers such as secured transport channel.

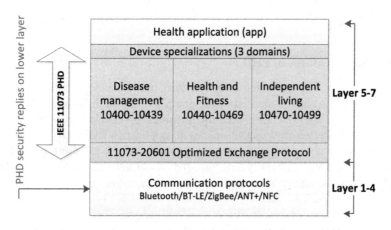

Fig. 4. IEEE 11073 PHD protocols

6 Future Areas of Study

6.1 Security and Quality of Sensor Device

When a patient is equipped or implanted with sensors, there must be a way to verify that the sensor device will work properly as malfunctions or invalid data will critically affect the treatment or prescription by the caregiver. Also at a physical layer, there is a way of providing encryption with keys embedded within sensor chipsets which will be installed by manufacturers. This will make attacks harder, however, it is required to replace the key by reconfiguring keys stored in the memory when it has been compromised and listed in the blacklist. Portilla et al. proposed that both a hardware and software solution is more energy efficient than a software only solution for WSNs [54]. Embedding keys in the device's memory will require more storage capacity. Also, implementing security mechanisms requires extra bandwidth to transfer data which brings up the issue of power capacity limitations [3]. Future areas to consider may include utilizing combinations of both preloading keys and generating keys on the device which has been shown to increase efficiency [26], as well as solving issues of power capacity limitations. Such solutions may include wireless charging or self-generation of power [55].

6.2   Privacy

The question of how to manage the separation of user information and health data has not yet been addressed. As the health information may be processed and used by various parties such as caregivers and health service provides, government agencies for each purposes in homogeneous or heterogeneous networks, it is crucial to protect the identification and confidentiality of patients. One option to prevent identifying information could be to store personal information and health data in physically separated networks and to implement a median device between them with strong firewall and security functions applied.

6.3   Security Measures in PHD

There are currently no plans to implement security mechanisms under the IEEE 11073 PHD work group. Although the PHD work group focuses on the application layer and accordingly, does not deal with security measures on the lower layers, it is still important to provide security mechanisms for the application layer as some threats such as DoS can occur at any layer. A study is required on how to ensure the PHD data transfer with underplayed security structure, and how it interacts with various mHealth networks with standardized and complied protocols at lower layers.

6.4   Compatibility and Standardization of Security Protocols Versus Application Protocols

Collected health data has little value until it has been properly processed and analyzed by algorithms to create meaningful data for physicians. For this purpose, it is better to collect more information across heterogeneous networks rather than less. With various standards and technologies being utilized by multiple vendors, the interoperability of WSN devices within a homogeneous network is an important requirement to consider as it affects security. In order to process health information collected across heterogeneous networks, the data format should be processed by a MC to focus on efficiency. As mHealth technology covers end to end networks from WSN to the caregiver's terminal which is including various entities of standard bodies such as IEEE, ITU-T and IETF, it is envisaged that a couple of popular standards may be used in the long term rather than various and incompatible standards. This will rely upon the cooperation and efforts of vendors to participate and discuss on agreements. Ultimately it will be up to the end users to influence and decide which standards to be used. While there are many proprietary routing protocols being used within WSN, it is required to include this in international standard category such as IEEE/ISO so that manufacturers are able to adopt at higher layers such as transport and upwards.

6.5   Unique Identifiers as an Authentication Mechanism

Over an extended period of time, certain patterns from the data collected by sensors may arise which is specific to an individual. For instance, metabolic patterns of an individual may become apparent and be used with other collected data to act as a "fingerprint" for authentication purposes. Utilizing a person's physiological, biological and metabolic characteristics for use in security mechanisms can be a possible area of study in the future to consider [26]. Sensor nodes can also be verified using its pattern of battery consumption. It is unlikely that other sensors will have the same pattern and this can be used to verify that the data came from the authentic sensor. An abnormal change in this pattern could indicate a malfunction or an attack which can be used as a prompt to manually check the device.

6.6   User Centeredness

It is important that the patient is able to have a level of control over their own information [3] such as the ability to stop the transmission of data to a health service provider for privacy purposes. Patients should be able to control the collected data and to whom it is provided even though the data can be owned and maintained by a caregiver or hospital in the form of medical records. This is particularly important as mHealth is extending to wearable devices for the general public for fitness, dietary and other health purposes with the release of the Apple Watch as well as other Android devices. Users of these devices should have the ability to benefit from the information that they provide such as being able to track and view real time data collected by the MC. For example, being able to track their own weight data against mean weight patterns in their geographic area and ages will help improve their willingness to exercise. A diabetic may be able to see the trends of food consumption and relevant criteria of other diabetics in order to help make an informed decision to improve eating habits.

6.7   Intelligent Sensors with QoS

Apart from sensors attached in or on a body, sensors may be installed as part of furniture or a room and designed to wirelessly monitor information such as body temperature and other health data of the person inside. These sensors have the potential to be smarter than sensors on the body as they have greater access to power and other resources whilst out of the body. By expanding the WBAN network to include a defined physical space rather than the dynamic area around a person only, sensors do not necessarily have to be in or on the body which may be intrusive to the wearer while they are in that space such as a hospital room. This will expand security capabilities as well as increasing QoS issues. QoS can also be implemented with smart sensors which will have computational and power capacity. For example, information related to vital signs should be transmitted with priority over other traffic using the same connection such as internet of things and personal computers.

7 Conclusion

The threats of mHealth networks have been addressed from a layered approach, taking into consideration some commonly applied and standardized security mechanisms. This article illustrated that the increasing popularity of NSA Suite B Cryptography is trending amongst both the government and private sectors which can also be used by mHealth with Suite E which is modified to suit smaller devices with lower power consumption. IEEE 11073 PHD protocols used by mHealth currently do not address security issues in their PHD standard documents. It is up to the vendors to provide the security implementations. As security threats are present at all layers, it is important that further studies in all layers of protocols are conducted to address the risks of attacks. For example, encryption keys can be embedded into the chipset by the manufacturer to enhance layer 1 security.

WBAN and WSN security provide a personal level of security, as opposed to large scale threats in a homogeneous network at the MC and the caregiver's network. This risk will become even greater if the network combines with other heterogeneous networks to share, process and store collected data. This area is beyond the scope of WBAN and requires an overall approach to designing and implementing network security solutions at the public network service provider's level.

BT-LE is popular in many handheld devices and provides a more robust and cost efficient technology than classic Bluetooth technology. BT-LE consumes much less power as it has sleep mode and uses fewer channels. This aspect is important for mHealth WBANs, as a low energy consumption communication protocol allows for more resources to be dedicated to security related purposes.

As reviewed with security mechanisms, communication protocols and algorithms continue to evolve towards focusing on improving energy efficiency such as BT to BT-LE and Suite A/B to Suite E. Low energy consumption will be a core characteristic that will affect the development and security of mHealth technologies.

At the same time, the motivation of attacks targeting WBAN may not provide enough justification to implement high standard security measures which increases the battery consumption of sensor devices. Instead, it may be better to utilise the power capacity for enhanced collection and transfer of health information. Furthermore, not everyone will require high security measures such as the general public or in developing countries where people may be more interested with other features such as having reliable access to health services. It is important to provide different levels of mHealth security so that users can choose the level to suit their needs, just as consumers have the right to access better health services at their own will.

References

1. Barnaby Jack. http://en.wikipedia.org/wiki/Barnaby_Jack
2. The Good Hacker Barnaby Jack Dies. http://www.thedailybeast.com/articles/2013/07/26/the-good-hacker-barnaby-jack-dies.html. Accessed 17 Dec 2014

3. Adibi, S.: Link technologies and blackberry mobile health (mHealth) solutions: a review. IEEE Trans. Inf. Technol. Biomed. **16**(4), 586–597 (2012)
4. Rushanan, M., Rubin, A.D., Kune, D.F., Swanson, C.M.: SoK: security and privacy in implantable medical devices and body area networks. In: 2014 IEEE Symposium on Security and Privacy, pp. 524–539, May 2014
5. Citrix. Mobile Analytics report (2015)
6. Android Central. How to use the Heart Rate Monitor on the Galaxy S5. http://www.androidcentral.com/how-use-heart-rate-monitor-galaxy-s5. Accessed 11 Feb 2015
7. mHealth news. Are you ready for sensors in healthcare? http://www.mhealthnews.com/content/infographic-are-you-ready-sensors-healthcare. Accessed 11 Feb 2015
8. FierceMobileHealthcare. mHealth devices must auto-collect data from cloud, sensors (2014). http://www.fiercemobilehealthcare.com/story/mhealth-devices-must-auto-collect-data-cloud-sensors/2014-01-30. Accessed 11 Feb 2015
9. Keeping valuable algorithms secret. http://security.stackexchange.com/questions/14671/keeping-valuable-algorithms-secret. Accessed 13 Jan 2015
10. Attack (computing). http://en.wikipedia.org/wiki/Attack_(computing). Accessed 20 Jan 2015
11. FIPS 140-2. http://en.wikipedia.org/wiki/FIPS_140-2. Accessed 20 Jan 2015
12. Project Ubertooth. http://ubertooth.sourceforge.net. Accessed 23 Dec 2014
13. Ubertooth Schedule. http://www.shmoocon.org/schedule#ubertooth/. Accessed 24 Dec 2014
14. Adibi, S., et al.: A multilayer non - repudiation system: a suite-B approach
15. Saleem, S., Ullah, S., Kwak, K.S.: A study of IEEE 802.15.4 security framework for wireless body area networks. Sensors (Basel) **11**(2), 1383–1395 (2011)
16. Gagandeep, G., Aashima, A.: Study on Sinkhole attacks in wireless Ad hocnetworks. Int. J. Comput. Sci. Eng. **4**(6), 1078–1085 (2012)
17. PalSingh, V., Anand Ukey, A.S., Jain, S.: Signal strength based hello flood attack detection and prevention in wireless sensor networks. Int. J. Comput. Appl. **62**(15), 1–6 (2013)
18. X.800: Security architecture for Open Systems Interconnection for CCITT applications. http://www.itu.int/rec/T-REC-X.800-199103-I/en. Accessed 20 Jan 2015
19. Confidentiality, Integrity, Availability: The three components of the CIA Triad. http://security.blogoverflow.com/2012/08/confidentiality-integrity-availability-the-three-components-of-the-cia-triad/. Accessed 19 Jan 2015
20. Uluagac, A.S., Lee, C.P., Beyah, R.A., Copeland, J.A.: Designing secure protocols for wireless sensor networks. In: Li, Y., Huynh, D.T., Das, S.K., Du, D.-Z. (eds.) WASA 2008. LNCS, vol. 5258, pp. 503–514. Springer, Heidelberg (2008)
21. X.805: Security architecture for systems providing end-to-end communications. http://www.itu.int/rec/T-REC-X.805-200310-I/en. Accessed 20 Jan 2015
22. Sunyaev, A., Dehling, T., Taylor, P.L., Mandl, K.D.: Availability and quality of mobile health app privacy policies. J. Am. Med. Inform. Assoc. 1–4 (2014)
23. Crytographic Protocol. http://en.wikipedia.org/wiki/Cryptographic_protocol. Accessed 12 Jan 2015
24. Garloff, K.; Symmetric vs. asymmetric algorithms (2000). http://users.suse.com/~garloff/Writings/mutt_gpg/node3.html. Accessed 11 Feb 2015
25. Jarmusz, S.: Symmetric vs. Asymmetric Encryption: Which Way is Better? http://blog.atmel.com/2013/03/11/symmetric-vs-asymmetric-encryption-which-way-is-better/. Accessed 11 Feb 2015
26. Irum, S., Ali, A., Khan, F.A., Abbas, H.: A hybrid security mechanism for intra-WBAN and inter-WBAN communications. Int. J. Distrib. Sens. Netw. **2013**, 1–11 (2013)
27. Faisal, M., Al-Muhtadi, J., Al-Dhelaan, A.: Integrated protocols to ensure security services in wireless sensor networks. Int. J. Distrib. Sens. Netw. **2013**, 1–13 (2013)

28. Krohn, R., Metcalf, D.: mHealth Innovation: Best Practices from The Mobile Frontier, p. 204. HIMSS, Chicago (2014)

29. Ullah, S., Mohaisen, M., Alnuem, M.A.: A review of IEEE 802.15.6 MAC, PHY, and security specifications. IJDSN **2013** (2013)

30. IEEE Standards Association. 802.15.6 - IEEE Standard for Local and metropolitan area networks - Part 15.6: Wireless Body Area Networks (2012)

31. Toorani, M.: On Vulnerabilities of the Security Association in the IEEE 802.15.6 Standard, Jan 2015

32. Zheng, J., Jamalipour, A.: Wireless Sensor Networks: A Networking Perspective, pp. 1–489. Wiley, Hoboken (2008)

33. Toorani, M., Shirazi, A.A.B.: LPKI - a lightweight public key infrastructure for the mobile environments. In: 2008 11th IEEE Singapore International Conference on Communication Systems, ICCS 2008, pp. 162–166 (2008)

34. Sahoo, P.K.: Efficient security mechanisms for mHealth applications using wireless body sensor networks. Sensors (Basel) **12**(9), 12606–12633 (2012)

35. Nasser, N., Chen, Y.: SEEM: secure and energy-efficient multipath routing protocol for wireless sensor networks. Comput. Commun. **30**(11–12), 2401–2412 (2007)

36. Australian Government Department of Defence. DSD approval for the use of Suite B cryptography for CONFIDENTIAL and above. http://www.asd.gov.au/publications/dsdbroadcast/20130100-suite-b-crypto-approved.htm. Accessed 31 Dec 2014

37. Sanderson, R.: Trusted Computing Using IPsec Minimum Essential Interoperability Protocols (2011)

38. NSA Suite B Cryptography. http://en.wikipedia.org/wiki/NSA_Suite_B_Cryptography. Accessed 31 Dec 2014

39. Cisco Next-Generation Cryptography: Enable Secure Communications and Collaboration

40. Zaverucha, G.; ECQV Implicit Certificates and the Cryptographic Suite for Embedded Systems (Suite E)

41. Cryptographic Suite for Embedded Systems (Suite E). http://tools.ietf.org/html/draft-campagna-suitee-01. Accessed 03 Feb 2015

42. Vanstone, S., Campagna, M.: A cryptographic suite for embedded systems suite E. In: 6th ETSI Security Workshop

43. Security service (telecommunication). http://en.wikipedia.org/wiki/Security_service_(telecommunication). Accessed 20 Jan 2015

44. ANT+. http://en.wikipedia.org/wiki/ANT+. Accessed 18 Dec 2014

45. ANT (network). http://en.wikipedia.org/wiki/ANT_(network). Accessed 11 Feb 2015

46. What is ZigBee? http://www.wisegeek.org/what-is-zigbee.htm. Accessed 24 Dec 2014

47. Crosby, G.V., Ghosh, T., Murimi, R., Chin, C.A.: Wireless body area networks for healthcare: a survey. IJASUC **3**(3) (2012)

48. Bluetooth Low Energy Technology Makes New Applications Possible. http://www.connectblue.com/press/articles/bluetooth-low-energy-technology-makes-new-applications-possible/. Accessed 13 Jan 2015

49. How Bluetooth Works. http://electronics.howstuffworks.com/bluetooth2.htm. Accessed 24 Dec 2014

50. Nilsson, R., Saltzstein, B.: Bluetooth Low Energy vs. Classic Bluetooth: Choose the Best Wireless Technology for Your Application. Medical Electronics Design (2012)

51. Bluetooth vs. Bluetooth Low Energy: What's the Difference? http://www.link-labs.com/bluetooth-vs-bluetooth-low-energy/. Accessed 24 Dec 2014

52. ISO/IEEE_11073. http://en.wikipedia.org/wiki/ISO/IEEE_11073. Accessed 01 Feb 2015

53. IEEE. IEEE Std 11073-00103 Section 5.4 (2012)
54. Portilla, J., Otero, A., de la Torre, E., Riesgo, T., Stecklina, O., Peter, S., Langendörfer, P.: Adaptable security in wireless sensor networks by using reconfigurable ECC hardware coprocessors. Int. J. Distrib. Sens. Netw. **2010**, 1–12 (2010)
55. Inductive Charging. http://en.wikipedia.org/wiki/Inductive_charging. Accessed 05 Jan 2015

An Efficient Detection Mechanism Against Packet Faking Attack in Opportunistic Networks

Majeed Alajeely[✉], Asma'a Ahmad, Robin Doss, and Vicky Mak-Hau

School of Information Technology, Deakin University, Melbourne, Australia
malajeel@deakin.edu.au

Abstract. Security is a major challenge in Opportunistic Networks (OppNets) because of its characteristics, such as open medium, dynamic topology, no centralized management and absent clear lines of defense. A packet dropping attack is one of the major security threats in OppNets since neither source nodes nor destination nodes have the knowledge of where or when the packet will be dropped. In our previous novel attack (Packet Faking Attack [1]) we presented a special type of packet dropping where the malicious node drops one or more packets and then injects new fake packets instead. In this paper, we present an efficient detection mechanism against this type of attack where each node can detect the attack instead of the destination node. Our detection mechanism is very powerful and has very high accuracy. It relies on a very simple yet powerful idea, that is, the packet creation time of each packet. Simulation results show this robust mechanism achieves a very high accuracy, detection rate and good network traffic reduction.

Keywords: Opportunistic networks · Security · Packet dropping attacks · Denial-of-service · Malicious node detection

1 Introduction

Opportunistic networks (OppNets) refer to a number of wireless nodes that opportunistically communicate with each other in the form of "Store-Carry-Forward" when they come into contact with each other without proper network infrastructure. Due to these characteristics, OppNets have gained significant research attention due to the security and privacy challenges that have emerged. A packet dropping attack is one of the major security threats in OppNets. It can be classified as a denial of service attack (DoS) where the malicious node drops all or some of the packets. This attack is one of the most difficult DoS attacks since neither the source node nor the destination node has the knowledge of where or when the packet will be dropped. Packet dropping can degrade the performance of the network and may obstruct the propagation of sensitive data. It is a significant challenge to deal with such an attack since the unreliable wireless communication and resource limitations can result in communication failure and result in the wrong prediction about the presence of a packet dropping

© Springer International Publishing Switzerland 2015
R. Doss et al. (Eds.): FNSS 2015, CCIS 523, pp. 84–100, 2015.
DOI: 10.1007/978-3-319-19210-9_6

attack. Moreover, a node's resources, such as energy and bandwidth can be the real reasons behind packet dropping. A power shortage or communication failure such as physical damage can make a node unavailable. Therefore, it is difficult to recognize whether packets were dropped due to a security attack or for non security reasons. Dropping packets can lead to an increase in the number of packet retransmissions, transfer time, response time and network overhead. However, there is no doubt about the malicious behavior if the node drops some legitimate packets and then injects fake packets to replace them. In this case the malicious node obviously has enough resources to do this.

In packet faking attack [1] malicious node can selectively drop some packets and inject fake packets so it can maintain the original total number of packets originated from the sender node. The existing packet dropping defense mechanism, such as the multipath routing based mechanisms [2–6], reputation based mechanism [7], data provenance based mechanisms [8], acknowledgement based mechanisms [9–11], are inefficient as in OppNets we have no end to end connections and usually have no alternative paths from the sender to the destination or vice versa. Network coding based mechanisms [12], are inefficient as the destination nodes should have a copy of all neighbors packets/messages so it can decode its message, which is difficult to achieved in OppNets. Watchdog and pathrater mechanism [13–18] are inefficient for detecting this type of attack as the detection idea is based on the calculation of the total number of transmitted/received packets. Encryption techniques [19] are inefficient as well, as we required the use of a secret key, which is difficult to manage in OppNets since we have no centralized management. Hashing can be used with a limitation in OppNets to maintain packet integrity [11] as malicious nodes can drop and then inject fake packet with its hash value so the legitimate nodes can't recognize it. It is difficult also to send the hash values separately as we can't always find alternative paths in OppNets due to its characteristics of being an open medium with dynamic topology.

Our mechanism is very accurate for detecting this type of attack as we rely on the packet creation time of each packet.

Contribution: The main contributions of this work is an efficient detection mechanism against packet faking attack in OppNets. Our method is distributed and limits the propagation of the fake packets over the network.

The remainder of this paper is organized as follows. In Sect. 2, we present related work. In Sect. 3, we present an overview on the efficient detection mechanism against packet faking attack. In Sect. 4, we present our mathematical model. In Sect. 5, we present our simulation results and in Sect. 6, we present our conclusion and future work.

2   Related Work

Defence mechanisms for packet dropping attacks can use multipath routing based mechanisms where packets are divided into a number of groups and then sent to a destination in more than one path [2–6].

In E-HSAM [2], a security improvement mechanism is proposed where the packets that go through a path with a malicious node are redirected to an alternative path. However, in OppNets this variety is not always available since there is no end to end connection and no alternative path available all the time. This technique results in network overhead and difficulty in identifying malicious nodes. Moreover, this technique might be vulnerable to route discovery attacks.

In [3], the authors used multipath data forwarding only when a Neighbor Watch System detected a malicious node, while single path data forwarding was used in normal operation in order to reduce power consumption. The authors in [4], proposed a packet dropping detection mechanism based on cooperative participation at the network-bootstrapping phase. Alternative routing was used to avoid malicious nodes or non-trust paths. However, this solution leads to network overhead.

S. Lee et al., [5] proposed an on-demand routing protocol by establishing and using multiple routes. This protocol uses a per-packet allocation scheme to spread data packets into multiple paths. This will utilize available network resources and prevent nodes from being traffic congested.

Y. Lu et al., [6] proposed a distributed, scalable and localized multipath search protocol for discovering multiple node-disjoint paths between the sink and source nodes. The authors also proposed a load balancing mechanism to spread the traffic over the discovered paths.

Acknowledgement based mechanisms can also be used for detecting a packet dropping attack [9–11]. This is based on authenticated acknowledgment from the intermediate nodes and the destination within a specific time. The source or destination can detect a malicious node.

A. Baadache et al., [11] proposed a mechanism for detecting a packet dropping attack where the intermediate node acknowledges the reception of the packets. A source node used this acknowledgment to construct a Merkle tree, and then compared the value of the tree root with precalculated value. If these values are equal then no packets were dropped in that path, otherwise there was packet dropping. However, this technique can detect a path with a malicious node but is unable to detect the malicious node, therefore it looks for an alternative path for retransmission, thus resulting in network overhead.

Network coding based mechanisms can be used for detection and defence as in [12], where a mitigation scheme to evaluate the impact of the selective packet dropping attack in DTN is proposed by using network coding. In this scheme the destination node measures the delivery ratio and send it back to the sender. The sender then begins adjusting the redundancy factor dynamically to mitigate against the degradation in the delivery ratio caused by the attack. Theoretical analysis and experimental simulations help to identify some characteristics of the impact of packet dropping on the routing performance, such as delivery ratio, delivery cost and delivery latency. These are degraded if the majority of nodes behave as packet droppers or selfishly. In addition, the impact of non-forwarding of messages reduces the delivery cost, while the behavior of dropping messages increases the delivery cost.

Data provenance based mechanisms [8] can be used to identify malicious nodes where the characteristics of the watermarking based secure provenance transmission mechanism and the inter-packet timing characteristics are exploited to achieve this goal. There are three stages to this technique. The first detects lost packets using the distribution of the inter-packet delay. The second identifies the present of the attack by comparing the empirical average packet loss rate with the natural packet loss rate of the data flow path, and finally the technique identifies a malicious node or link then isolates it by transmitting more provenance information along with the sensor data. However, this technique is not very accurate because it does not detect the exact malicious node in the entire path or link. The impact of TCP packet dropping attacks and detection methods is explored in [20]. Three dropping mechanisms are investigated. These are periodic packet dropping (PerPD), Retransmission packet dropping (RetPD) and Random packet dropping (RanPD). Statistical based analysis (TDSAM) used for detection of these kinds of attacks are based on the NIDESETAT algorithm running on the ftp client side. However, only one detection technique is proposed in this work without any defence mechanism.

Watchdog and Pathrater mechanism is also used for detecting malicious attacks [13,14,16–18]. Watchdog is a technique for monitoring the behaviour of neighbour nodes in order to classify nodes as either legitimate or malicious. Pathrater uses the input of watchdog to select the best path to the destination.

In [13], watchdog and pathrater are used to improve throughput in a mobile ad hoc network. In the watchdog stage, the sender node detects the misbehaving node by overhearing the neighbour node and comparing the message transmission with the saved copy on its buffer and checks if it's matching. If matching, this means the node is not malicious and the message copy on the buffer will be deleted. If the sender node does not hear for a certain time the watchdog will increment the failure tally of that neighbour node. If that tally exceeds the threshold value, the node will then be recorded as a misbehaving node. Each node runs the pathrater phase to determine the best path with the highest metric by combining the information from the watchdog with the link reliability data to calculate the best path. According to the information from the watchdog and pathrater, each node will build a rating table for other known nodes on the network to use for future transmissions. However, the watchdog technique is not that efficient in case of the presence of ambiguous collisions, receiver collisions, limited transmission power, false misbehaviour, or collusion.

To solve the weakness of watchdog, authors in [14] proposed ExWatchdog to enhance the intrusion detecting system for discovering malicious nodes. ExWatchdog has the ability to detect malicious nodes that can partition the network by untruthfully reporting other nodes as malicious. Each node builds a table with the number of received packets and the number of forwarded packets. When a node receives a report about the misbehaviour of some node, the source of the communication starts sending a message to the destination to check if the number of received and forwarded packets are equal. If equal, the node that reported the other node as malicious is actually malicious itself.

The work in [16] uses the same idea of a watchdog mechanism where a node can act as a monitor node if it can overhear the radio signal of two nodes on the same routing path. The mechanism can also oversee the data transmission that comes from these two nodes. When these two nodes send packets to each other, the monitoring path node backs up the data packets and oversees the transmission behaviour of the receiver node. If the receiver node truly sends out the packet to another node, the monitor node will remove the packet from its buffer. When the monitor node detects packets stored in its buffer over a threshold time, the monitor node will try to find an alternative path to the destination and retransmit the data packet.

S. Jianhua et al., [18], proposed a reputation based mechanism for detecting a packet dropping attack. This mechanism used direct observation and indirect or second hand information to achieve full reputation weight. Nodes can be excluded from the network if it has low reputation weight. To prevent fault tolerance, the authors used historical reputation. Fuzzy logic was used to improve the performance by dealing with the fact that packet dropping can be heterogeneous.

TBDSR [17] is an enhancement of the Dynamic Source Routing protocol where each node maintains a trust table of opinion towards other nodes as either belief, disbelief or uncertainty. At the beginning stage of the network, each node has the default opinion (uncertain) towards other nodes but after some successful or failed transmissions between nodes, this opinion changes gradually to belief or disbelief. Also, nodes can exchange trust information about each other and then use the trust combination algorithm to calculate new opinion by combining all of the recommendations.

In [7], a reputation based mechanism for analyzing the performance of packet dropping policies is used. The packet dropping mechanism is based on the packets weight, where the packets' weight is calculated based on the inter-contact time between nodes. In [19], a mechanism for detecting and tracing packet dropping in malicious nodes with selfish or blackhole behavior was proposed for DTN networks. Nodes are required to keep record of the packets sent and received during data exchange when they contact with each other and verify the confidentiality by using initiators public key. An encryption algorithm is used to detect the malicious nodes during the data exchange.

3   Overview on the Efficient Detection Mechanism Against Packet Faking Attack

In a packet dropping/modification attack, malicious nodes may drop or modify the packets. The existing mechanisms used to find the number of dropped packets or the number of new injected fake packets are based on the calculations of the total transmitted/received packets. These mechanisms are inefficient to detect the attack when malicious nodes drop some packets and then inject new fake packets instead of them. In our previous work [1], we called this attack a "Packet Faking Attack". Our novel fake packets detection mechanism against this attack was based on the destination nodes. The new detection mechanism is node by node based where each legitimate node can run the algorithm to detect fake packets directly. Propagation of fake packets through the network is prevented as any legitimate nodes can detect and drop fake packets. This efficient detection mechanism is very powerful and accurate. It is relies on a very simple yet powerful idea, that is "Packets Creation Time" of each packet. When a message reaches a legitimate node, the node can compare the packet creation time of each received packet. The node can then detect the fake packet based on a different creation time, as all packets in the same message should have the same creation time or be very close (with a difference of Δt).

3.1   Assumptions

In our approach we make the following two assumptions:

1. The sender node should automatically include the packets' creation time within each packet sent.
2. A malicious node has the ability of dropping legitimate packets and then inject fake packets instead of them but has no ability to modify the packets contents including the packets creation time.

Based on these two assumptions, a legitimate node will learn all of the nodes along packets' path, including the packets creation time. Figure 1 shows the packets path where c8 is the source of the message, c9 is the destination of the message and t16, t15, w14 are intermediate nodes.

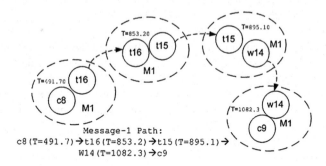

Message-1 Path:
c8 (T=491.7)→t16 (T=853.2)→t15 (T=895.1)→
W14 (T=1082.3)→c9

Fig. 1. Packets path with packets creation time

3.2   Attack and Detection Scenario

In a fake packet attack, malicious nodes can drop one or more packets (but not all the packets), and instead of them, inject fake packets with the current time of the malicious node. The legitimate node will calculate and find the fake packets. Figure 2 shows the packets' path of message 1 (c8 → t16 → t15 → w14 → c9), where node t15 drops one packet at time T = 860.2 and then injects a fake packet instead of it.

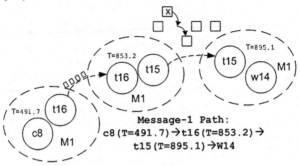

Fig. 2. Packet dropping/injecting at malicious node (t15)

We have two phases in Algorithm 1. In phase one, we checked all packets to find and selected the lowest packet creation time. When the legitimate node receives all the packets including Packets' Creation Time (PCT) for each packet, it will accurately start to detect any fake packets by sorting the packet creation time of all received packets and then choosing the smallest value in the list. We will consider that smallest value as a legitimate (PCT).

In phase two, we are detecting fake packets. The algorithm will continuously check all packets to distinguish and count all fake and true packets. All packets should have the same (PCT) or a very slight difference (Δt). When the malicious node drops packets, it will inject fake packets instead of them at the current malicious node time, therefore the fake (PCT) will always be higher than the original packet creation time of legitimate packets. We may find more than one fake packet creation time (PCT) depending on the number of malicious nodes on the packet's path as we may have more than one malicious nodes sending to each other. If all packets have the same creation time $\pm \Delta t$ then there will be no fake packets and no malicious nodes.

As mentioned earlier, in this attack, malicious nodes drop some packets and instead of them, inject fake packets. Our algorithm is based on the assumption

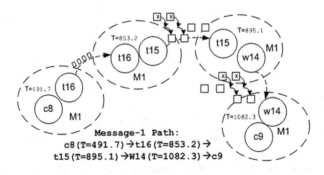

Fig. 3. Different sequence packets dropping/injecting on two malicious nodes path

---

Algorithm 1. Detecting fake packets

1: READ: packetsCreationTime.
2: **Phase 1**: Select lowest packet creation time
3: For all packets
4: Sort packetsCreationTime[i]
5: lowestPacketCreationTime = packetsCreationTime[0]
6: packetsAreLegitimate = true
7: **Phase 2**: Detect fake packet(s)
8: For all packets
9: **if** packetsCreationTime[i] = (lowestPacketCreationTime ± Δt) **then**
10:     legitimatePacketsCounter++
11: **else**
12:     fakePacketsCounter++
13:     packetsAreLegitimate = false
14: **end if**
15: **if** packetsAreLegitimate **then**
16:     No fake packets and no malicious node, Exit
17: **end if**

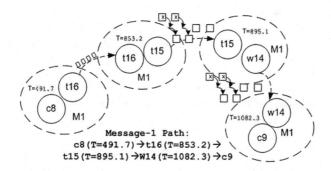

Fig. 4. Same sequence packets dropping/injecting on two malicious nodes path

we have at least one legitimate packet at the legitimate node side which has the lowest packet creation time. We can then rely on it and compare it with other packet creation times to find fake packets. However, if "all received packets" are fake or the "same packet sequence" is faked twice or more, then our algorithm will compare it according to the lowest packet creation time to find the fake packets in that message. However, in this case one or more fake packets will be missed and categorized as legitimate. We can see this case in Figs. 3 and 4. In Fig. 3, we have two malicious nodes on the same path and each one drops/injects different packet sequences. Malicious node (t15) first drops two packets and then sends all four packets to another malicious node (w14). The second malicious node (w14) drops the last two packets and then sends all four packets to the destination (c9) so it will receive four fake packets. In Fig. 4, malicious node (t15) drops/injects the first two packets, and then the malicious node (w14) drops/injects two packets in the same sequence (first two packets), and then sends out four packets to the destination (c9). Legitimate node (c9) will not be able to detect the fake packets of malicious node (t15) in either scenarios. It can only detect the fake packets of malicious node (w14), and it will recognize the fake packets of (t15) as legitimate packets. However, there is a high probability we can detect the missed fake packets of malicious node (t15) on the other paths, as we will see in the simulation results. The only way to detect all fake packets is to have one or more legitimate packets on the legitimate node side. When we transmit a large number of packets, we will have a better chance of achieving these two conditions, as we will see in the mathematical model.

4   Mathematical Model

In order to calculate the probability of detecting the fake packets of all malicious nodes on the packets' path, let us assume,

- n be the total number of hops;
- m be the number of malicious hops;
- k be the number of packets;
- p be the probability that a packet be changed at a malicious hop;
- α be the probability of at least one packet surviving all malicious hops (i.e., Probability of accurate detection).

The probability of a packet unchanged at a malicious node is given by $(1-p)$, for p the probability of a packet changed at the malicious node. Now, the probability of a packet unchanged in a path with m malicious node(s) is given by:

$$(1 - p)^m \tag{1}$$

Therefore, the probability of a packet being changed in a path with m malicious nodes is given by:

$$1 - (1 - p)^m \tag{2}$$

Now, the probability of having j packets unchanged but the rest of the k packets changed in a path with m malicious nodes is given by:

$$[(1 - p)^m]^j \, [1 - (1 - p)^m]^{k-j} . \tag{3}$$

Notice that there are $\binom{k}{j}$ combinations of obtaining j objects out of k. Hence the overall probability of exactly j out of the k packets unchanged in a path with m malicious nodes is given by:

$$\binom{k}{j} [(1 - p)^m]^j \, [1 - (1 - p)^m]^{k-j} \tag{4}$$

Now, let α be the probability of at least one packet surviving all malicious hops, which is equal to $1-$ the probability of all packets changed. We have that:

$$\alpha = 1 - [\, 1 - (1 - p)^m]^k \tag{5}$$

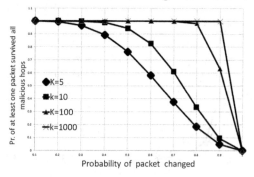

Fig. 5. Probability of at least one packet survived all malicious hops in a 2 malicious hop path

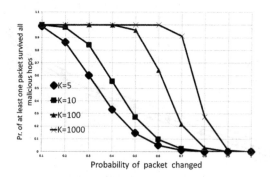

Fig. 6. Probability of at least one packet survived all malicious hops in a 5 malicious hop path

Observe that to increase α, whilst p and m are held constant, one can increase k, the number of packets. In Figs. 5, 6 and 7, we can see the probability of at least one packet surviving all malicious hops in a path with 2, 5 and 20 malicious hops. We can achieve a high probability of receiving legitimate packets α when the number of malicious nodes is low in the packet's path, then it starts to drop with an increase in the malicious nodes. We can observe the value of α is affected by the number of malicious hops, because when we have two malicious hops the probability of receiving legitimate packets will be high even if the value of p is high. This is because we only have two hops on that path. The value of α decreases when the number of malicious nodes increases.

Our algorithm relies on the probability of at least one unchanged packet on all hops "α" so we can use the packet creation time of that unchanged packet for detecting the fake packets. We need to keep this probability α as high as possible by optimizing the number of packets k sent in each transaction with reference to the changing packet probability p.

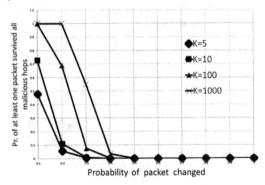

Fig. 7. Probability of at least one packet survived all malicious hops in a 20 malicious hop path

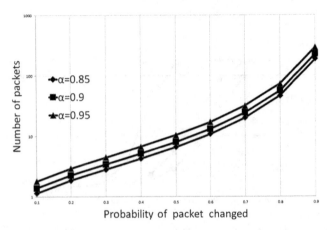

Fig. 8. Number of packets needed to achieve $\alpha = (0.85, 0.90, 0.95)$ in a path with two malicious nodes

As in Eq. 5, the probably of having at least one packet surviving all malicious hops, i.e. α is given as:

$$\alpha = 1 - \left[1 - (1-p)^m\right]^k$$

Hence,

$$1 - \alpha = \left[1 - (1-p)^m\right]^k,$$

and therefore

$$\log(1-\alpha) = k \log\left[1 - (1-p)^m\right],$$

which implies that

$$k = \frac{\log(1-\alpha)}{\log\left[1 - (1-p)^m\right]}.$$

Figures 8, 9 and 10 show the relationship between the number of packets and the probability of at least one packet survived all malicious hops in different

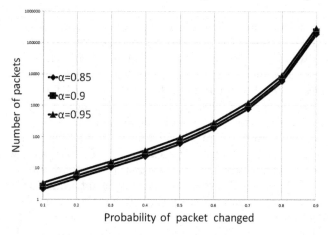

Fig. 9. Number of packets needed to achieve $\alpha = (0.85, 0.90, 0.95)$ in a path with five malicious nodes

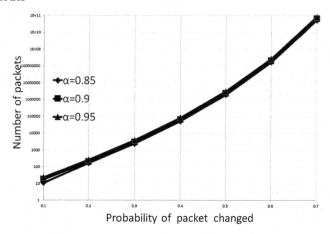

Fig. 10. Number of packets needed to achieve $\alpha = (0.85, 0.90, 0.95)$ in a path with twenty malicious nodes

path lengths. When the number of malicious nodes increases, the probability of packet changes p in the path of malicious nodes will increase as well. In this case, we will be required to send a large number of packets k so we can achieve a high probability (0.85–0.95) of receiving at least one legitimate packet α in order to achieve a high accuracy of detecting fake packets.

5   Simulation Settings

To test our algorithm, we implemented a scenario in the ONE simulator [21] using the Epidemic protocol. The simulation was defined to last for 1 h, with 0.5 s of update intervals. Bluetooth was chosen for connectivity with a transmit range of 10 m for node radio devices, and transmit speeds of 1000 kbps. There are 12 active nodes composed of cars and pedestrians. Pedestrians and cars have up to 50 MB of RAM for storage. Pedestrians move at random speeds between 1 and 1.5 m/s, cars drive only on roads and move at speeds between 10–50 km/h, with wait times of 0–120 s. MapBasedMovement is used for pedestrians and cars, with a network area of 4500 × 3400 m. Nodes move randomly on roads and walkways with a movement warm-up for 10 s. There are 3 groups of trams, with 2 trams in each group. MapRouteMovement is used for trams to follow a constructed tram line. Trams drive at speeds of 7–10 m/s with a wait time of 10–30 s at each configured stop. In addition to the Bluetooth interface, a group of trams uses the high speed interface with a transmit range of 1000 m and a transmit speed of 10 mbps. Messages are generated every 1–5 min per node, with message sizes between 50 k and 100 k, and a message time to live of 5 h. We used the simulator's output as a dataset, and randomly corrupted the dataset based on the number of malicious nodes. We then fed the corrupted dataset to our algorithm. Two programs were written using C++. The first program reads the dataset file and then corrupts it by making legitimate nodes malicious by changing the packet creation time for randomly chosen packets and nodes. The second program implements the algorithm, and begins by taking as input the output dataset file generated by program 1. The second program is run to get the algorithm results of the metrics calculations. We also ran the simulator for an average of 30 times to represent each point on the graphs in Figs. 11 and 13.

5.1 Simulation Results and Analysis

We have used three metrics for evaluating our algorithm,

1. Fake packet detection accuracy: The ratio of the total number of fake packets detected to the total number of actual fake packets.
2. False negative rate: The percentage of fake packets have been incorrectly classified as a legitimate packet.
3. Network traffic reduction: The ratio of the total number of fake packets detected on the destination nodes side to the total number of the fake packets detected on the node by node side.

In our scenario, we have assumed the source nodes are not malicious as the source node always sends packets with the same creation time. As in a Catabolism attack, the malicious node drops some of the packets, and instead of them injects fake packets with the current malicious node time. Dropping and injecting will be on one or more nodes on the same packets' path. In our calculations, we assume we have at least one legitimate packet so we can use it as a benchmark comparison.

In Fig. 11, we can see the packet detection accuracy of our algorithm can achieve 100 % accuracy when the percentage of malicious nodes is less than 5 %. This is because there is a good chance for destinations to receive legitimate packets, especially when source nodes transmit large numbers of packets. When

the number of malicious nodes increases, the accuracy slightly starts to drop as
fake packets may be missed when two or more malicious nodes drop and inject
packets into the same packet sequence on the same path, as illustrated in Fig. 4.
However, our algorithm results show the packet detection accuracy does not drop
below 78 %, even when 100 % of intermediate nodes act as malicious nodes. This
is due to the low probability of having two or more malicious nodes dropping
and injecting in the same packet sequence on the same path. In addition, the
probability of receiving all packets as fake is also low, especially when the sender
sends a large number of packets. In our efficient detection mechanism we always
achieved better packet detection accuracy as fake packets will not propagate
through the network till it reaches the destination. Any legitimate nodes can stop
fake packet propagation, in contrast, our old detection mechanism [1] can detect
fake packets only through destination node. Figure 12 shows the networks traffic
reduction in our enhance detection mechanism compare to the old detection
mechanism [1]. Overall we have achieved good traffic reduction as each legitimate
node can detect fake packets and then stop fake packet from propagation through
the network.

As we can see in Fig. 3, we may categorize fake packets as legitimate when
we have more than one malicious node sending to each other on the same path
where each malicious node fakes a different sequence of packets. This results in
having all the received packets at the legitimate node as fake packets. In Fig. 13,
we can see a zero false negative rate for our algorithm when we have less than
2 % malicious nodes. This is because of the small number of malicious nodes
and the probability of receiving all packets as fake will be very low. The false

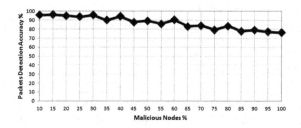

Fig. 11. Fake packet detection accuracy as the number of malicious nodes increases

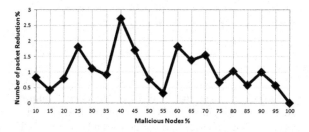

Fig. 12. Network traffic reduction

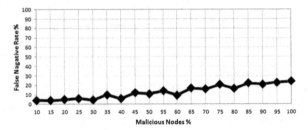

Fig. 13. False negative rate as the number of malicious nodes increases

negative rate starts to increase slightly till it reaches a maximum of 22 %, and the number of malicious nodes also increase as the probability of receiving all packets as fake also rises.

6   Conclusion and Future Work

Security is a major challenge in OppNets due to its characteristics, such as open medium, dynamic topology, dependence on cooperative techniques, no centralized management, and absent clear lines of defense. With the absence of an end to end connection, packet dropping attacks have become one of the hardest security threats in OppNets. In addition, neither source nor destination nodes have knowledge of when or where a packet will be dropped in a packet dropping attack.

In our previous novel attack (Packet faking attack [1]) we presented a special type of packet dropping where the malicious node drops one or more packets and then injects new fake packets instead. In this paper, we present an efficient defence mechanism against this type of attack where each node can detect the attack instead of the destination node. Our detection mechanism is very powerful and has very high accuracy. It relies on a very simple yet powerful idea, that is, the packet creation time of each packet. Simulation results show this robust mechanism achieves a very high accuracy, detection rate and good network traffic reduction. A lot of work remains to be done as we still do not have a complete solution for a packet dropping attack. Developing new routing protocols with a mechanism for detecting the dropping of all the packets or some of the packets and modifying these is a real challenge for the future.

References

1. Alajeely, M., Ahmad, A., Doss, R., Mak-Hau, V.: Packet faking attack: a novel attack and detection mechanism in OppNets. In: 2014 IEEE Tenth International Conference on Computational Intelligence and Security (CIS), pp. 638–642, November 2014

2. Obaidat, M., Woungang, I., Dhurandher, S., Koo, V.: Preventing packet dropping and message tampering attacks on AODV-based mobile ad hoc networks. In: International Conference on Computer, Information and Telecommunication Systems (CITS), pp. 1–5, May 2012

3. Lee, S., Choi, Y.: A resilient packet-forwarding scheme against maliciously packet-dropping nodes in sensor networks. In: Proceedings of the Fourth ACM Workshop on Security of Ad Hoc and Sensor Networks, pp. 59–70, October 2006

4. Sen, J., Chandra, M., Balamuralidhar, P., Harihara, S., Reddy, H.: A distributed protocol for detection of packet dropping attack in mobile ad hoc networks. In: IEEE International Conference on Telecommunications and Malaysia International Conference on Communication, pp. 75–80, May 2007

5. Lee, S., Gerla, M.: Split multipath routing with maximally disjoint paths in ad hoc networks. In: IEEE International Conference on Communications, vol. 10, pp. 3201–3205 (2001)

6. Lu, Y., Wong, V.: An energy-efficient multipath routing protocol for wireless sensor networks. Int. J. Commun. Syst. **20**(7), 747–766 (2007)

7. Ke, M., Nenghai, Y., Bin, L.: A new packet dropping policy in delay tolerant network. In: Twelfth IEEE International Conference on Communication Technology (ICCT), pp. 337–380, November 2010

8. Sultana, S., Bertino, E., Shehab, M.: A Provenance based mechanism to identify malicious packet dropping adversaries in sensor networks. In: Proceedings of the 2011 Thirty First International Conference on Distributed Computing Systems Workshops, pp. 332–338, June 2011

9. Zhang, X., Jain, A., Perrig, A.: Packet-dropping adversary identification for data plane security. In: Proceedings of the 2008 ACM CoNEXT Conference, December 2008

10. Carbunar, B., Ioannidis, I., Nita-Rotaru, C.: JANUS: towards robust and malicious resilient routing in hybrid wireless networks. In: Proceedings of the Third ACM Workshop on Wireless Security, pp. 11–20 (2004)

11. Baadache, A., Belmehdi, A.: Fighting against packet dropping misbehavior in multi-hop wireless ad hoc networks. J. Netw. Comput. Appl. **35**(3), 1130–1139 (2012)

12. Chuah, M., Yang, P.: Impact of selective dropping attacks on network coding performance in DTNs and a potential mitigation scheme. In: Proceedings of the Eighteenth International Conference on Computer Communications and Networks, pp. 1–6, August 2009

13. Marti, S., Giuli, T., Lai, K., Baker, M.: Mitigating routing misbehavior in mobile ad hoc networks. In: Proceedings of the Sixth Annual International Conference on Mobile Computing and Networking, pp. 255–265 (2000)

14. Nasser, N., Chen, Y.: Enhanced intrusion detection system for discovering malicious nodes in mobile ad hoc networks. In: IEEE International Conference on Communications, pp. 1154–1159, June 2007

15. Zouridaki, C., Mark, B., Hejmo, M., Thomas, R.: A quantitative trust establishment framework for reliable data packet delivery in MANETs. In: Proceedings of the Third ACM Workshop on Security of Ad Hoc and Sensor Networks, pp. 1–10, November 2005

16. Sun, H., Chen, C., Hsu, L., Chen, Y., Chen, Y.: Reliable data transmission against packet dropping misbehavior in wireless ad hoc networks. In: IET International Communication Conference on Wireless Mobile and Computing, pp. 419–424, November 2011

17. Vasantha, V., Manimegalai, D.: Mitigating routing misbehaviors using subjective trust model in mobile ad hoc networks. In: Proceedings of the International Conference on Computational Intelligence and Multimedia Applications, vol. 4, 417–422 (2007)
18. Jianhua, S., ChuanXiang, M.: A reputation-based scheme against malicious packet dropping for mobile ad hoc networks. In: IEEE International Conference on Intelligent Computing and Intelligent Systems (ICIS), vol. 3, 113–117 (2009)
19. Devi, K., Damodharan, P.: Detecting misbehavior routing and attacks in disruption tolerant network using itrm. In: International Conference on Current Trends in Engineering and Technology, pp. 334–337, July 2013
20. Zhang, X., Wu, S., Fu, Z., Wu, T.: Malicious packet dropping: How it might impact the TCP performance and how we can detect it. In: Proceedings of the 2000 IEEE International Conference on Network Protocols, pp. 263–272 (2000)
21. Keränen, A., Ott, J., Kärkkäinen, T.: The ONE simulator for DTN protocol evaluation. In: Proceedings of the Second International Conference on Simulation Tools and Techniques, pp. 1–10, March 2009

An Integrated Access Control Service Enabler for Cloud Applications

Tran Quang Thanh[1(✉)], Stefan Covaci[1], Benjamin Ertl[1],
and Paolo Zampognano[2]

[1] Technical University Berlin, Berlin, Germany
{tran,stefan.covaci,benjamin.ertl}@tu-berlin.de
[2] Engineering Ingegneria Informatica S.p.A., Rome, Italy
paolo.zampognaro@eng.it

Abstract. Cost reducing, ubiquitous access, are foreseeable benefits when organizations outsourcing applications, services to the cloud. However, security is current major challenge that limits their widespread deployments. In this paper, a RESTful security service enabler is proposed to provide authentication, authorization and audit logging services for cloud application developers, by leveraging several important security standards (e.g. OAuth, XACML). Specifically, a prototype of this enabler is ongoing developed based on our requirement investigation in the health care domain and related Generic Enabler technologies in the FI-PPP (Future Internet Public Private Partnership) FIWARE Project.

Keywords: Access control · Cloud · eHealth · Future internet · Security

1 Introduction

Migrating applications to the cloud is getting a lot of interests in many organizations by its given benefits in term of flexibility, scalability and cost effective. Cloud technology also changes the way of how organization applications and services are developed: from software-enabled to API-enabled. Considering as the evolution of SOA (Software Oriented Architecture), API technology enables organizations to better support their application developers and to introduce their applications services to wider range of customers and partners. As critical applications and sensitive data are moving to the cloud, accessible through given APIs, it becomes clear that proper security solutions should be in place to protect them from malicious usages.

In this paper, an integrated access control service enabler is introduced to help cloud application developers when implementing and deploying their services. By consuming exposed APIs, developers save a lot of time when implementing security logics as required credentials, access policies and decision support engines are managed outside their applications. In our solution, all security functionalities including identity provisioning, authentication, authorization and audit logging are provided as REST APIs [1]. In addition to that, several important security standards are adopted (e.g. SAML [2], XACML [3], OAuth [4], SCIM [5] and OpenID Connect [6]). It is worth to mention that our proposed enabler is flexible enough, not only on how it will be implemented (as different existing software components can be reused), but also on the capability deploy

© Springer International Publishing Switzerland 2015
R. Doss et al. (Eds.): FNSS 2015, CCIS 523, pp. 101–112, 2015.
DOI: 10.1007/978-3-319-19210-9_7

in different service domains. As illustration, a prototype of this enabler has been ongoing developed and evaluated in the context of FI-STAR project [7].

This paper is organized as follows. Section 2 gives an overview of relevant standards and works. The architecture, APIs and service functionalities are presented in Sect. 3. A prototype of this enabler is discussed in Sect. 4 based on our requirement investigation in the health care domain and related Generic Enabler technologies in the FI-PPP (Future Internet Public Private Partnership) FIWARE Project [8].

2   Background

OAUTH [4] (Open Authorization framework) is the evolving standard to secure API access. OAuth allows users (resource owner) to grant third-party applications (client) accessing data (resource server) without sharing credential (e.g. password). The client can be a native mobile application, a desktop application, a server-side or browser-based web application. The abstract flow of current OAuth version 2.0 is shown in the Fig. 1. The client interacts with resource owner to get authorization grant and use this to authenticate and get an access token from authorization server (which owns the user identities and credentials). Such token is then used to request resource access. The access token has often limited rights and can be revoked any time.

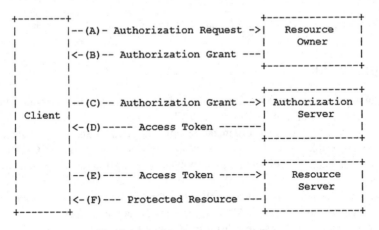

Fig. 1. OAuth2 abstract protocol flow

OAuth has widespread adoption by many service providers (e.g. Google, Twitter, FaceBook, GitHub etc.). The current version 2 (OAuth2) keeps the overall architecture but is not compatible with previous versions (OAuth 1.0 and OAuth 1.0a). **OpenID Connect** [6] defines a simple identity layer on top of the OAuth2. It allows Clients to verify the identity of the End-User based on the authentication performed by an Authorization Server, as well as to obtain basic profile information about the End-User in an interoperable and REST-like manner. The current version of Open ID Connect is 1.0 and it is not compatible with previous OpenID versions.

SCIM [5] System for Cross domain Identity Management (former as Simple Cloud Identity Management) defines a RESTful protocol for identity management operations. It consists of three major components: SCIM Core schema, REST API (for exchange user-related resources via XML or JSON) and binding (e.g. SAML binding). OAUTH2 is recommended for SCIM API authentication and authorization. SCIM has widely supported by Google, Ping, and Salesforge etc.

SAML [2] The Security Assertion Mark-up Language (SAML) is an XML-based framework that allows identity and security information to be shared across security domains. SAML is also the industry standard for the SSO mechanism for cloud and/or enterprise applications. SAML 1.0 and 1.1 has specified by OASIS (Organization for the Advancement of Structured Information Standards) but the today's SAML 2.0 is the convergence of three standards: SAML 1.1, Liberty Alliance Identity Federation Framework (ID-FF) and Shibboleth.

XACML [3] eXtensible Access Control Markup Language (XACML) is developed by OASIS to standardize the authorization decisions in enterprise applications. XACML defines a XML-based policy language, a request/response scheme and access control architecture. The decision based architecture is presents in Fig. 2 with different components such as PEP (Policy Enforcement Point) or PDP (Policy Decision Point). Many organizations are using XACML and the latest version is 3.0

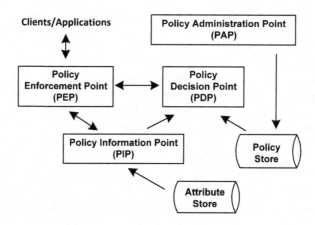

Fig. 2. XACML reference architecture

SYSLOG [9] is a de factor message logging standard for many years. It is widely adopted for logging network and security event by the capability to separate software that generates messages, storage systems and reporting and analyzing solutions. The latest technical specification was published in 2009 by IETF with some important enhancements.

Related Works: The concept of "Enabler" came from the Future Public Private Partnership program (FI-PPP) [10] by European Commission to accelerate the development and adoption of Future Internet technologies. As specified, an enabler is a technological component that provides set of APIs and interoperable interfaces to support a concrete set of functions. There are many research projects and partners involved in the program. In the FI-PPP, FIWARE [8] is the core project that specified and implemented a lot of general-purpose enablers (GE) that common to almost usage areas. Such GEs are categorized into main technical chapters: Cloud Hosting, Data & Context Management, Internet of Thing (IoT), Application, Advanced Middleware and Interface to Network and Device and Security. FI-PPP has also supported some use case projects in several important domains such as SAFECITY (smart city), FINESCE (smart energy), FINEST (transport) and FITMAN (manufacturing) [10]. In these projects, besides leveraging the usage of existing FIWARE GEs, they have also introduced new specific enablers (SE). About two hundreds GEs and SEs have been specified and the number will continuously increase as the program is still evolving. The enabler in this work is designed based on set of software components (enablers) including the two related FIWARE GEs: Identity Management GE (IDM) [11] and Authorization PDP GE [12]. The integrating approach provides several advantages, not only better functionality support, but also more flexible and convenience. The detail is further discussed in the next section.

3 Architecture

Developers prefer to spend time on business logic rather than security aspect. Utilizing existing security supported modules, software components is often the choice, especially for non-security developers. For their access control requirement, they either embed the authorization logic within the code (e.g. using an authentication/authorization security framework) or outsource to another external component (e.g. Identity and Access Management - IAM or IDM). By adopting the latter approach, not only the ease-of-implement, time-saving target are achieved, but also making applications easier to maintain, evolve and more flexible to adapt with new requirements especially when they will be deployed in the cloud environment. In this section, an "Integrated Access Control Enabler" (IAC) is described which takes into account most-wanted security requirements from cloud application developers by combining the Authentication, Authorization and Auditing (AAA) services and leveraging several selected enterprise and cloud security standards. AAA are often the required functionalities in any application for security reason. Figure 3 gives an overview of the high level architecture of the IAC. In order to keep our enabler cloud-ready, flexible and easy-of-implement, following design principles are adopted:

- *API-centric:* Service functionalities are exposed through a powerful set of REST APIs. REST architecture style is widely adopted by its given benefits to application/ service developers such as simple (e.g. using HTTP GET, POST, PUT and DELETE for Create, Retrieve, Update and Delete operations), standard-aligned (using standards such as HTTP, URI, XML and JSON) and protocol independent (not only coupled to HTTP). As shown in Fig. 3, different groups of APIs are provided including: Authentication APIs (identifying and authenticating), Authorization APIs (deciding whether resource access is allowed), Audit Logging APIs (collecting access log for subsequent review or malicious usage detection) and Provisioning APIs (managing identity, access control policy).

– *Standard-aligned:* Selected security standards are investigated and taken into account: Authentication (SAML, OAuth2, and OpenID Connect), Authorization (OAuth2, XACML), Audit Log (Syslog) and Identity Provisioning (SCIM).
– *Modular & Layered:* As shown in the architecture, the IAC enabler can be built based on five main functional blocks (enablers). The interactions between them are through APIs or standard protocols. Detail information of such enablers are described as follows:

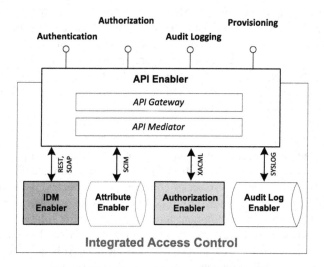

Fig. 3. High level architecture of IAC enabler

The front-end **API Enabler** controls which APIs are available and how to access them. It consists of two modules: *API Gateway* and *API Mediator*. The former protects exposed APIs from unauthorized attacks and misuses through different mechanisms such as input validation, rate limiting and token-based access control. The latter interacts with back-end enablers to handle the API request. Depending on the back-end capability, there are two types of mediator behaviors: Redirect and Translator. The redirect behavior is applied when an API request can be served by a back-end enabler. In this circumstance, the API mediator replies the API request (or route it) with guiding information about new service end-point. For example, when the back-end "IdM Enabler" supports OAuth, all the OAuth requests to the front-end will be redirected to it. With other APIs that can not directly served by any back-end enabler, the translation is required as the front-end needs to handle API requests by interacting with back-end enablers through their given specific APIs. Such translation can be simple (e.g. REST-to-SOAP) or more complex (e.g. requiring multiple APIs correlation).

There are four main service enablers in the back-end: (OAuth-supported) IDM Enabler, (XACML) Authorization Enabler, (SCIM) Attribute Enabler and (Syslog) Audit Log Enabler.

- **IDM Enabler:** any OAuth-supported Identity Management System. The IDM E-nabler should implement common OAuth 2.0 grant flows: authorization code grant, resource owner password credentials grant, implicit grant and client credentials grant. It is recommended to comply with existing security standards (Sect. 2) and to provide administration tool for identity life-cycle management. Many existing IdM solutions can be used as IDM Enabler including any implementation of FIWARE IdM GE [11] or other open source solutions (e.g. WSO2 IS [13]).
- **Authorization Enabler:** any XACML authorization engine. This enabler provides functionality of several components in the XACML access control architecture (Fig. 2) such as the policy decision point (PDP), policy administration point (PAP) and policy store (PRP). The PDP gives authorization decision based on various attributes and access policies. Through the PAP interface, administrators can manage access policies those are stored at PRP. Like the IDM, beside commercial solutions (e.g. Axiomatics Policy Server [14]), some open source candidates are also available such as SunXACML [15], FIWARE Authorization PDP [12] or WSO2 IS [13].
- **Attribute Enabler:** a secondary user attribute management and storage. It is an optional component as its functionality can be part of the IDM enabler. However, as many IDMs support only a fix set of common user attributes, the requirement to support other specific attributes is fulfilled by using this enabler. Supporting different types of attributes is important for any access control solution to be flexible enough to adapt with requirements from different service domains. LDAP or RDBMS can be used for data storage and management APIs are recommended to be complied with SCIM standard [5].
- **Audit Log Enabler:** any Syslog server and storage. However, this enabler leverages Syslog standard to collect only sensitive access events (e.g. authentication, authorization activities). Such logging information will help maintaining permanent evidence of all authorized and unauthorized access to protected resources.

Table 1 summarizes service interfaces that should be supported by any implementation of this enabler.

In the IAC, the token-based access control model is adopted to provide access control service. In order to access protected resources, cloud applications/services must present an access token (OAuth2 token). Our enabler offers two options to check whether or not to grant the resource access:

- *Coarse-grained access control:* Only the OAuth access token is checked and if it is valid (e.g. belonging to an authenticated user), the authorized decision is granted.
- *Fine-grained access control:* Both the token and other attributes of the token owners are checked. This is achieved by adopting XACML Attribute Based Access Control (ABAC) and Policy Based Access Control (PBAC) model.

Figure 4 presents a common scenario that using the access control service: A user uses a client (web, desktop, mobile application) to access cloud resource. First, he need to

Table 1. Service interfaces

Interface	Description
iOAuth	This interface supports four main OAuth2 flows as described in the OAuth2 specification RFC 6749: authorization code grant, resource owner password credentials grant, implicit grant and client credentials grant
	This interface supports SAML Assertion OAuth flow, an ongoing extension of OAuth2 by IETF to support identity federation. Legacy systems often adopt SAML token for authentication
	Providing CRUD APIs to manage OAuth applications (CRUD: Create, Retrieve, Update, Delete)
	Providing APIs for access token validation
iOpenIDConnect	OpenID Connect authentication interface. OpenID Connect defines a simple identity layer on top of the OAuth 2.0. Supporting this interface is optional
iSCIM	Providing SCIM APIs (System for Cross-Domain Identity Management Protocol) to manage identity
iPDP	Providing REST APIs to evaluate XACML authorization request (Policy Decision Point interface)
iPAP	Providing REST APIs to manage XACML access control policies (Policy Administration Point interface)
iAuditLog	Providing REST APIs to manage authorized and unauthorized access to protect resources

authenticate with the Access Control Service to get an access token and then includes such token in the resource request. A specific module, PEP (Policy Enforcement Point), which can be part of the resource or located another intermediate security component (e.g. security gateway/proxy), will intercept the resource request and check with the access control service in order to grant or deny the access by applying the coarse-grained or fine-grained approach. Flexibility, reusability are several foreseeable benefits when applying such token-based access control approach as access policies are specified and validated separately from where they are enforced.

In addition to that, several emerging cloud-centric solutions are also integrated into our enabler including: SCIM-based Identity Provisioning and OAuth-based Federated Authentication.

SCIM-Based Identity Provisioning: When outsourcing applications to cloud, enterprise and organization often want a simple solution that can leverage existing identities (e.g. from their legacy IDM systems) to give them access to cloud applications. Such credential (with all required attributes) must be provisioned/synchronized to the cloud using manual, just-in-time or proprietary approach. SCIM, the current evolving provisioning protocol, is adopted as it fulfills such requirement in standard way and using REST. Moreover, beside standard attributes in the core schema, SCIM allow supporting new attributes by specifying them in an extension schema (Fig. 5).

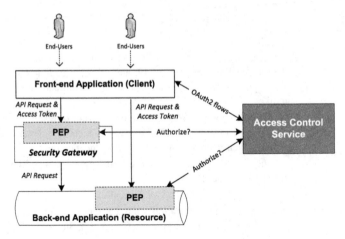

Fig. 4. Token-based access control model

```
{
  "userName":"test",
  "password":"fistar",
  "name":{"familyName":"Tran","givenName":"Quang Thanh"},
  "addresses":{"country":"Germany","streetAddress":"Kaiserin Augusta Allee 31","postalCode":"10589"},
  "phoneNumbers":[{"value":"4321","type":"mobile"},{"value":"1234","type":"other"}],
  "ims":[{"value":"tran@skype.com","type":"skype"}],
  "emails": [{"value":"tran@mail.tu-berlin.de","type":"work"}],
  "profileUrl":"av.tu-berlin.de/thanh",
  "preferredLanguage":["deutsch","english"],
  "fistarExtension":
    {
      "emergency":"inactive",
      "relatedPerson": ["http://fistar.test/Users/person1","http://fistar.test/Users/person2"],
      "gender":"male",
      "dateOfBirth":"1981-01-01",
      "careProvider":"Hospital A",
      "device":["device1","device2"]
    }
}
```

Fig. 5. Example of SCIM core and specific attributes

Feature 5 describes how we extend the SCIM to support required specific attributes for our emergency use cases in the healthcare domain. Attributes inside green rectangle are the core SCIM attributes and those inside the red one are specific.

OAUTH-Based Federated Authentication: As an open authorization framework, OAuth also allows client application requesting the access token using an existing proof of authentication (federated authentication). Such feature is important as it can offer access control service to utilize federated identities (managed by another trusted identity provider). In our enabler, the SAML 2.0 Bearer Assertion Profiles for OAuth 2.0 specification [16] is taken into account as many existing identity providers using SAML assertion as user claim. Figure 6 explains how it works.

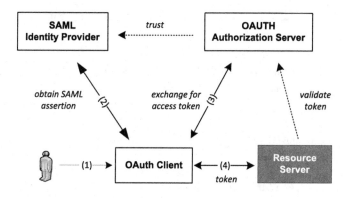

Fig. 6. SAML grant type for OAuth

(1) User requests access to protected resource from OAuth client (e.g. web, desktop or mobile application)
(2) User authenticates and obtains SAML assertion from a local SAML Identity Provider
(3) Client requests to OAuth AS to exchange the SAML assertion for an OAuth access token by using the SAML Grant type for OAuth grant flow. The OAuth AS needs to trust the SAML Identity Provider
(4) Received token is added to the API call to the (SaaS) resource.

4 Implementation and Result

In this section, an implementation of the proposed access control enabler is presented and currently under evaluation in the context of FI-STAR project [7]. Health care sector has been underway the major transition from specialist centered hospital to distributed patient centric. More patients will be treated over internet in their home, outside hospital. The transformation, in a one hand, is essential to make patient treatment more efficient, on the other hand, to help reducing the cost. Leveraging innovation technologies such as cloud computing will offer the ubiquitous data access and significant economic benefits.

The IAC enabler aligns well with the current healthcare standards as they are also interested in our selected security standards (e.g. OAuth2, SAML, Syslog etc.). We have investigated several related works such as IHE profiles [17] or HL7 FHIR specifications (Health Level 7 - Fast Healthcare Interoperability Resources) [18]. The former are specified by IHE (Integrating the Healthcare Enterprise), an initiative by healthcare professionals and industry, to improve the way computer systems in healthcare share information. In the latter, health care domain adopts REST for their resources specification. Through several human-related resources, various specific attributes can be selected to incorporate into our enabler implementation in order to adapt with requirements from healthcare organizations. Table 2 gives a first look of the

Table 2. Common SCIM and FHIR patient attributes

SCIM	FHIR patient resource
Core schema:	
Id, username	Identifier
Name	Name
PhoneNumbers	Telecom
Addresses	Address
PreferredLanguage	Communication
Photo	Photo
Active	Active
FI-STAR extension schema:	
Gender	Gender
BirthDate	BirthDate
CareProvider	CareProvider
...	...

potential mapping between our current supported SCIM user attributes with FHIR Patient Resource.

A prototype of the IAC enabler is ongoing developed in the context of FI-STAR project [7]. The current beta version is published at [19]. In this version, the API Enabler is implemented using Java programming language and Spring framework [20]. For the back-end enablers, several open source software components are selected such as WSO2

Fig. 7. Testing a SCIM API

Identity Server [13] and RSYSLOG [21]. It is worth to mention that the current implementation is flexible as all interactions among our components are through web APIs and standard protocols. It can be deployed in the cloud, on customer premise or even in the user computer. Figure 7 describes a SCIM API that allows getting user profile by given SCIM ID. We can see a lot of supported user attributes in the response message. Further information about supported APIs (e.g. user guide document, sample code) as well as upcoming updates will be continuously updated at [19].

5 Conclusions

Implementing security logic is always the complex part in any application. In this paper, an integrated access control service enabler is proposed to help cloud application developers mitigating such challenge. Moreover, several widespread security standards are taken into account to fulfill emerging security requirements including identity provisioning, federated authentication and flexible access control. In addition to that, by applying the standard and modularity design principle, the proposed enabler is flexible enough, not only on how it will be implemented (as its building blocks can be made use of existing software components), but also on the capability to deploy in different service domains. Specifically, a proof-of-concept prototype has been developed based on the requirements from healthcare domain in the context of FI-STAR project. For the future work, selected privacy enhancing technologies such as privacy preserving authentication, pseudonymization will be investigated and developed.

Acknowledgment. The authors are members of the Future Internet – Social Technological Alignment Research (FI-STAR) project, which is part of the Future Internet Private Public Partnership (FI-PPP) run by the European Commission.

References

1. REST API Tutorial. http://www.restapitutorial.com
2. SAML Specifications. http://saml.xml.org/saml-specifications
3. OASIS eXtensible Access Control Markup Language. https://www.oasis-open.org/committees/tc_home.php?wg_abbrev=xacml
4. OAuth 2.0 Authorization Framework. http://tools.ietf.org/html/rfc6749
5. System for Cross-domain Identity Management (SCIM). http://www.simplecloud.info
6. Open ID Connect. http://openid.net/connect
7. FI-STAR: Future Internet Social and Technological Alignment Research. https://www.fi-star.eu
8. FIWARE: Open APIs for Open Minds. http://www.fiware.org
9. The Syslog Protocol. https://tools.ietf.org/html/rfc5424
10. Internet-enabler Innovation in Europe. http://www.fi-ppp.eu/projects/
11. FIWARE Identity Management Open Specification. https://forge.fiware.org/plugins/mediawiki/wiki/fiware/index.php/FIWARE.OpenSpecification.Security.IdentityManagement

12. FIWARE Authorization PDP Specification. http://forge.fiware.org/plugins/mediawiki/wiki/fiware/index.php/Access_Control_GE.Authorization.Open_RESTful_API_Specification
13. WSO2 Identity Server. http://wso2.com/products/identity-server/
14. Axiomatics Policy Server. http://www.axiomatics.com/solutions/products/authorization-for-applications/axiomatics-policy-server.html
15. Sun XACML implementation. http://sunxacml.sourceforge.net/index.html
16. SAML 2.0 Profile for OAuth 2.0 Client Authentication and Authorization Grants. http://tools.ietf.org/html/draft-ietf-oauth-saml2-bearer-23
17. Internet User Authorization Profile (IUA). http://wiki.ihe.net/index.php?title=Internet_User_Authorization
18. Fast Healthcare Interoperability Resources. http://www.hl7.org/implement/standards/fhir/resourcelist.html
19. Security & Privacy ICA (Integrated Access Control). http://catalogue.fi-star.eu/enablers/securityprivacy-iac
20. Spring Boot framework. http://projects.spring.io/spring-boot/
21. RSYSLOG: The Rocket-fast System for Log Processing. http://www.rsyslog.com

Authentication Scheme for REST

Luigi Lo Iacono and Hoai Viet Nguyen[(⊠)]

Cologne University of Applied Sciences, Cologne, Germany
{luigi.lo_iacono,viet.nguyen}@fh-koeln.de

Abstract. REST has been established as an architectural style for designing distributed hypermedia systems. With an increased adoption in Cloud and Service-oriented Computing, REST is confronted with requirements not having been central to it so far. Most often the protection of REST-based service systems is, e.g., solely ensured by transport-oriented security. For mission-critical enterprise applications securing data in transit only, is, however, not a sufficient safeguard. This introduces a vital demand for REST Security, which is currently an active research and development topic, focusing on one specific instantiation of REST merely, though, namely on HTTP.

This paper augments REST by an authentication scheme, while remaining on the same level of abstraction as the architectural style itself. The introduced authentication scheme for REST is then mapped to HTTP. Based on this concrete instantiation, an empirical study is conducted in order to analyse the current state of the art in authentication techniques for REST-ful HTTP. The developed scheme and its HTTP instantiation in particular offer a methodical framework for assessing and comparing the available work, which shows to be incompatible and incomplete in terms of the provided protection. Moreover, this generic authentication scheme can be used to deduce other concrete means related to existing and upcoming technologies for implementing REST-based systems.

Keywords: REST · REST security · Authentication

1 Introduction

Representational State Transfer (REST) [13] has been introduced as a guideline for designing large scale distributed hypermedia systems. The adaptation of REST in Cloud and Service-oriented Computing induces an increased utilization in enterprise environments. Such deployments have high security demands. A common safeguard for REST-based systems is the usage of Transport Layer Security (TLS) [11]. As the name implies, TLS shields data during transit only. Supporting the design of layered systems considering intermediate systems, transport-oriented security permits only a very limited protection. Moreover, using transport security as one and only pillar has been proved to be insufficient [5,7,24].

End-to-end security mechanisms for REST-based systems are gaining importance. Messages in REST own specific characteristics which must be considered

© Springer International Publishing Switzerland 2015
R. Doss et al. (Eds.): FNSS 2015, CCIS 523, pp. 113–128, 2015.
DOI: 10.1007/978-3-319-19210-9_8

before being able to develop integrated and comprehension security concepts. Unlike other related approaches such as SOAP [16], REST is not bound to any specific technology stack [14]. Another different property is the communication over a Uniform Interface. This REST constraint defines that a message consist of a set of data elements which can be based on different standards and data formats. HTTP [12] is, e.g., the most common protocol for REST-based applications and is composed of three technologies: (1) the HTTP itself, which defines the meta data, (2) the URI [6] specification representing the resource identifier and (3) the resource representation which can be any kind of data format such as JSON [10], XML [8] or HTML [19]. All these elements are equally important for the receiver of the message. Tampering one of them causes a different server-side and client-side processing. Hence, protecting only the body with approaches like XML-Security [30], if XML is used, or JavaScript Object Signing and Encryption (JOSE) [20], if JSON is used, is insufficient, since the meta data and the resource identifier play a central role for processing the REST message [15]. Based on these facts, many techniques focussing on the authenticity of REST messages have been evolved, recently.

However, these mechanisms only targets on HTTP-based REST applications. HTTP is merely one technical instantiation of the Uniform Interface and does not fit with all scenarios. The Internet of Things (IoT) domain, which has low-power requirements, uses the binary protocol Constrained Application Protocol (CoAP) [29] to implement REST architectures. In order to provide authenticity and integrity shields for the message exchange of all REST-based systems, a universal and technology-neutral concept is needed.

This paper introduces such an approach by augmenting the principles of REST with an integrated authentication scheme. Based on this scheme, a mapping to any technical foundation becomes feasible in a structured way governed by the abstract notation. This work maps the presented approach to HTTP in order to conduct an empirical state of the art analysis of current REST-based HTTP authentication techniques.

2   REST-Ful Message Authentication

The *Uniform Interface* is one of the basic REST constraints [13]. It specifies that REST messages are composed of meta data, a resource identifier and a resource representation. Meta data is grouped in three categories: control data, resource meta data and resource representation meta data. Control data is meta information specifying the intention of a message. This can be either the action of a request or the meaning of a response. Moreover, control data is used to parametrise messages and to overwrite default behaviours. Examples for the former type of control data include authentication information. The latter type is commonly utilised to perform cache controls or to redirect clients. The resource identifier represents a unique identifier of a resource. The client uses this identifier together with the control data to access or manipulate a resource. Resources by themselves are never exposed to the outside world. Clients can only retrieve a distinct representation of a resource or can manipulate a resource through a representation. Resource representations vary in terms of data formats according to the needs of client and service. Descriptive information on a resource is provided by resource meta data. Clients can use resource meta data to ask whether partial resource access is supported. Moreover, specific responses on status requests, e.g., contain resource meta data to describe allowed actions on a resource. A specification of the properties of a resource representation such as its type, encoding, language and length is contained in the group of resource representation meta data.

These three REST message elements forming the Uniform Interface can be implemented by different standards and are equally important for the message processing. Hence, a REST security scheme needs to consider them all. Protecting only the message body is insufficient, since malicious changes to the meta data or the resource identifier would still be feasible inducing a different treatment of the message regardless whether the resource representation is protected or not [15]. Such a violation could be a tampering of the request action. In a practical relevant attack an update request could be changed to become a delete request instead. Another possible vulnerability might result from a manipulation of the resource identifier redirecting the request to another resource. Likewise, the spoofing of other resource or resource representation meta data might provoke further client- or server-side misbehaviour.

To avoid such attack vectors, all the three REST message elements must be—from the viewpoint of an authentication scheme—integrity protected and authenticated. This paper contributes a generic scheme to authenticate a REST message which considers all crucial message elements. In order to lay the ground for a comprehensive REST authentication, a formal description of REST messages and an identification of authentication relevant parts in such messages need to be specified first.

2.1 Formal Description of REST Messages

Since REST is constrained to the client-server model in conjunction with the request-response model, it is always the client issuing a request message to which the addressed server replies with a response message. Thus, a REST message is either a request or a response. The request message space is denoted by R_c (were c stands for client) and the response message space is referred to as R_s (were s stands for server). The whole REST message space R is henceforth defined as follows:

$$R := R_c \cup R_s \tag{1}$$

The meta data space M is defined as the union of resource meta data M_r, resource representation meta data M_b and control data M_c:

$$M := M_r \cup M_b \cup M_c \tag{2}$$

The control data set M_c is composed of the union of the set of request actions M_{ca}, the set of response meanings M_{cm}, the set of message parametrisation M_{cp} and the set of data to overwrite the default processing of a message M_{co}:

$$M_c := M_{ca} \cup M_{cm} \cup M_{cp} \cup M_{co} \tag{3}$$

A REST message $r \in R$ consists of two parts: a header containing meta data and a body comprising a resource representation. With H denoting the header and B the body space, the structure of a REST message is defined as

$$r := h||delimiter||b, \{(r, h, b) : r \in R \wedge h \in H \wedge (b \in B \vee b \in \emptyset)\}, \tag{4}$$

where *delimiter* is a set of characters separating the header from the body and $||$ representing the concatenation operation. Note, that the actual embodiment of the delimiter depends on the concrete REST-ful protocol. In case of a binary protocol, the delimiter set might even be empty. For the sake of readability but without the loss of generality, the following explainations will focus on text-based protocols only, since these protocols include additional challenges in terms of the ordering, normalisation and separation of header fields. To obtain an according description for binary protocols, these aspects can simply be omitted.

A header h holds a subset $\dot{M} \subset M$ of the meta data entities. If h is part of a request message, it additionally includes a resource identifier $i \in I$, where I defines the set of resource identifiers. Because of this:

$$h := \begin{cases} (\dot{M}, i), & \text{if } r \in R_c, \\ (\dot{M}), & \text{if } r \in R_s. \end{cases} \tag{5}$$

The constitution of h can further be concretised by the following requirements:

1. A message $r \in R$ comprising a resource representation must include at least the two resource representation meta data entities $m_{bl} \in M_b$ and $m_{bt} \in M_b$ describing the length and the media type of the contained resource representation respectively.
2. A request $r \in R_c$ must contain one control data element $m_{ca} \in M_{ca}$ and one resource identifier i describing the action and the target of the action.
3. A response $r \in R_s$ must contain one control data element $m_{cm} \in M_{cm}$ expressing the meaning of the response.

2.2 Message Parts to Be Authenticated

As these header entries are considered security-relevant, they need to be part of h as a prerequisite. These entities form the information which is crucial to the message processing and therefore needs to be signed. Hence, these header elements are taken from h to shape the header to be signed denoted as $\tilde{h}$. This means that $\tilde{h}$ must contain at least the header entries defined in the requirements specified previously. The limitation of the signature coverage to $\tilde{h}$ instead of h as a whole is driven by efficiency considerations. Note, that $\tilde{h}$ varies depending on whether it is part of a request or response, the action of the request, the meaning of the response and whether the message contains a resource representation or not. The variability of $\tilde{h}$ can be especially substantiated by the request actions. Depending on the objective of the action, each of them may require a different set of meta data. However, the REST definition of Roy Fielding does not specify any concrete action. Since the intention of the uniform interface constraint is—among others—to define actions for manipulating and accessing resources, a set of reasonable methods can still be deduced which includes reading, creating, updating and deleting of resources. The following requirements define additional construction rules for $\tilde{h}$ based on the afore derived actions:

4. A read request must contain at least one resource representation meta data element $m_{br} \in M_b$ describing the desired media type being requested.
5. A creation request must contain a resource representation.
6. An update request must contain a complete or partial resource representation.
7. A delete request does not require any additional prerequisite header entities until further requirements.

Further requirements in terms of header entries contained in $\tilde{h}$ are a matter of the technical instantiation of REST and the application domain.

Based on these abstract notations, the following subsections introduce a signature generation and verification scheme for REST messages.

2.3   REST Message Signature Generation

Algorithm 1 defines a method for ensuring the authenticity and integrity of REST messages by generating a digital signature over the body and security-vital header entries. The latter are given by the requirements defined in Sects. 2.1 and 2.2. Note, that eventual error conditions are not made explicit due to readability reasons.

Algorithm 1. REST message signature generation

Input: REST message r, description $desc$ of the application-specific to be signed header entries, signature generation key k
Output: Signature value sv, time-variant parameter tvp
1: $b \leftarrow getBody(r)$
2: $h \leftarrow getHeader(r)$
3: $\tilde{h} \leftarrow getTbsHeaders(h)$
4: $\tilde{h} \leftarrow \tilde{h} \| getTbsHeaders(h, desc)$
5: $tvp \leftarrow generateTimeVariantParameter()$
6: $tbs \leftarrow tvp$
7: $i \leftarrow 0$
8: **while** $i < |\tilde{h}|$ **do**
9:    $tbs \leftarrow tbs \| delimiter \| normalize(\tilde{h}_i)$
10:    $i \leftarrow i + 1$
11: **end while**
12: $tbs \leftarrow tbs \| delimiter \| hash(b)$
13: $sv \leftarrow sign(k, tbs)$

The signature generation algorithm requires a REST message r, a signature generation key k and a description $desc$ that contains application-specific header fields to be appended to $\tilde{h}$. The latter argument is especially needed for RESTful protocols that are text-based. Such protocols usually identify header fields not by their (fixed) location in the message structure as binary protocols do, but by a standardised key. Moreover, the size of the string values is not constant, allowing for a higher flexibility, but requiring some form of delimiter in order to distinguish the entries from each other. Hence, for text-based REST-ful protocols a description needs to be provided, defining what additional header fields to include into the signature and in what sequence. After obtaining the body b and the header h from the message r, the function in line 3 must ensure that all required header entries are included in h in order to be able to construct $\tilde{h}$. Then eventually specified additional header fields are appended to $\tilde{h}$ according to the policy defined by $desc$. In order to avoid replay attacks, the signature generation algorithm continues with the creation of a fresh time-variant parameter tvp. This parameter is the first element to be assigned to the tbs variable, which is gradually filled with the data to be signed. These two steps must not be omitted even when a concrete instantiation of this scheme already includes a time-variant parameter in $\tilde{h}$, since between message generation and signature generation might exist a considerable time spread. All header fields contained in $\tilde{h}$ are normalised and concatenated to tbs. In order to tie the resource representation b to $\tilde{h}$ inducing the integrity of the conjunction of security-relevant header entries and body, it needs to be appended to tbs as well. The resource representation b is therefore hashed by a cryptographic hash function and the resulting hash value is attached to tbs. Note, that in case a message does have an empty resource representation, a hash of an empty body is computed and added to tbs. The next statement signs the crafted tbs with a signature generation key k. Algorithm 1 outputs the generated signature value sv and the time-variant parameter tvp.

With these two outputs, an authentication control data element $m_{cpa} \in M_{cp}$ can be generated, containing the signature algorithm name sig, the hash algorithm name $hash$, a key id kid, the time-variant parameter tvp, the signature value sv and the presence and order of additional header entries given by $desc$. This control data element m_{cpa} needs ultimately to be embedded into the respective message r. Since resource representations can vary, m_{cpa} must be integrated into the header h of the message r in order to remain data format independent.

2.4   REST Message Signature Verification

Algorithm 2 specifies the signature verification procedure for REST messages. As for the signature generation algorithm, the distinction between a binary and text-based transfer protocol instantiations is not considered explicitly. In case of the utilisation of a binary protocol, some of the otherwise required artefacts are not present. Note, that again for readability reasons, any handling of errors is omitted.

The signature verification algorithm requires a signed REST message r as input and it returns a boolean value expressing the validation result. From the signed message r the required parts are extracted, including the message body b and the message header h. From h the authentication control data header m_{cpa} can be obtained next, which consists of the concatenated values sig, $hash$, kid, tvp, sv and $desc$. After building $\tilde{h}$ in line 5, the next statement appends the

---

Algorithm 2. REST message signature verification

Input: Signed REST message r
Output: Boolean signature verification result $valid$
1: $b \leftarrow getBody(r)$
2: $h \leftarrow getHeader(r)$
3: $m_{cpa} \leftarrow getAuthorisationControlData(h)$
4: $(sig, hash, kid, tvp, sv, desc) \leftarrow split(m_{cpa})$
5: $\tilde{h} \leftarrow getTbsHeaders(h)$
6: $\tilde{h} \leftarrow \tilde{h}\|getTbsHeaders(h, desc)$
7: $tbs \leftarrow tvp$
8: $i \leftarrow 0$
9: **while** $i < |\tilde{h}|$ **do**
10:     $tbs \leftarrow tbs\|delimiter\|normalize(\tilde{h}_i)$
11:     $i \leftarrow i + 1$
12: **end while**
13: $tbs \leftarrow tbs\|delimiter\|hash(b)$
14: $valid \leftarrow verify(kid, tbs, sv)$

---

additional header entries to $\tilde{h}$ according to *desc*. Then the header fields in $\tilde{h}$ are iterated in the same manner—and especially the same order—as during the signature generation process to build *tbs*. With *tbs* and the signature verification key id *kid*, the verification of the signature value *sv* can be performed. The boolean verification result is assigned to the variable *valid*, which represents the output of the signature verification procedure.

3   REST-Ful HTTP Message Authentication

HTTP [12] is a stateless, text-based application layer transfer protocol. It builds the technical foundation of the Web and represents the most prominent instance of the REST concept [13]. This section applies the introduced REST message authentication scheme to HTTP in order to emphasise how it can be instantiated in the context of a concrete REST-ful technology. Further adoptions of the generic authentication scheme for REST to other REST-ful technologies can be carried out likewise resulting in equally protected environments. One example is CoAP [29] which gains traction as REST-ful protocol for resource-restricted environments.

3.1   REST-Ful HTTP

An HTTP message r is text-based and it is either a request issued by a client ($r \in R_c$) or a response returned by a server ($r \in R_s$). It consists of two parts: a header and a body. If present, the body contains a resource representation. The header part consists of a start line and a set of header fields. The start line of a request contains an HTTP method, a request-target and an HTTP version number. The HTTP method represents the action of a request whose action space M_{ca} is defined as follows:

$$M_{ca} := \{GET, POST, PUT, PATCH, DELETE, HEAD, OPTIONS\}$$

Most often, the request-target is a resource identifier i defined according to the URI [6] specification describing the location of the resource being requested. The HTTP version number declares the version of the protocol and the format of a message. In other words, it is a reference to parametrise a message. Therefore, it counts as control data element of M_{cp}.

A response start line begins with an HTTP version number followed by a status code and a reason phrase. The status code including the reason phrase is the meaning of the response and its space is defined as follows:

$$M_{cm} := \{100 \text{ Continue}, \ldots, 200 \text{ OK}, \ldots, 300 \text{ Multiple Choices}, \ldots,$$
$$400 \text{ Bad Request}, \ldots, 500 \text{ Internal Server Error}, \ldots\}$$

The header fields represent the remaining meta data of a message. The HTTP specification defines a large number of them which cannot be listed all at once. Hence, the following equation lists only few HTTP header fields which are elements of resource meta data M_r, resource representation meta data M_b, control data to override the default behaviours M_{co} and control data to parametrise message M_{cp}.

$$M_r := \{\text{Allow}, \text{Vary}, \text{Accept-Ranges}, \ldots\}$$
$$M_b := \{\text{Content-Length}, \text{Content-Type}, \text{Accept}, \ldots\}$$
$$M_{co} := \{\text{Cache-Control}, \text{Pragma}, \text{Location}, \ldots\}$$
$$M_{cp} := \{\text{Authorization}, \text{Date}, \text{Cookie}, \ldots\}$$

An HTTP message may include a resource representation that can be in any kind of data format. REST-ful HTTP clients and services commonly use JSON [10], XML [8] or HTML [19]. The delimiter to separate the header from the body is specified by the character sequence carriage return and line feed. Based on this instantiation, a mapping and extension of the requirements specified in Sects. 2.1 and 2.2 to HTTP messages can be conducted as follows:

1. An HTTP message containing a resource representation must include a Content-Length header field (m_{bl}) specifying the length and a Content-Type header field (m_{bt}) defining the media type of the resource representation.
2. An HTTP request must contain a method (m_{ca}) and a URL (i) within the start line describing the action and the target of the action.
3. An HTTP response must contain a status code followed by a reason phrase (m_{cm}) describing the meaning of the response.
4. An HTTP GET and HEAD request must contain an Accept header field (m_{br}) declaring the media type of the resource representation being requested.
5. An HTTP POST request must contain a resource representation.
6. An HTTP PUT request must contain a complete resource representation and a PATCH request must contain a partial resource representation.
7. An HTTP DELETE request does not require any additional prerequisite header fields until further requirements.
8. An HTTP message must contain a valid HTTP version number within the start line.

9. An HTTP message without a resource representation must denote the empty body with a Content-Length header field value 0 unless it is a response to a HEAD request.

10. An HTTP message must contain a Connection header field to instruct the endpoint about the connection management.

11. An HTTP request must contain a Host header field describing the host and the port of the targeted server.

12. An HTTP GET, HEAD, OPTIONS, DELETE request and a response with the status code 204 must not contain a resource representation.

13. An HTTP response to POST request and a response with the status code 301, 302, 303 or 307 intending to redirect a client to another resource must contain a Location header field with a URL as its value.

14. An HTTP response to a HEAD request must contain the same header fields as a response to a GET request.

15. An HTTP response to an OPTIONS request must contain an Allow header field declaring the allowed methods for a resource.

3.2 REST Message Authentication Applied to REST-Ful HTTP

All these requirements define the construction rules for $\tilde{h}$ in HTTP and have to be considered by the signature generating as well as verification procedures. Moreover, an authenticated REST message must contain an Authorization or equivalent header field storing the authentication control data element (m_{cpa}). Note, that this header entry is not included in $\tilde{h}$ and therefore remains unprotected, since it is generated after the signature computation of the message. If a violation of these prerequisites is detected, the according procedure has to judge the message as syntactically incorrect and needs to interrupt the processing.

The two templates shown below illustrate the adoption of Algorithm 1 to HTTP. Note, that the *delimiter* is implemented as a line break denoted as "\n" and the concatenation operator is the common string concatenation operation symbolised by '+'.

tbs string template for HTTP request	*tbs* string template for HTTP response
tvp + "\n" + UpperCase(Method) + "\n" + RequestTarget + "\n" + UpperCase(Version) + "\n" + LowerCase(Header0) + "\n" + ... LowerCase(HeaderN) + "\n" + Base64URL(hash(Body))	tvp + "\n" + UpperCase(Version) + "\n" + StatusCode + "\n" + LowerCase(Header0) + "\n" + LowerCase(Header1) + "\n" + ... LowerCase(HeaderN) + "\n" + Base64URL(hash(Body))

Assuming that the following example request and response messages require to be authenticated,

Example HTTP request message	Example HTTP response message
GET /resources/1 HTTP/1.1 Host: example.org Accept: application/json Content-Length: 0 Connection: keep-alive	HTTP/1.1 200 OK Content-Length: 19 Content-Type: application/json Server: Apache Connection: keep-alive Cache-Control: max-age=3600 {"REST":"Security"}

then each of the two strings to be signed *tbs* is constructed to:

tbs string of example HTTP request	*tbs* string of example HTTP response
2014-11-21T15:26:43.483Z	2014-11-21T15:26:45.351Z
GET	HTTP/1.1
/resources/1	200
HTTP/1.1	keep-alive
application/json	19
keep-alive	application/json
0	max-age=3600
example.org	CCGO5_fRG44ZYQTD6uMPmX8ksFkV12T3u
47DEQpj8HBSa-_TImW-5JCeuQeRkm5NMp	↪EUo_P6j5F2M
↪JWZG3hSuFU	

Note, that the header fields in $\tilde{h}$ are contatenated according to the alphabetical order of the header field names and not by the header field values. The second thing to note is that the example request contains only the required header fields and the response adds one additional header entry—the Cache-Control field—to $\tilde{h}$. To inform the verifier about this signature input extension, the signer includes the according description *desc*. The description is denoted as *addHeaders* (see next table) and contains a semicolon seperated list of additional headers to be covered by the signature apart from the required ones. If no additional headers are appended as in the example request, then the value is set to null. Also note, that the response leaves out the Server header field, since this meta data item is not crucial from an authenticity viewpoint.

The constructed string to be signed *tbs* is UTF8 encoded and then signed. Header entries in HTTP must be text, hence a transformation of the binary signature value to a text-based equivalent is required. This implementation uses a URL-safe Base64 transformation [23], because the standard Base64 encoding produces characters which are not allowed in the value of HTTP header fields:

$$sv = \text{Base64URL}(sign(k, \text{UTF8}(tbs)))$$

The final step incorporates the text-encoded signature value *sv* along with the associated authentication information to the newly defined Signature header field. From the standardised set of HTTP header fields none semantically matches the authentication content.

Authenticated example HTTP request	Authenticated example HTTP response
GET /resources/1 HTTP/1.1	HTTP/1.1 200 OK
Host: example.org	Content-Length: 19
Accept: application/json	Content-Type: application/json
Content-Length: 0	Server: Apache
Connection: keep-alive	Signature: sig=RSA/SHA256,hash=SHA256,
Signature: sig=RSA/SHA256,hash=SHA256,	↪ kid=https://example.org/cert,
↪ kid=https://myid.org/cert,	↪ tvp=2014-11-21T15:26:45.351Z,
↪ tvp=2014-11-21T15:26:43.483Z,	↪ addHeaders=Cache-Control,sigValue=<*sv*>
↪ addHeaders=null,sigValue=<*sv*>	
	{"REST":"Security"}

4   Related Work

The insufficient protection provided by transport security means in REST-based systems has already been identified as major shortcoming. Hence, some attempts

Table 1. Analysis of related work in HTTP message authentication

HTTP AuthN Approaches	AuthN Information in Header	Timestamp Required	Meta Data Required / Extensible	Content Hash Required	Content Hash Algorithm	Signature Algorithm	AuthN of Request / Response
Amazon [4]	● (or URL)	●	●/●	●	SHA256	HMAC-SHA256	●/○
Google [3]	● (or URL)	●	◑/○	○	MD5	HMAC-SHA{1,256}	●/○
HP [2]	●	●	◑/○	○	MD5	HMAC-SHA1	●/○
Microsoft [1]	●	●	◑/○	○	MD5	HMAC-SHA256	●/○
Signing HTTP Messages [9]	●	●	●/●	○	...	RSA-SHA56, HMAC-SHA256, ECDSA-SHA256	●/◑
OAuth 1 [17]	●	●	●/○	○	−	RSA-SHA1, HMAC-SHA1, Plaintext	●/○
OAuth 2 MAC Tokens [26]	●	○	●/●	○	...	HMAC-SHA{1,256}	●/○
Signing an HTTP Request for OAuth [25]	−	○	○/●	○	HMAC-SHA{256, 512}	Algorithms defined in JWA [21]	●/○
Serme et al. [28]	●	−	−/−	●	−	−	●/●
Lo Iacono et al.	●	●	●/●	●	...	...	●/●

have been developed to address this gap. This section evaluates the current state in REST message authentication which currently boils down to HTTP message authentication only. Guided by the contributions introduced in the Sects. 2 and 3 the related work is subsequently analysed in a methodic manner in order to infer its conformance with the requirements laid in Sect. 2. The related work is composed of practical approaches used in productive environments, (draft) standards and academic publications. The results are summarised in Table 1.

The Cloud storage services of Google [3], HP [2] and Microsoft [1] require a valid signature in any HTTP request in order to grant access to the functionalities provided by the REST-APIs. At the core of the signing process of all three services, a string to be signed is constructed by concatenating the HTTP method with the resource path including the query (unless HP which makes use of the resource path only) and a fixed set of header fields. Independent of the exact composition of these sets, only the timestamp entry is mandatory. All other specified header fields—including for instance the Content-Type or Content-MD5 entries—are optional. In case a foreseen header field is missing in the request message, an empty value is appended to the string instead. The signature value of the in this way constructed string is enriched with further signature-related meta data. This generated authentication information is finally inserted into the Authorization header. Google supports an alternative option which allows to incorporate the authentication information inside the query part of the URL.

The defined sets of header fields to be considered of each provider do not include all header fields contained in $\tilde{h}$, as defined in Sects. 2 and 3. Missing meta data includes for instance the Host and the Connection header fields. These omissions enable an adversary to redirect the message to another system or to manipulate the connection management. Moreover, the providers do not stringently require considering a hash of the body in signature computation. Clients can create a Content-MD5 header field to integrate a hash of the body in the signature, but they do not have to. Integrating a hash value covering the resource representation into the string to be signed is a vital requirement in order to provide the integrity of the whole REST message. Ignoring this opens the door for spoofing the resource representation. The last but not least observed disadvantage is the lack of mutual authentication, due to leaving the response out of the protection sphere. Thus, a client cannot proof the authenticity of a response providing the surface for man in the middle attacks.

The Amazon Simple Storage Service (S3) also requires the authentication of service requests over HTTP [4]. Like for the other three cloud storage providers, S3 clients have to concatenate the HTTP method, the resource path including the query and a set of header fields to a string to be signed. The authentication procedure of Amazon offers, however, more flexibility as it allows adding header fields to the signature computation as required by the application. This is realized by a list which specifies the header fields required to be appended before signing or verifying. When this list is used, the request must contain at least the Host header field, a header field containing a timestamp and the x-amz-sha256 header field which stores a SHA-256 hash of the body. The list is then stored together with signature value and the remaining authentication information either within the Authorization header field or in the URL. Based on this list, the S3 service checks what header fields are covered by the signature. If one of the required fields is not contained in the list, the service terminates the message processing.

Since the signature coverage can be extended, application specific meta data can be added. The other benefit is the required hash of the body in the signature generation. Amazon sets, however, the Host header entry, a timestamp and the x-amz-sha256 header field as mandatory only. Consequently, further important meta information such as the Content-Length, Content-Type and Connection header field are not considered. Thus, an attacker is able to manipulate the resource representation and the connection, if these header elements have not been signed. With the aid of the list, an adversary can extract what has been signed and what not. If the Content-Length and Content-Type header field are not in the list, a replacement of the resource representation with another resource representation with the same hash value is feasible. Taking the two aforementioned header fields into account is crucial to mitigate such attacks. By this, the attacker has to find a resource representation that has the same hash value, size and media type as the actual body. Also, Amazon's HTTP authentication scheme suffers from not taking the response into account.

A standard dealing with the authentication of HTTP message is the *Signing HTTP Messages* draft of the IETF [9]. Similar to the discussed proprietary approaches, a signer has to concatenate the HTTP method, the resource path including the query and a set of headers to a string to be signed. The concatenation order of the header fields is determined by the signer which creates a corresponding list. Together with the signature algorithm, the key id and signature value, this list is embedded in the Authorization or the newly defined Signature header field. Using this list, however, is not required. An absent list results in considering the Date header field in the signature generation only. Consequently, a present list must contain at least a Date entry. Besides this header field, the proposal does not consider additional meta data relevant to ensure

HTTP message authentication. A client can optionally add more header entries to the signature string if required and aware of the consequences of a too narrow protection sphere. Furthermore, the draft does not require incorporating a hash of the body in the signature computation. Moreover, it does not make clear, how a server needs to authenticate a response. Signing the response is mentioned at the beginning of the draft, but in the rest of the specification it is not elaborated any further.

The OAuth v1 specification of the IETF [17] has an inherent support for protecting a request by a signature. The signature string is the concatenation of the HTTP method, the resource path including the query, the Host header field and a set of OAuth v1 specific parameters. The latter parameters consist of a realm, a key id which is called consumer key, an OAuth token, a timestamp and a nonce. OAuth v1 does not enable to add any other parameter or header field in the signature. The authentication information is stored in the Authorization header entry. Like the other approaches discussed so far, the authenticity of the request is considered solely. No means for signing a response have been defined.

In contrast to the first version, OAuth v2 does not include any security means on its own [18]. That is why it is not present in Table 1. Instead, the security is merely based on TLS. If a message-oriented protection is yet required, OAuth v2 can be augmented by either the *OAuth MAC Tokens* [26] specification or by the extension *A Method for Signing an HTTP Requests for OAuth* [25]. The OAuth MAC Tokens draft demands to sign the HTTP method, the resource path including the query and at least the Host header field. Further meta data can be considered by defining a list similar to some of the previously discussed approaches. The resulting signature value has to be included into the Authorization header field.

The second OAuth v2 extension *A Method for Signing an HTTP Requests for OAuth* uses JSON Web Signature (JWS) [22] to guarantee the authenticity of HTTP messages. The JWS object used in this specification owns a set of members which contains the method, the host including the port, the resource path, the query, the headers, an HMAC authenticator of the body and a timestamp. Using JWS as the pillar can be a stable groundwork, since it is a well advanced IETF draft for signing JSON objects which is already used in many applications. However, the main drawback of this specification lies in the fact that all mentioned JSON members are optional. Even though most of these elements are vital to guarantee the authenticity and integrity of an HTTP message, none of them is set as mandatory for the signature. Also, this draft does not state any information whether the JWS object is stored in a header or in the body.

The common problem of both OAuth versions is the tight coupling to the actual application domain of these authorisation frameworks. As a result, adopting these standards to other contexts is not feasible in a straightforward manner. As with the other approaches, the major disadvantage of the OAuth protocols is that they do not specify a protection of the response.

Serme et al. [28] introduced the first approach which addresses this shortcoming and proposes a REST-ful HTTP security protocol which signs the request as well as the response. Their proposal introduces new header fields expressing the certificate ID, the hash algorithm and the signature algorithm name. The signature is a concatenation of the body, the URL, the hash algorithm name, the signature algorithm name, the certificate ID and a set of header fields forming a string to be signed. The generated hash and signature values are stored in separated, newly defined header fields each.

One drawback of [28] is the missing reference implementation. The paper provides only two pseudo code notations of the signature generation and verification. The algorithms do not clearly state whether a timestamp or the HTTP method is considered in the processing. Moreover, they do not clarify the order of the concatenation or some form of policy which retains the order. Likewise, the approach does not specify which header must be protected. That is, it is not clear whether all headers must be signed or a subset of them is sufficient.

5   Conclusions and Outlook

This paper contributes a generic authentication scheme for REST. It enables in the first place to analyse the requirements and characteristics of REST message authentication while abstracting from the specifics of particular technologies suitable to implement REST-based systems. Moreover, such an abstract authentication scheme serves as a guideline to deduce concrete authentication protocols and frameworks in a methodic manner, ensuring a security baseline provided by the generic scheme. Since HTTP/URI is currently the most common set of technologies used to implement REST-based systems, the proposed REST message authentication scheme can be used to derive a concrete instantiation for HTTP/URI. While additional REST-ful protocols and standards evolve—as it is the case with CoAP in context of resource-restricted environments—, an adoption to these evolving technologies can be performed likewise.

Due to the dominating presence of HTTP/URI for implementing REST-based systems, the creation of an authentication scheme for REST-ful HTTP has been carried out following the abstract definitions given by the proposed REST authentication scheme. This has been conducted in order to show the mapping to a particular technology by example and to emphasize the benefits of the REST authentication scheme.

The strength of the contributed authentication scheme for REST is not only rooted in the fact that it enables the instantiation of tangible authentication schemes for concrete REST-ful technologies in a methodical manner. It furthermore allows, e.g., to guide the analysis of the available state of the art in a systematical way. Based on the derived HTTP instantiation this has been conducted with the related work in HTTP authentication. The findings of the empirical analysis reveals that none of the investigated approaches comply with the requirements provided in Sect. 3 (see Table 1). The main weaknesses lie in the fact that important meta data are either not protected or their protection is left optional. Moreover, most of the available works do not include safeguards for the response message.

The results of this work highlight that a bunch of enhancements are still required in order to deploy and operate REST-based systems in mission-critical environments in a safe manner. This paper focusses on the core REST constraints, but leaves cacheability out of considerations so far. This topic will be elaborated in subsequent studies. Furthermore, the streaming-based transfer of resource representation will be studied. Also, future work will apply the contributed scheme to other REST-ful protocols such as CoAP and will analyse the interplay with other Web-based security specifications such as OAuth [17,18], OpenID Connect [27] and JOSE [20].

References

1. Authentication for the Azure Storage Services (2014). http://msdn.microsoft.com/en-us/library/dd179428.aspx
2. HP Helion Public Cloud Object Storage API Specification (2014). https://docs.hpcloud.com/publiccloud/api/object-storage/
3. Migrating from Amazon S3 to Google Cloud Storage (2014). https://cloud.google.com/storage/docs/migrating
4. Signing AWS Requests By Using Signature Version 4 (2014). https://docs.aws.amazon.com/general/latest/gr/sigv4_signing.html
5. The Heartbleed Bug (2014). http://heartbleed.com/
6. Berners-Lee, T., Fielding, R., Masinter, L.: Uniform Resource Identifier (URI): Generic Syntax. RFC 3986, IETF (2005). http://www.ietf.org/rfc/rfc3986.txt
7. Bhargavan, K., Delignat-Lavaud, A., Fournet, C., Pironti, A., Strub, P.Y.: Triple handshakes and cookie cutters: breaking and fixing authentication over TLS. In: 35th IEEE Symposium on Security and Privacy (S&P) (2014)
8. Bray, T., Paoli, J., Sperberg-McQueen, C.M., Maler, E., Yergeau, F.: Extensible Markup Language (XML) 1.0, 5th edn. Recommendation, W3C (2008). http://www.w3.org/TR/2008/REC-xml-20081126
9. Cavage, M., Sporny, M.: Signing HTTP Messages. Internet-draft, IETF (2014). http://tools.ietf.org/html/draft-cavage-http-signatures-03
10. Crockford, D.: The application/json Media Type for JavaScript Object Notation (JSON). RFC 4627, IETF (2006). http://www.ietf.org/rfc/rfc4627.txt
11. Dierks, T., Rescorla, E.: The Transport Layer Security (TLS) Protocol Version 1.2. RFC 5246, IETF (2008). http://tools.ietf.org/html/rfc5246
12. Fielding, R., Gettys, J., Mogul, J., Frystyk, H., Masinter, L., Leach, P., Berners-Lee, T.: Hypertext Transfer Protocol - HTTP/1.1. RFC 2616, IETF (1999). http://www.ietf.org/rfc/rfc2616.txt
13. Fielding, R.: Architectural styles and the design of network-based software architectures. Ph.D. thesis, University of California, Irvine (2000). https://www.ics.uci.edu/fielding/pubs/dissertation/top.htm
14. Fielding, R.: REST APIs must be hypertext-driven (2008). http://roy.gbiv.com/untangled/2008/rest-apis-must-be-hypertext-driven
15. Gorski, P., Lo Iacono, L., Nguyen, H.V., Torkian, D.B.: Service security revisited. In: 11th IEEE International Conference on Services Computing (SCC) (2014)
16. Gudgin, M., Hadley, M., Mendelsohn, N., Moreau, J.J., Nielsen, H.F., Karmarkar, A., Lafon, Y.: SOAP Version 1.2 Part 1: Messaging Framework, 2nd edn. W3C Recommendation, W3C (2007). http://www.w3.org/TR/soap12-part1/

17. Hammer-Lahav, E.: The OAuth 1.0 Protocol. RFC 5849, IETF (2010). https://tools.ietf.org/html/rfc5849
18. Hardt, D.: The OAuth 2.0 Authorization Framework. RFC 6749, IETF (2012). https://tools.ietf.org/html/rfc6749
19. Hickson, I., Berjon, R., Faulkner, S., Leithead, T., Navara, E.D., O'Connor, E., Pfeiffer, S.: HTML5 - A vocabulary and associated APIs for HTML and XHTML. Recommendation, W3C (2014). http://www.w3.org/TR/html5/
20. IETF JOSE Working Group: Javascript Object Signing and Encryption (JOSE) (2014). http://datatracker.ietf.org/wg/jose/
21. Jones, M.: JSON Web Algorithms (JWA). Internet-draft, IETF (2015). https://tools.ietf.org/html/draft-ietf-jose-json-web-algorithms-40
22. Jones, M., Bradley, J., Sakimura, N.: JSON Web Signature (JWS). Internet-draft, IETF (2015). https://tools.ietf.org/html/draft-ietf-jose-json-web-signature-40
23. Josefsson, S.: The Base16, Base32, and Base64 Data Encodings. RFC 4648, IETF (2006). https://tools.ietf.org/html/rfc4648
24. Meyer, C., Somorovsky, J., Weiss, E., Schwenk, J., Schinzel, S., Tews, E.: Revisiting SSL/TLS implementations: new bleichenbacher side channels and attacks. In: 23rd USENIX Security Symposium (USENIX Security) (2014)
25. Richer, J., Bradley, J., Tschofenig, H.: A Method for Signing an HTTP Requests for OAuth. Internet-Draft, IETF (2014). https://tools.ietf.org/html/draft-richer-oauth-signed-http-request-01
26. Richer, J., Mills, W., Tschofenig, H.: OAuth 2.0 Message Authentication Code (MAC) Tokens. Internet-Draft, IETF (2014). http://tools.ietf.org/html/draft-ietf-oauth-v2-http-mac-05
27. Sakimura, N., Bradley, J., Jones, M., de Medeiros, B., Mortimore, C.: OpenID Connect Core 1.0. Specification, OpenID Foundation (2014). http://openid.net/specs/openid-connect-core-1_0.html
28. Serme, G., De Oliveira, A.S., Massiera, Julien, R.Y.: Enabling message security for RESTful services. In: 19th IEEE International Conference on Web Services (ICWS) (2012)
29. Shelby, Z., Hartke, K., Borman, C.: The Constrained Application Protocol (CoAP). RFC, IETF (2014). https://tools.ietf.org/html/rfc7252
30. W3C: XML Security Working Group (2013). http://www.w3.org/standards/xml/security

Transmission Channel Switching Based on Channel Utilization in ROD-SAN

Takeo Hidaka$^{(\boxtimes)}$, Daiki Nobayashi, Yutaka Fukuda,
Kazuya Tsukamoto, and Takeshi Ikenaga

Kyushu Institute of Technology, Fukuoka, Japan
`j108093t@mail.kyutech.jp`

Abstract. In the future, wireless sensor and actuator networks (WSANs)
are expected to provide frameworks for various services such as the Internet of things (IoT) and machine-to-machine (M2M) communications. To
efficiently provide such services, WSANs require high response levels as
well as power saving functionalities. To facilitate this, we apply radio-on-
demand (ROD) technology to the wireless local area network (WLAN)
proposed in our previous work in order to create a WSAN that provides
low latency and reduced power consumption. In a WSAN that incorporates ROD technology, each sensor node has a dedicated wake-up receiver
that is used to receive wake-up signals. Since a sleeping sensor switches
to active mode when it receives a wake-up signal from its neighboring sensors, the method used to select an appropriate channel is a very
important consideration. Herein, we propose a channel selection scheme
that can provide the effective sensor node channel utilization by using
the channel utilizati on average. Then, based on simulations, we show
how our scheme is capable of decreasing node transmission delays while
simultaneously increasing a packet delivery ratio.

Keywords: WSAN · ROD-SAN · Channel switching

1 Introduction

Wireless sensor and actuator networks (WSANs), which are constructed by linking sensor and actuator nodes, are expected to provide frameworks for a variety
of future services, such as the Internet of things (IoT) and machine-to-machine
(M2M) communications. In such networks, where actuators work to control sensors, WSAN activities require rapid responses to time-dependent events, which
means that they normally perform sensing and control actions at high occurrence
rates. This results in significant network power consumption levels. These high-
speed demand response actions require high response performance and highly
efficient power-conservation technologies.

In WSANs, power saving is typically achieved via duty cycling. However,
due to the trade-offs involved, this method cannot facilitate both power reduc-
tions and high responsiveness. For example, when a node has a long set sleep
period, power conservation is achieved, but the responsiveness is degraded. Thus,

© Springer International Publishing Switzerland 2015
R. Doss et al. (Eds.): FNSS 2015, CCIS 523, pp. 129–138, 2015.
DOI: 10.1007/978-3-319-19210-9_9

a method in which each node can provide high responsiveness to communications demands while conserving power when idle is essential.

Accordingly, in an effort to apply radio-on-demand (ROD) [1] technology to WSANs, we have been working to develop radio-on-demand sensor and actuator network (ROD-SAN) technology. In ROD-SANs, each sensor node has a dedicated wake-up receiver that receives wake-up signals. This wake-up receiver operates continuously at ultra low power, even when the node is in a sleep state. When a wake-up receiver receives a wake-up signal from a neighboring node, the nodes switch to the active state in order to communicate. Additionally, since wake-up signals also include directions on which channel is to be used for communication with destination nodes, ROD-SAN nodes can efficiently utilize these multiple channels, and thus potentially facilitate both high responsiveness and power conservation. However, if multiple nodes use the same channel, packet losses and transmission delays increase significantly as a result of packet collisions. This is particularly true if each node behaves in the selfish manner. Thus, the method used when selecting an appropriate channel is a very crucial issue.

In this paper, we propose a new channel selection scheme. Our proposed scheme effectively alleviates channel collisions by instructing nodes to use a channel-switching index based on the average channel utilization and evenly distributes the traffic load among all available channels. Thus, each node can use available channels uniformly and autonomously. Through simulation experiments, we will also show how our scheme can not only decrease node transmission delays, but also increase a packet delivery ratio.

The remainder of this paper will proceed as follows: In Sect. 2, we introduce related work. In Sect. 3, we describe the ROD-SAN concept in detail. An outline of our proposed method is given in Sect. 4. In Sect. 5, the simulation model and results are provided, and in Sect. 6 we give our conclusions.

2   Related Works

WSANs are required to handle various types of traffic with different communication quality requirements. For example, sensor nodes must forward not only sensing data, but also control message to the actuators.

2.1   Works Related to Power Conservation

Coordinated sampled listening (CSL) and receiver initiated transmission (RIT), the two sub-modes discussed in IEEE 802.15.4 e/d [2], allow low duty cycle devices to access a network in order to reduce power consumption. In CSL, each sensor nodes send wake-up packets before sending data packets. In contrast, each sensor node sends a data request packet according the duty cycle when RIT is used. These methods effectively reduce wireless sensor network (WSN) power consumption. However, these schemes cannot facilitate power conservation and high responsiveness simultaneously. If the duty cycle interval is small, power consumption increases due to frequent wake up operations. Therefore, we believe that WSANs should have a function that allows them to wake-up on-demand.

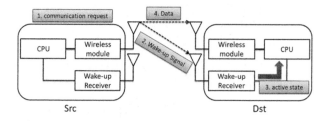

Fig. 1. Node with ROD-SAN

2.2 Works Related to Response Performance

Numerous methods for reducing WSN packet collision and transmission delay have been proposed [3–6]. In the single-sink multi-hop [7] method, the authors proposed parallel and block data transfer with multiple channels for fast data transfer. The multi-channel lightweight medium access control (MC-LMAC) [8] method also uses multiple channels to provide high throughput. These methods have shown the effectiveness of media access control across multiple channels. However, they do not discuss effective channel selection, so a scheme such as ROD-SAN is required.

3 ROD-SAN

ROD-SAN was developed to provide on-demand access in a WSAN, thereby facilitating both high responsiveness and power-consumption via implementation of a channel selection scheme using the wake-up receiver. In ROD-SAN, each node has a wake-up receiver corresponding to IEEE 802.15.4 d/g/e with a 920 MHz bandwidth [2], which is the wireless standard for WSANs. These wake-up receivers consume very low amounts of power and immediately activate the sensor if a wake-up signal from a neighboring node is detected. Therefore, a ROD-SAN enabled node can facilitate power conservation while maintaining high responsiveness.

3.1 Overview

Figure 1 shows an overview of a ROD-SAN node, each of which uses a radio module to send a wake-up signal to the next hop before sending a data packet. When the wake-up receiver of the next hop node receives the wake-up signal, that node immediately switches from sleep to active state and awaits data packets. ROD-SAN nodes can also communicate using multiple channels because the wake-up signal includes node identification and channel information. If the destination node flows along an appointed channel, the source node transmits the data to the destination node, and the destination node then transitions from active to sleep state. Therefore, ROD-SAN nodes facilitate high responsiveness and power conservation by transitioning from the sleep to active state only when communicating with other nodes.

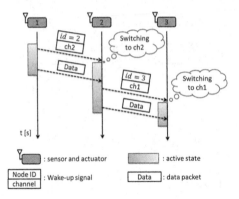

Fig. 2. Channel control process

3.2 Multiple Channel Correspondence

ROD-SAN nodes can also communicate using multiple channels. This feature is implemented by embedding a forwarding address node identifier and channel information into the wake-up signal. Figure 2 shows the channel control process. First, before beginning communication, Node 1 sends a wake-up signal to Node 2. This wake-up signal includes the information that Node 2 is to operate on Channel 2 (ch2). After scanning that information, Node 2 switches to ch2. Next, after transmitting the data packet to Node 2, Node 1 transitions to sleep state. If the packet received by Node 2 has to be forwarded to another node, Node 2 transmits it to a neighboring node or the destination node. Then, after scanning the wake-up signal for channel information, the next node implements communication over the designated channel. This process shows that ROD-SANs can use multiple channels because channel control can be easily achieved by embedding a forwarding address node identifier and channel information into the wake-up signal.

4 Proposed Method

In this paper, we propose a transmission channel switching method that uses a wake-up receiver to reduce channel interference by spreading the load equally over multiple channels. We report on the calculation method used for the wake-up receiver in Sect. 4.1, and describe the transmission channel switching method in Sect. 4.2.

4.1 Wake-Up Receiver Calculation

In a WSAN, all nodes normally communicate using a single-channel because the adjustment control in the multiple channels is complex. Additionally, when using radio signals to communicate, adjustments must be made between source and destination nodes. Furthermore, if numerous nodes are required to use the same channel to communicate, packet loss and transmission delay may increase due to channel interference when using carrier sense multiple access with collision avoidance (CSMA/CA). However, since the wake-up receiver is capable of capturing signals on all available channels, devising a proposal whereby using multiple channels can be used by numerous nodes to simultaneously reduce channel interference and power consumption would offer numerous benefits.

ROD-SANs perform captures based on channel conditions and achieve easy channel control by accessing channel and destination node identification information from the wake-up signals. First, the ROD-SAN transmits a wake-up signal to a node in the sleep state. Based on the length of the wake-up signal, the destination node then autonomously decides which channel is to be used. Furthermore, ROD-SAN nodes can calculate and assess the channel situations based on the signal length because the wake-up receiver can capture all channels currently in use. This demonstrates that ROD-SANs have the ability to assess channel utilization and achieve easy channel control.

4.2   Transmission Channel Switching Method

In this paper, we propose average-channel-utilization-based channel switching (ACS), which is a transmission-channel switching method based on channel utilization that will be described below.

First, the ACS calculates the average channel utilization of all channels from the overall utilization of each channel. It then determines how to use radio resources effectively by determining which nodes should be switched to other channels based on their probability of use in relation to average channel utilizations. In addition, ACS reduces packet loss and transmission delay because this method reduces channel interference through the efficient use of radio resources.

Figure 3 shows an overview of our proposed method. Each node calculates the utilization of each channel, u_{ch}, when it transmits data. After each node has calculated the u_{ch} value, they then calculate the average channel utilization, u_{ave}. If the channel utilization for each node is less than $u_{ave} + \alpha$ (any given value), they resolve that there is a low probability of occurring channel interference and transmit the data without switching channels. In contrast, if the utilization of the channel that each node is greater than $u_{ave} + \alpha$, they resolve that there is a high probability of occurring channel interference and transmit the data only after switching channels. In a ROD-SAN, autonomous distribution is achieved because all nodes that use channels with utilization levels in excess of $u_{ave} + \alpha$ switch to other channels. Each node decides, autonomously, whether to switch channels using Eq. (1).

$$p = \frac{u_{ch} - u_{ave}}{u_{ch}} \qquad (1)$$

Each node switches channels so that high load channels approach the u_{ave} by switching to channels with a utilization probability p. Furthermore, each node randomly switches from the channel being used by choosing a switching

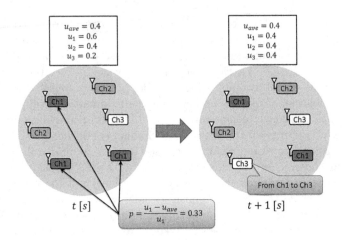

Fig. 3. Overview of our proposed method

destination channel from channels that have utilization rates of less than $u_{ave}+\alpha$. This allows ACS to achieve high responsiveness via the efficient use of radio resources.

5   Performance Analyses

In this section, we report on the simulation used to evaluate the effectiveness of our proposed method. A description of the simulation models used, along with the channel utilization, delivery ratio, and transmission delay results are presented and discussed below. We then discuss the results of the simulation.

5.1   Simulation Models

Table 1 lists the simulation parameters, and Fig. 4 shows the simulation models. We constructed the simulation environment with device settings from 5 to 40, coordinator settings from 4 to 39, and a PAN coordinator. We placed nodes at random within a 400 m square, set the flow distance at 30 m, and then set the traffic to be random from 1 kb/s to 20 kb/s. Next, we compared our proposed ACS method with the "Fixed" method, in which each node continues to use randomly chosen channels. We also compared our ACS method with the "Low" method, in which nodes using channels that exceed the average channel + α switch to a channel with a lower-than-average channel utilization.

5.2   Performance Evaluation of Delivery Ratios

Figure 5 shows the delivery ratio of each method. The horizontal axis shows the number of nodes, and the vertical axis shows the delivery ratio. The x of the "Low-ax" and "ACS-ax" were set to any given value α. In the figure, the delivery

Table 1. Simulation parameters

Name	Parameter
Simulator	QualNet 6.1
Simulation time	60 s
Number of nodes	$10 \sim 80$
Communication distance	30 m
Number of hops	1 hop
Transmission rate	250 kb/s
Number of channels	6
Radio interface	IEEE 802.15.4
Transport protocol	UDP
CBR rate	$1 \, kb/s \sim 20 \, kb/s$
Size of CBR packets	40 Byte

ratio of "Low" is approximately 75 %, and that of "Fixed" is approximately 82 % for 80 nodes. These methods have the potential to concentrate numerous nodes in one channel, thereby drastically decreasing their delivery ratios. In contrast, "the ACS" method can improve the delivery ratio. As a result, we conclude that ACS can effectively use multiple channels, and thus can significantly reduce channel interference.

5.3   Transmission Delay Performance Evaluation

Figure 6 shows the transmission delay of each method. The horizontal axis shows the number of nodes, and the vertical axis shows the transmission delay. In this figure, ACS and "Low" have significantly reduced transmission delays. "Fixed," on the other hand, has significantly increased transmission delays because this method is not able to switch to other channels. Nodes with low channel utilization do not occur channel interference, but channel interference is frequently occurred at all nodes with high channel utilization. In contrast, "ACS" and "Low" can reduce transmission delays because they can switch to other channels, thus avoiding channel interference. This result demonstrates the effectiveness of reducing transmission delay by proposed method.

5.4   Performance Evaluation of the Number of Channel Switching Operations

Figure 7 shows the number of channel switching operations by each method. The horizontal axis shows the number of nodes, and the vertical axis shows the number of channel switching operations. As we can see in the figure, with the "Low" method, the number of channel switching operations increases as the number of nodes increases. In particular, for 80 nodes, the number of channel switching

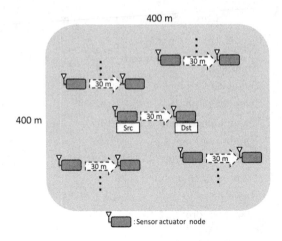

Fig. 4. Simulation models

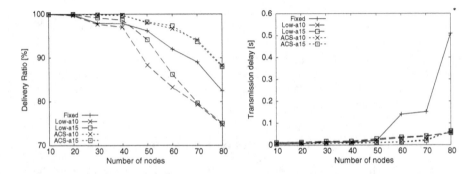

Fig. 5. Delivery ratio results   **Fig. 6.** Transmission delay results

operations increases to 1800. Because all nodes with higher average channel utilizations are able to determine when the channel load is high, they can switch to other channels whenever necessary. Thus, all nodes switch channels frequently without converging. However, the "ACS" method also reduces the number of channel switching operations as the number of nodes increases. Because our proposed method switches channels according to probability based on the average channel utilization, this method can reduce the number of channel switching operations to approximately 50.

5.5   Channel Utilization Performance Evaluation

Figures 8, 9 and 10 show the transition between channel utilizations. The horizontal axis shows the elapsed time of a simulation and the vertical axis shows the channel utilization. Figure 8 shows results for the "Fixed" method, Fig. 9 for the "Low" method, and Fig. 10 shows the results for the "ACS" method. In Fig. 8

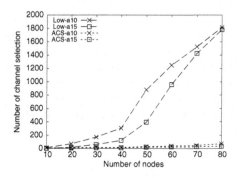

Fig. 7. Number of channel switching operations

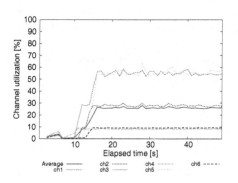

Fig. 8. "Fixed" channel utilization example

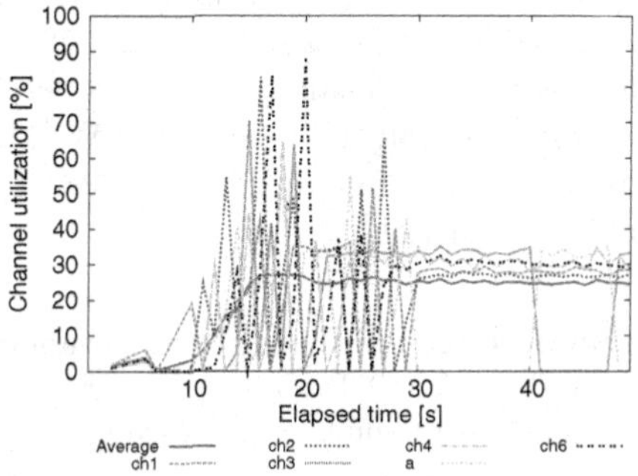

Fig. 9. "Low" channel utilization example

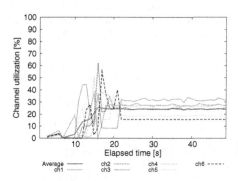

Fig. 10. "ACS" channel utilization example

"Fixed" shows significant differences in each channel's utilization. The channel utilization of ch1 and ch2 both increase to approximately 60%. However, the channel utilizations of ch4 and ch6 increase to only approximately 10%. This demonstrates that the "Fixed" method does not use multiple channels effectively.

Furthermore, in Fig. 9, we can see that the "Low" method is even less capable of using multiple channels than the "Fixed" method because all nodes using channels that exceed the $u_{ave} + \alpha$ switch to channels with lower than average channel utilizations. Contrastingly, the "ACS" method achieves a value nearly equivalent to that of the average channel utilization because, using probabilities, it switches from an excessive channel utilization to the average channel utilization. Therefore, it can be said that "ACS" uses multiple channels effectively.

6 Conclusions

In this paper, we reported on of the improved power-conservation and high responsiveness of ROD-SANs in WSANs. In response to concerns that ROD-SAN technology may occur channel interference frequently between nodes, we proposed a new transmission channel switching method that reduces channel interference by using a wake-up receiver to spread the communication load equally over multiple channels. We then demonstrate the effectiveness of this method. In our future work, we plan to verify the effectiveness of our method in multihop network.

Acknowledgement. This work is supported by the Strategic Information and Communications R&D Promotion Programme (SCOPE) funded by Ministry of Internal Affairs and Communication, Japan.

References

1. Tang, S., Yomo, H., Kondo, Y., Obana, S.: Wake-up receiver for radio-on-demand wireless LANs. EURASIP J. Wirel. Commun. Netw. **42**, 1–13 (2012)
2. IEEE 802.15.4. http://www.ieee802.org/15/pub/TG4.html
3. Akyidiz, I.F., Melodia, T., Chowdhury, K.R.: A survey on wireless multimedia sensor networks. Comput. Netw. **51**(4), 921–960 (2007)
4. Yick, J., Mukherjee, B., Ghosal, D.: Wireless sensor network survey. Comput. Netw. **52**(12), 2292–2330 (2008)
5. Yigitel, M.A., Incel, O.D., Ersoy, C.: QoS-aware MAC protocols for wireless sensor networks: a survey. Comput. Netw. **55**(8), 1982–2004 (2011)
6. Durmaz Incel, O.: A survey on multi-channel communication in wireless sensor networks. Comput. Netw. **55**(13), 3081–3099 (2011)
7. Tomonori, N., Moinzadeh, P., Mechitov, K., Ushita, M., Makihata, N., Ieiri, M., Agha, G., Spencer, B.F., Fujino, Y., Seo, J.-W.: Reliable multi-hop communication for structural health monitoring. Smart Struct. Syst. **6**(5), 481–504 (2010)
8. Durmaz Incela, O., van Hoeselb, L., Jansenc, P., Havingac, P.: MC-LMAC: a multi-channel MAC protocol for wireless sensor networks. Ad Hoc Netw. **9**(1), 73–94 (2011)

Malware Biodiversity Using Static Analysis

Jeremy D. Seideman[1](✉), Bilal Khan[2], and Antonio Cesar Vargas[3]

[1] The Graduate Center, City University of New York, New York, USA
jseideman@gradcenter.cuny.edu
[2] Department of Mathematics and Computer Science, John Jay College,
CUNY, New York, USA
bkhan@jjay.cuny.edu
[3] NacoLabs Consulting, LLC, New York, USA
cesar@nacolabs.com

Abstract. Malware is constantly changing and is released very rapidly, necessarily to remain effective in the changing computer landscape. Some malware files can be related to each other; studies that indicate that malware samples are similar often base that determination on common behavior or code. Given, then, that new malware is often developed based on existing malware, we can see that some code fragments, behavior, and techniques may be influencing more development than others. We propose a method by which we can determine the extent that previously released malware is influencing the development of new malware. Our method allows us to examine the way that malware changes over time, allowing us to look at trends in the changing malware landscape. This method, which involves a historical study of malware, can then be extended to investigate specific behaviors or code fragments. Our method shows that, with respect to the method in which we compared malware samples, over 64 % of malware samples that we analyzed are contributing to the biodiversity of the malware ecosystem and influencing new malware development.

1 Introduction

When studying *malware*, it is tempting to treat it as artificial life [27]; whether or not malware can actually be considered artificial life is a study on its own. When studying artificial life, though, concepts from biology are used to aid in measurement and analysis [34]. Our study of malware requires us to adopt some of those concepts from biology. We begin to build our method with these concepts. To start, we consider each malware sample as an *organism*.

Minor differences between organisms do not necessarily separate them into different species – two organisms can exhibit some differences and still be considered the same species. With malware, this is seen with *variants* – malware that is based on earlier malware with small changes. Looking at variants leads to a discussion of what actually constitutes relationships among malware [11]. As malware writers often reuse other code or infection techniques used in earlier malware, we can say that the earlier malware has an influence on later "offspring" malware, in

© Springer International Publishing Switzerland 2015
R. Doss et al. (Eds.): FNSS 2015, CCIS 523, pp. 139–155, 2015.
DOI: 10.1007/978-3-319-19210-9_10

this possible indirect fashion. As malware release rates are reported to be as high as 82,000 new malware samples per day [22], we can infer that there would be a lot of similarity between those new samples and existing ones, since malicious code is often based on existing code. Due to the way malware is released, we wanted to examine how malware samples relate to each other over time.

By definition, Malware interacts with, and has an effect upon, its "environment" – the infected system or systems upon which it operates [7,10]. In this study, that environment is the *ecosystem* in which our organisms exist. In biology, *biodiversity* can "refer to the number and size of populations in a community [20, p. 12]." Since that community can contain many different species, many ecologists prefer to examine communities based on their *species diversity*, which examines the number of species within the community and the number of members of each species [5, p. 1130]. The relationship of organisms with each other, with other organisms, and with other parts of the ecosystem is the organism's *ecological niche*, which represents not just a thing or a place, but the process as a whole including the things and the places [23, p. 72]. In our research, we see the side effects of malware, but they are not the same as the effects of living organisms. As a result, we will not see certain types of interaction between malware samples that we would see among biological organisms, such as competition between samples, despite the fact that this interaction is known to exist [27].

The ecosystem reflects the generalized state of computers as a whole, with the various operating systems, applications, and users and their associated vulnerabilities that can allow for malware infection. In effect, we are looking at malware through the lens of species diversity within an ecological niche that encompasses the collected computers in the world. Our definition of biodiversity, which will be explored below, therefore is more restrictive than the definition found in biology as we cannot reliably determine certain qualities about malware infection, such as the number of infected machines or the number of actual malware organisms.

Through a variety of methods, malware samples can be analyzed in order to see how they fit into this ecosystem. Malware analysis techniques are generally grouped into two types, static and dynamic, indicating how the samples are examined. Our study employs static analysis, as we are examining the malware binaries as they sit on disk. Our analysis method was partially inspired by previous studies, e.g. [16,17], which looked at fixed-width segments of binary code. Knowing that variants of malware are going to exhibit similar characteristics [32] allows us to group them together; while that particular study involved dynamic analysis of malware, the fact that malware behavior is a result of program code implies that variants of malware may have similar byte sequences.

The remainder of the paper is organized as follows: Sect. 2 discusses prior work related to our study, Sect. 3 explores our research method, Sect. 4 discusses our results, and Sect. 5 describes our findings and future directions for the work.

2 Prior Work

Often, malware is grouped together based on some sort of behavioral classification method; there are several ways to do this. Generally, the malware samples are analyzed dynamically, yielding a representation of their behavior, which can be used to determine the relationship between the samples. Lee and Mody classified malware by examining the behavior as a sequence of events that occur to the operating system, and then utilized several different methods to cluster similar malware together, creating families [18]. The goal of their research was to find a way to automate classification and use machine learning in order to produce more reliable clustering, in order to better defend against future malware.

Bailey, *et al.* devised a way to label malware that could provide a unified way to identify malware and respond to the shortcomings of many anti-virus systems, by profiling malware behavior on execution and examining the information overlap between those profiles [3]. Their results were quite promising, as they were able to consistently cluster malware into appropriate families. They were also able to show that anti-virus software often did not group malware together properly, and that different vendors would often group malware differently, which reduces the utility of anti-virus software in general. At the same time, Jacob, *et al.* promotes the use of behavioral detection to overcome shortcomings over other detection methods, while using several different grouping techniques to create families, but also does not discount the usefulness of static analysis to perform more detailed analysis [14].

Recently, the authors of [1] used Hidden Markov Models (HMMs) to classify malware. They state that similar malware will have similar behavioral profiles, and even though static methods are more efficient than dynamic methods, they do have limitations. Their method scores malware differences with an untrained HMM, clustered with k-means. Their method was able to easily differentiate between the malware families in their corpus, and they point out several improvements to their method that would also show promise, but conclude that their method would be useful in malware analysis. The authors of [33] have previously shown that the use of HMMs is useful in classifying similar malware even in the face of metamorphism, provided that malware samples are compared using a method that identifies code sequences that identify similar behavior, since even with metamorphic techniques, some of the code may remain the same and can be identified as such.

Seewald views the classification problem as one of machine learning, executing samples within a restricted execution environment, allowing for the recording of behavior [24]. He then tried several clustering algorithms to see if the clusters corresponded to the sample names, and to determine which clustering methods worked best. Bayer, *et al.* also examines several similar techniques; that study has shown positive results, demonstrating a highly efficient and accurate analysis and classification method of malware samples. They utilized several forms of behavior to create their profiles and create malware clusters, but also presented an efficient algorithm that avoids calculating all pairwise comparisons of samples in their data set [4].

All of this prior work shows the importance of classification by using behavior, and how classification is useful when performing analysis. None of them, however, explore the changing malware landscape over time and attempt to determine the influence of samples on the development of later samples. Our study will serve to examine the relationship between related samples in order to determine whether or not samples are creating "offspring" samples, whether they are variants or completely new types of malware.

One of the major influences for our study was the work by Karim, *et al.* which built phylogeny models based upon static analysis of malware samples, using both fixed-width code segments and permutations of those code segments. From there, they also employed some clustering techniques and were able to build a phylogenetic tree to compare detection rates of anti-virus programs in order to verify if their classification was correct [16]. Another major influence was the work by Kolter and Maloof, who also used fixed-width code segments, analyzing the frequencies that occurred in their data set in order to select those that were most relevant [17]. Their data set, which was made of benign and known malicious samples, and then samples from the wild, was then analyzed with several different methods to see how well their system could detect an unknown malware sample. Again, these studies did not take into account the temporal dimension, so the influence of samples over time could not be seen.

There has been other work that uses the concept of ancestor-descendant relationships between malware samples. One of particular interest is the work of Darmetko, *et al.*, which sought to use artificial intelligence techniques to determine relationships between malware samples in a lineage. Their method was able to correctly identify lineages to a high degree and correctly identify parent-child relationships in cases when they were known (which was a feature of their malware corpus). Their approach, however, did not take into account the temporal dimension, opting instead to use structures within the individual samples in order to identify parent-child relationships [8].

The work of Jang, *et al.* is also of interest as it also seeks to automatically determine software lineage. Their work represents the parent-child relationship with a straight line lineage and a directed acyclic graph, by employing a variety of methods – both static and dynamic – to determine the difference between samples. Their difference measurements included the use of n-grams of code. Their results also showed a high-degree of accuracy in identifying these relationships. They decided upon this approach instead of using phylogenetic trees because they felt that their method provided better metrics to judge the quality of their results [15]. As our method uses existing data about our malware corpus to build phylogenetic trees, we are able to use this existing data along with the relationships that we determine in order to perform our analysis.

3   Method

Our method of analysis is applied to a historical study of malware. We start by determining the relationship between those samples and then creating a data structure that represents that relationship. We can then use a time line to determine how samples contribute to the biodiversity of the malware ecosystem.

3.1   Malware Corpus

As we are engaged in a historical study of malware, we required a tagged and dated malware corpus for our analysis. We used the VX Heavens malware corpus [31] as our source. Using a custom email submission engine, we submitted the samples to VirusTotal [30], obtaining the labels that various anti-malware software would assign each sample. Taking a list of discovery dates from Symantec's Threat Explorer [28] we removed samples for which we had no discovery date, leaving us with a corpus, $\mathcal{M}$, of $N = 32,573$ samples. When $\mathcal{M}$ is sorted chronologically by discovery date, we refer to the jth malware sample, where $j \in \{1...N\}$, as M_j. The discovery date of sample M_j is denoted by $Date(M_j)$. We refer to the set of malware discovered on date d as $\mathcal{M}_d$.

3.2   Static Analysis

We analyzed our corpus with a static analysis technique. Our comparison method is based on the methods presented by Karim, et al. [16] and Kolter, et al. [17], where n-grams of bytes are extracted from each sample. However, instead of weighting the importance of an n-gram using TFxIDF or Information Gain as in those studies, we opted to use the n-gram distribution of bytes within the sample.

For every malware sample M_j, we computed the n-gram frequency probability distribution, $H_n(M_j) : P_n \to [0,1]^1$, where P_n is the set of n-grams. We chose a value of $n = 4$ for our study, based partially on the previous work which showed the best results at that value of n. Furthermore, many x86 machine code instructions are four bytes or less (with the average being around two bytes [12]), increasing the chance that an extracted n-gram contains an entire instruction when $n = 4$. As the maximum size of an instruction is 15 bytes [13], any instructions requiring multiple sequences of four bytes will appear together in multiple samples if the same instruction is used. Using a larger n would not give a better result as the n-grams would likely contain multiple instructions, reducing their usefulness. As we are scanning the entire file, the n-grams can also include non-instruction bytes. The distribution gives us the list of interleaved n-grams and the frequency of each.

For each pair of malware samples, M_a and M_b, we computed the cosine similarity based on their n-gram distributions, $A = H_4(M_a)$ and $B = H_4(M_b)$. Using A and B as vectors, cosine similarity uses the angle θ between them as a measure of similarity [26]. Using cosine guarantees the similarity ranges from 0 to 1. To calculate the distance between two samples as represented by cosine similarity, we subtracted the similarity from 1:

$$D(M_a, M_b) = 1 - \cos(\theta) \tag{1}$$

---

[1] In other words, $H_n(M_j) : P_n \to \{y|0 \le y \le 1, y \in \mathbb{R}\}$.

where $\cos(\theta)$ is calculated as the ratio of the **dot products** of the two vectors to the product of the **Euclidean lengths** of the vectors [9]:

$$\cos(\theta) = \frac{A \cdot B}{\|A\|\|B\|} = \frac{\sum_{p \in P_4} (A_p \times B_p)}{\sqrt{\sum_{p \in P_4} (A_p)^2} \times \sqrt{\sum_{p \in P_4} (B_p)^2}} \tag{2}$$

in order to get the distance between two files, so that identical files (which would have $\theta = 0$ between them) have a distance of 0, while two completely different files have a distance of 1. For example, Trojan.Win32.Deltree.b and Virus.Boot.Havoc.l are very different as evidenced by a cosine difference of 0.983270. On the other hand, Virus.DOS.Spanska.1120.a and Virus.DOS.PS-MPC.748 are very similar, as their cosine difference is 0.000379.

We found that computing the distance between all possible pairs would be too time-consuming, so we pruned the number of required comparisons by only comparing samples to those that appeared earlier in time. We also noticed variability in the sizes of the samples and decided to reduce the number of comparisons by only comparing samples that are within a certain size threshold of each other, the rationale being that even if two samples are similar based on their n-gram distributions, they are probably not closely related if they are vastly different in size. We felt that by restricting the comparisons, we would be able to obtain more meaningful results. We selected a size threshold of 25 % for our dataset, and only compared samples that were within a 25 % binary size difference from each other.

It is important to note that all static analysis methods, including cosine similarity, are weak against obfuscation [3], where a sample's binary code can be changed through encryption and compression, and polymorphism and metamorphism [19,21], where samples alter their infectious payload in order to avoid matching known signatures of their infection, yielding malware which can be functionally similar but have different internal structures [33]. Polymorphic malware alters the routines used to decrypt the encrypted payload (which means that static techniques would work on the decrypted payload), while metamorphic malware alters the actual program code, through techniques like code substitution, garbage instruction insertion and subroutine permutation. Malware generation kits allow malware creators to perform these operations and others on malware code to create "new" malware that would be difficult to detect using static analysis but still maintain the same or similar behavior.

3.3   Tree Building

To demonstrate the relationship between pairs of malware, we constructed a phylogenetic tree. Samples were ordered by discovery date and added to the tree in order, so that we could see their ancestor-descendant relationship. The tree was built up incrementally by attaching each sample to the node in the tree with which it had the lowest distance. At time i we constructed tree $T_i = (V_i, E_i)$

from tree $T_{i-1} = (V_{i-1}, E_{i-1})$, using malware samples $\mathcal{M}_i$ that appeared on that day[2]:

$$V_i = V_{i-1} \cup \mathcal{M}_i \tag{3}$$

and

$$E_i = E_{i-1} \cup \{(x,y)|x \in \mathcal{M}_i \wedge y \in V_{i-1} \wedge D(x,y) \text{ is minimal.}\} \tag{4}$$

such that M_j connects to V_{i-1}^a, a vertex in tree T_{i-1} for malware sample M_a, the closest sample that appeared before M_j. The tree generated is unique to the distance metric employed; the choice of a different distance metric will produce a different tree as the relationships between samples would be measured and expressed differently.

Our method does not take into account a threshold distance value, above which a new sample should become a new root node within a forest instead of being attached to an ancestor. Ongoing research is exploring different ways to identify better methods to attach nodes to the tree, in order to identify more accurate clusters of malware that help illustrate better ancestral relationships.

There were cases where there were samples that were larger than older samples in the corpus. In these cases, if they had a size difference larger than the 25 % threshold we used to prune the number of comparisons, we had no distance measurements and were unable connect them to an existing node in the tree. These nodes would then become the root of a new tree, thus turning our tree into a forest. For example, when Trojan.Win32.FormatAll.d appeared, there were no existing samples that were within the size difference threshold for it to attach to, so it formed the root of a new tree within the forest.

3.4   Stasis Criteria

If a node does not appear to spawn any offspring, it may be a "dead-end" in terms of development in the ecosystem. When a node is no longer contributing to the biodiversity of the ecosystem, we declare the node as "in stasis." The *stasis coefficient* at time i is represented as X_i. We calculate X_i by selecting a *stasis criterion*, which helps us define when a sample is to be placed in stasis. As a stasis criterion, we chose the *current mean* of the age difference between parent and child; our stasis coefficient was calculated as:

$$X_i = mean(Date(M_v) - Date(M_u)|(M_u, M_v) \in E_i) \tag{5}$$

Nodes in the tree or forest can have zero or more children. We defined $Child(M_j, i)$ as the set of children of M_j at time i, directly connected to M_j and appearing in the corpus after M_j. We then say that a node is *in stasis* if the difference between the sample's discovery date and the current date is greater than the stasis criterion, and the sample has not produced any offspring that

---

[2] Any nodes that appeared on the same day were added to the tree at the same time, since we could not determine the order in which the samples were discovered beyond the discovery date.

are *not* in stasis at time i. We check the node's children since, despite the age of the node, if it produced children that are not in stasis it is contributing to the overall biodiversity. At a given time i, the set of nodes that are in stasis, S, is defined as:

$$S_i = \{M_x \in V_i | i - Date(M_x) > X_i \wedge \forall M_y \in Child(M_x, i), i - Date(M_y) > X_i\} \tag{6}$$

Stasis differs from extinction in that stasis does not permanently remove the node from the ecosystem. In order to determine when a sample is no longer contributing to the biodiversity of the ecosystem, we use the stasis coefficient to calculate whether or not we should place a node in stasis at i. However, if a node in stasis at i spawns a child at time $i + \delta i$, we would no longer consider the node to be in stasis at $i + \delta i$.

It is important to note that placing a node in stasis has no effect on that node's parents or children. If a node is placed in stasis, it is possible for that node's parent or child to remain out of stasis; if we were to remove nodes in stasis from the tree, placing a node in stasis would split the tree into multiple components.

3.5   Biodiversity Calculation

Our biodiversity calculation is based on our determination of which nodes in the forest are contributing to the biodiversity at each time i on the time line. The set of nodes that are "alive" and contributing to the biodiversity of the ecosystem at each time i are those nodes that are not in stasis at i:

$$Alive_i = V_i \setminus S_i \tag{7}$$

The biodiversity, β, at time i is $0 \geq \beta_i \geq 1$ and is calculated as:

$$\beta_i = \frac{|Alive_i|}{|V_i|} \tag{8}$$

and is calculated at every time i and can then be analyzed for a data set. We can also examine the rate of change of β from one time point to another by taking the derivative of β. A β of 1 indicates that all nodes are alive. A β of 0 indicates that all nodes are in stasis. This can only happen if there is a time i on the time line where no new nodes were discovered and there have been no new nodes discovered for a time period longer than the time period calculated by X_i. In other words, it is a date on the time line that occurs during a period of no development, after more than X_i time has passed since the last sample was discovered.

4   Results

Our corpus consists 32,573 samples spread over 1,562 time points (where a time point is a date where malware samples appeared), ranging from 1 to 5,691 samples at each point, for an average of 20.85 samples appearing per time point.

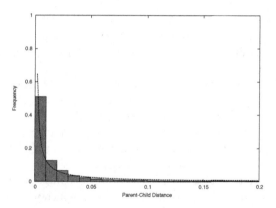

Fig. 1. Histogram of parent-child distances, using $D(M_a, M_b)$.

Our analysis was performed on the COS25 dataset – the comparison of samples using cosine similarity when the binary sizes were within 25 % of each other.

We calculated the pair-wise distances between samples and built the phylogenetic trees at each time i to calculate X_i and β_i. Overall, the average parent-child age difference was 806 days, with a standard deviation of 658 days. This means that samples can be more closely related to older samples than to more recent ones, suggesting the existence of infection techniques and code segments that are reused for a very long time. The average parent-child distance was 0.1149 with a standard deviation of 0.2483, indicating that child samples tend to be very similar to their parents. While there were some children that had a larger distance to their parent, this value indicates this was not the norm.

The frequencies of parent-child distances as determined by our cosine similarity distance measurement decay as expected by a power law. Figure 1 shows the frequency histogram, fit to $y = ax^b$ when $a = 0.0013$ and $b = -1.0066$.

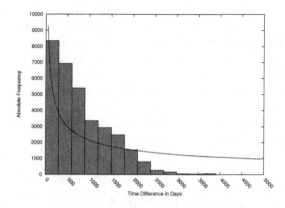

Fig. 2. Histogram of parent-child age differences.

We see that, while there are sample pairs that exhibit a larger parent-child distance, the majority of the parent-child distances are small. In the figure, we limit the x-axis to a value of 0.2 as only a tiny fraction of the parent-child distances were greater than 0.2.

Figure 2 is a histogram of the frequencies of parent-child age differences, including the best-fit curve $y = ak^b$, when $a = 62539.2$ and $b = -0.4892$. The distribution deviates from the best-fit curve but still demonstrates a decay. We saw more of the smaller age differences, with fewer large age differences. While there were occasional parent-child age differences that were exceedingly large, the fact that the majority of them were small suggests that new malware tends to be based on more recent malware that is in turn based on older samples. However, we know that the average parent-child age difference is large, which we see in the deviation of the distribution from the expected values. The majority of the parent-child age differences occur at a greater frequency than actually expected, skewing the average towards a higher number. While a node is more likely to attach to a more recent sample than an ancient one, we see a high number of instances of children attaching to an older parent than a more recent one.

Over the entire time line, the average β was 0.6412, with a standard deviation of 0.2041. In other words, 64.12 % of the samples were contributing to the biodiversity of the ecosystem. A high average β would mean the majority of the samples present at any time were spawning offspring. A lower average β does not necessarily mean the opposite – it could mean is that our malware ecosystem is similar to a natural one, and that samples that go into stasis do not return to the ecosystem. Rather, their offspring lead to future progeny – ancestral samples are eventually removed but their descendants remain to spawn new samples. Since our measure of biodiversity takes into account all of the samples that have *ever* appeared, we see that stasis limits the overall biodiversity, while still allowing for new lineages of malware samples.

4.1   Malware Offspring and Families

The phylogenetic tree tells us a variety of things about our data set. We can determine families, calculate node procreation rates and separate out those nodes which can be considered a "dead-end" in terms of malware development. For example, Virus.DOS.SillyC.217.d was released in 1993 and never spawned a child in the data set that we could link to, based on our method. We can then say that the code used in that sample did not appear to lead to further development of later samples.

We found that 22.9 % (7,463) of the nodes in our tree had child nodes, meaning 77.1 % of the nodes in the tree were leaf nodes. This does not mean that they were all dead-ends, though, only that at that time we did not have a child to attach to them. On the average, nodes with children had an out-degree of 4.33, with a standard deviation of 13.35.

The number of offspring that a malware sample produced appears to obey a power law distribution, as seen in Fig. 3, a histogram of the frequencies of the out-degrees of the nodes in our tree fit to $y = ax^b$ where $a = 0.2185$ and

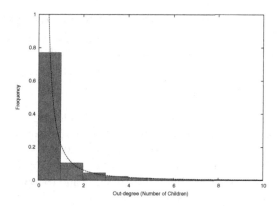

Fig. 3. Histogram of number of children for COS25.

$b = -1.8187$. Nodes with out-degrees greater than 10 represented a very small percentage of the frequencies and are absent from the histogram. As show in the figure, the majority of the nodes have an out-degree near the mean, which was expected, despite the low average out-degree and high standard deviation. There is a large amount of variability in the out-degrees present in our tree.

Of the nodes that produced children, there were several that produced a large number, although these samples were clearly outliers from what would be expected based on the frequency distribution of out-degrees. Table 1 shows the samples that have generated the greatest number of children, based on having the highest out-degree. This does not necessarily indicate that these samples are extremely long-lived; all of those children *could* have appeared soon after the parent. It could also mean that these samples were the progenitors of large families of malware, or that these samples were responsible for large branches of their respective families, leading to many descendants. What we do know is that a large number of children were spawned by this sample, something which can be explored further.

We found 276 root nodes in the forest – nodes that have an in-degree of 0, of which 111 of those are singletons (with no children). Singletons are dead-ends as they are not spawning anything. We cannot reliably connect them to other families

Table 1. Top 5 child-creating samples of COS25.

Sample	Discovery date	Children
Trojan-Dropper.Win32.Small.mj	20020404	508
Virus.DOS.PS-MPC.186	19920714	285
IM-Worm.Win32.Lewor.c	19971208	282
Trojan-Spy.Win32.Small.gc	20020504	267
Trojan-Downloader.Win32.Small.bmd	20020404	236

at this time because they were not compared to other samples due to size difference. The remaining 165 root nodes are in subtrees that represent malware families – groups of closely related malware that share common traits and ancestry.

4.2   Biodiversity Over Time

The biodiversity curve in Fig. 4 shows how the biodiversity in the ecosystem changed over time. The biodiversity is marked by periods of rapid increase and decrease. When samples appear in large numbers, we see the curve spike due to the arriving samples, and then remain either relatively flat before rapidly decreasing (due to stasis) or gradually decreasing (due to low malware development rates) as nodes are removed, changing the ratio of living nodes to total nodes. There are time when the biodiversity increases gradually, as the rate of new sample arrival exceeds the rate of stasis for old samples. This could be due to those samples attaching to a small number of existing nodes (leading to a smaller increase), or a larger number of existing nodes (leading to larger increase, as those older nodes would now remain "alive"). However, the second curve in the figure shows the total samples as they appear along the time line, and shows that while the biodiversity can correlate with new arrivals, increasing biodiversity and rapid malware development are not necessarily connected. We can see this between 2006–2008, where the number of samples is increasing, albeit slowly, while the overall biodiversity falls. This could be the result of those samples attaching to recent samples (placing older samples into stasis), while also causing the average parent-child age difference to fall, thus forcing even more samples into stasis.

Taking the derivative of the biodiversity curve shows us that generally, the biodiversity exhibits small percentages changes between days. This is shown in Fig. 5, which shows the daily changes in biodiversity, along with the number of new samples that appear each day. The small changes are to be expected as new samples were appearing all the time. However, we notice that there are occasional peaks and valleys in the graph, with the three largest of each

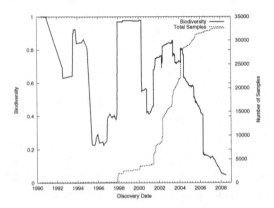

Fig. 4. Biodiversity curve of COS25 for current mean stasis criterion.

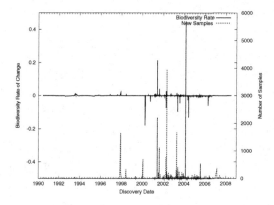

Fig. 5. Derivative biodiversity curve of COS25 for current mean stasis criterion.

summarized in Table 2. Peaks occur when a large number of samples appear due to the new nodes increasing the number of living nodes and a larger fraction of nodes are creating offspring. The valleys tend to occur towards the end of a period of low malware development, where more nodes are going into stasis than are appearing in the ecosystem.

In the peak and valley table, the "New" column refers to nodes that appeared that date. The "Alive" column includes both these new nodes and existing nodes that have not gone into stasis. Similarly, the "Total" column refers to all of the nodes that exist in the tree as of that day, both alive and in stasis.

We found there is no necessary correlation between and peak and a valley in our study; they do not appear in definite pairs. This is because the samples are increasing at a gradual rate punctuated by the occasional burst, but there is no regularity in the timing of those bursts. Figure 6 shows the total samples as it increases over our time line, while also showing the number of samples that appear at each time point. We suspect that the peaks in the graph correspond to

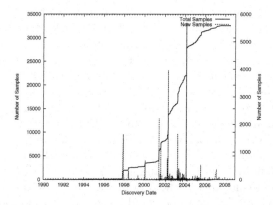

Fig. 6. Total samples and arriving samples, by discovery date.

Table 2. Top three peaks and valleys in COS25 derivative curve for current mean stasis criterion.

Discovery date	Type	Value	New	Alive	Total
20000406	Valley	−0.1786	1	2197	3535
20010608	Peak	0.2143	2206	4230	6230
20010817	Peak	0.0411	1116	5798	7763
20030514	Valley	−0.0953	32	14215	18636
20040219	Peak	0.0845	5691	22525	27841
20040603	Valley	−0.1305	1	17995	28353

some milestone in operating systems or applications development, as generally there is an increase in malware upon the discovery of an exploitable vulnerability, which would then drive the release of a patch to resolve it [2,6].

4.3   Effect of Malware Packers

A common technique by which malware evades static analysis methods is through the use of packers, such as UPX [29], which may make a sample appear similar to other samples that are packed using similar methods. In our corpus, we found 11,378 instances of packed malware – approximately 34.9 % of the samples. Examining the packed samples we found that the average distance between a packed sample and its parent was 0.0414, with a standard deviation of 0.1012. This smaller average and lower amount of variation indicates that our results are affected by the use of packers; packed malware tends to be more closely related according to our distance metric as they all exhibit a similar characteristic – the use of an unpacking routine to execute.

5   Conclusions

We have presented a method by which we can measure the biodiversity exhibited within an ecosystem. Our method determines whether or not a malware sample is exhibiting an effect on the overall ecosystem as measured by whether or not it has apparently spawned a variant or other descendant. We showed that generally, this measurement of biodiversity does not change much from one day to the next, but over the entire time line, we can see peaks and troughs, which can relate to the inconsistent development and release of malware. Our analysis shows rapid malware development exhibited in our corpus with a generally high level of biodiversity, which could indicate that malware samples are being written quickly, building on previously used techniques that remained successful over time. It is definitely worth examining how the observed biodiversity of the malware ecosystem compares to the overall state of software evolution; a similar study of known benign software would inform us how malware development relates to general software development.

This method can be adapted to examine and identify prevalent malware behavior and code techniques. Instead of looking at the biodiversity of the ecosystem as a whole, research can be done by which either a specific sample's offspring are tracked, or whether a specific feature remains prevalent and influences other development. Identifying prevalent behavior and code techniques can help defend against future infection because they can be used to aid in the differentiation between malicious and benign samples. In order to perform this kind of analysis, the overall method may require adjustment, but specifically the similarity measure between samples must be changed.

An important future direction for the use of this method is to perform a biodiversity analysis of our corpus using dynamic analysis techniques in order to examine samples at run-time. Statically, samples may appear similar but at execution time, those samples may appear very different. For packed or encrypted malware, examining the sample's payload at execution may show a large difference between samples that seemed similar from a static perspective. By examining samples at execution time, we can also compare the behavior that the samples exhibit, and determine the similarity between them based on the effects on the infected system. As a result, we will be able to construct a different phylogeny tree based on a different distance measurement, and examine how the resulting biodiversity calculation changes with respect to the method by which the samples are compared.

It is also important to note that a future study with this method can examine malware ecological niches in a more isolated fashion – while here we looked at the malware ecosystem as a whole, it is possible to restrict the environment such that we can look at certain factors that limit malware growth and propagation, namely OS conditions (such as OS version, sub-version, patch levels) and application vulnerabilities, both of which have been shown to have an effect on malware rates within ecosystems [25].

Finally, we can also examine the effect that changes in the data set can have on the calculations, whether we adjust the size threshold used in our comparison between samples, or take random samples of the data set and perform the same biodiversity calculations. As it is possible for a new feature to increase the size difference between a parent and child, we would like to see how new strains of malware differentiate from their ancestors, in order to better identify when we can consider a new version of malware as a new "species" in the ecosystem.

References

1. Annachhatre, C., Austin, T., Stamp, M.: Hidden markov models for malware classification. J. Comput. Virol. Hacking Tech., 1–15 (2014). http://dx.doi.org/10.1007/s11416-014-0215-x
2. Arora, A., Krishnan, R., Telang, R., Yang, Y.: Impact of vulnerability disclosure and patch availability - an empirical analysis. In. Third Workshop on the Economics of Information Security (2004). http://citeseerx.ist.psu.edu/viewdoc/summary?doi=10.1.1.81.9350

3. Bailey, M., Oberheide, J., Andersen, J., Mao, Z.M., Jahanian, F., Nazario, J.: Automated classification and analysis of internet malware. In: Kruegel, C., Lippmann, R., Clark, A. (eds.) RAID 2007. LNCS, vol. 4637, pp. 178–197. Springer, Heidelberg (2007). http://dx.doi.org/10.1007/978-3-540-74320-0_10

4. Bayer, U., Comparetti, P.M., Hlauschek, C., Krügel, C., Kirda, E.: Scalable, behavior-based malware clustering. In: Proceedings of NDSS 2009 (2009). http://www.isoc.org/isoc/conferences/ndss/09/pdf/11.pdf

5. Campbell, N.A.: Biology, 4th edn. The Benjamin/Cummings Publishing Company Inc., New York (1996)

6. Cencini, A., Yu, K., Chan, T.: Software Vulnerabilities: Full-, Responsible-, and Non-Disclosure (2005). http://www.cs.washington.edu/education/courses/csep590/05au/whitepaper_turnin/software_vulnerabilities_by_cencini_yu_chan.pdf

7. Cohen, F.: Computer virus: theory and experiments. Comput. Secur. **6**, 22–35 (1987). http://www.cs.washington.edu/education/courses/csep590/05au/whitepaper_turnin/software_vulnerabilities_by_cencini_yu_chan.pdf

8. Darmetko, C., Jilcott, S., Everett, J.: Inferring accurate histories of malware evolution from structural evidence. In: The Twenty-Sixth International FLAIRS Conference (2013)

9. Dot Products (2009). http://nlp.stanford.edu/IR-book/html/htmledition/dot-products-1.html

10. Filiol, E., Helenius, M., Zanero, S.: Open problems in computer virology. J. Comput. Virol. **1**(3–4), 55–66 (2006). http://dx.doi.org/10.1007/s11416-005-0008-3

11. Gheorghescu, M.: An automated virus classification system. In: Virus Bulletin Conference, pp. 294–300, Oct 2005

12. Ibrahim, A., Abdelhalim, M.B., Hussein, H., Fahmy, A.: Analysis of x86 instruction set usage for Windows 7 applications. In: 2010 2nd International Conference on Computer Technology and Development (ICCTD), pp. 511–516 (2010)

13. Intel Corporation: Intel® 64 and IA-32 Architectures Software Developer Manuals (2013). http://www.intel.com/content/www/us/en/processors/architectures-software-developer-manuals.html/

14. Jacob, G., Debar, H., Filiol, E.: Behavioral detection of malware: from a survey towards an established taxonomy. J. Comput. Virol. **4**(3), 251–266 (2008)

15. Jang, J., Woo, M., Brumley, D.: Towards automatic software lineage inference. In: Proceedings of the 22nd USENIX Conference on Security, pp. 81–96. USENIX Association (2013)

16. Karim, M.E., Walenstein, A., Lakhotia, A., Parida, L.: Malware phylogeny generation using permutations of code. J. Comput. Virol. **1**(1–2), 13–23 (2005)

17. Kolter, J.Z., Maloof, M.A.: Learning to detect and classify malicious executables in the wild. J. Mach. Learn. Res. **7**, 2721–2744 (2006). http://www.jmlr.org/papers/v7/kolter06a.html

18. Lee, T., Mody, J.J.: Behavioral classification. In: Proceedings of EICAR 2006, pp. 1–17, May 2006

19. Li, Z., Sanghi, M., Chen, Y., Kao, M.Y., Chavez, B.: Hamsa: fast signature generation for zero-day polymorphic worms with provable attack resilience. In: Proceedings of the 2006 IEEE Symposium on Security and Privacy. pp. 32–47 (2006). http://doi.ieeecomputersociety.org/10.1109/SP.2006.18

20. Mader, S.S.: Inquiry into Life (Customized for Brooklyn College), 9th edn. The McGraw-Hill Companies Inc., Primis Custom Publishing, New York (1999)

21. Newsome, J., Karp, B., Song, D.X.: Polygraph: automatically generating signatures for polymorphic worms. In: Proceedings of the 2005 IEEE Symposium on Security and Privacy, pp. 226–241 (2005). http://doi.ieeecomputersociety.org/10.1109/SP.2005.15

22. Annual Report Panda Labs - 2013 Summary (2013). http://press.pandasecurity.com/wp-content/uploads/2010/05/PandaLabs-Annual-Report_2013.pdf

23. Salthe, S.N.: Evolutionary Biology. Holt, Rinehart and Winston Inc., New York (1972)

24. Seewald, A.K.: Towards autmating malware classification and characterization. In: Proceedings of Sicherheit 2008, pp. 291–302 (2008). http://alex.seewald.at/files/2008-01.pdf

25. Seideman, J., Khan, B., Ben Brahim, G.: Determining vulnerability resolution time by examining malware proliferation rates. In: 2013 9th International Wireless Communications and Mobile Computing Conference (IWCMC), pp. 1678–1682 (2013)

26. Singhal, A.: Modern information retrieval: a brief overview. IEEE Data Eng. Bull. **24**(4), 35–43 (2001)

27. Spafford, E.H.: Computer viruses as artificial life. Artif. Life **1**(3), 249–265 (1994)

28. Threat explorer - spyware and adware, dialers, hack tools, hoaxes and other risks (2012). http://www.symantec.com/security_response/threatexplorer/

29. UPX: the Ultimate Packer for eXecutables - Homepage (2010). http://upx.sourceforge.net/

30. VirusTotal (2008). http://www.virustotal.com

31. VX heavens (2010). http://vxheaven.org/

32. Wagener, G., State, R., Dulaunoy, A.: Malware behaviour analysis. J. Comput. Virol. **4**(4), 279–287 (2008)

33. Wong, W., Stamp, M.: Hunting for metamorphic engines. J. Comput. Virol. **2**(3), 211–229 (2006). http://dx.doi.org/10.1007/s11416-006-0028-7

34. Woodberry, O.G., Korb, K.B., Nicholson, A.E.: Testing punctuated equilibrium theory using evolutionary activity statistics. In: Korb, K., Randall, M., Hendtlass, T. (eds.) ACAL 2009. LNCS, vol. 5865, pp. 86–95. Springer, Heidelberg (2009)

IoT and Supply Chain Traceability

Wei Zhou[1,3](✉) and Selwyn Piramuthu[2,3]

[1] Information and Operations Management, ESCP Europe, Paris, France
wzhou@escpeurope.eu
[2] Information Systems and Operations Management, University of Florida,
Gainesville, FL 32611-7169, USA
selwyn@ufl.edu
[3] RFID European Lab, Paris, France

Abstract. Real-time and item-level traceability is critical in many
industries such as the food, health care, and pharmaceutical industries.
However, it's still not clear how traceability, especially at the item level
and in real time, could impact supply chain health, safety, and environment (HSE) control. In this research-in-progress, we investigate this
rarely-studied problem based on IoT (Internet of Things) automatic
tracking/tracing technologies. We first introduce a theoretic framework
of three traceability levels: physical flow traceability, business process
traceability, and performance traceability. We extend this framework by
adopting a Bayesian causal network model for decision support.

1 Introduction

Health, Safety & Environment (HSE) plays a more and more important role
in modern supply chain management. To guarantee certain HSE standard, an
effective supply chain traceability information system holds the key that accurately monitors relevant business processes and moving subjects. Traditional
tracking methods, such as periodic bar code scanning and check points, provide segmental information that is incomplete. In recent years IoT technologies,
such as RFID, enables an automatic supply chain tracking/tracing capability on
almost zero operational cost. Many companies have started utilizing RFID to
track real time inventory information and to monitor human resource activities.
IoT technology has enabled supply chain traceability with complete information
that traditional technology couldn't achieve. Probably because of its novelty,
there is no systematic and theoretic framework that captures all perspectives
in supply chain traceability. We are motivated to investigate this problem by
introducing a qualitative framework that include three different levels of supply
chain traceability needs and a quantitative model to extend it.

Supply chain traceability with complete information is critically important
in some fields, such as the food, health care, and pharmaceutical industries.
Health, safety and environment have long been a key issue there. For an instance,
undesirable contamination in the cold chain, such as food poisoning, could cause
serious short-term and long-term health effects on consumers. Early discovery
and recall of possible contaminated items in the cold chain is vitally important to

© Springer International Publishing Switzerland 2015
R. Doss et al. (Eds.): FNSS 2015, CCIS 523, pp. 156–165, 2015.
DOI: 10.1007/978-3-319-19210-9_11

maintain service quality, brand reputation, and public confidence. While existing literatures on supply chain traceability has remained largely open in these fields, we are urged to answer the following research question: (1) how traceability can be defined in a supply chain, (2) the key perspectives of supply chain traceability, physical traceability, process traceability, and performance traceability and (3) an effective decision support system for supply chain traceability.

Traditionally, perfect information is rarely available in supply chain management. Due to cost and technology constraints, normally only a fraction of supply chain subjects can be tracked yet with incomplete spatial-temporal tracking information. RFID has the capability to track and trace items in real-time at item-level [29]. However, so far most RFID implementation remains at the pallet-level rather than at the item-level mostly due to cost constraints. We propose a Bayesian causal network to model the process traceability based on either complete or incomplete tracing data. Based on Bayesian networks, series of cause-effect relationships can be precisely discovered and presented in the form of Bayesian probabilities. For example, when we find a contaminated food product at a retailer, we would immediately ask whether it is a single case or if it is a part of a large scale of contamination. Then, for large scale, where is the origin and most importantly, where are the other contaminated products. We proceed with the food contamination problem that may be caused by various reasons, such as bacterial contamination, genetically modified organisms (GMOs) contamination, etc.

The remainder of this paper is organized as follows: Sect. 2 presents a brief overview of relevant literature. Section 3 introduces several examples of traceability. A general traceability model is proposed in Sect. 4. Analysis and discussions are also presented in Sect. 4. Section 5 concludes the paper with a brief discussion on the insights garnered and their implications.

2   Literature Review

Traceability in cold chain and food manufacturing can range from internal (or part of the production chain) to the entire supply chain that include the raw material supply to the final consumption market [20]. Regattieri et al. [27] introduces a general framework of food products traceability that consists of product identification, traceability tools, product routing and data. They also discuss various tracing technologies such as alphanumerical codes, bar codes, and radio frequency identification (RFID). Issues such as fatal bacterial contamination or genetically modified organisms (GMOs) seriously demand the industry to accurately trace the production and transportation in the cold chain. Miraglia et al. [19] provides an overview on regulatory perspective associated with GMO items, associated sampling strategy, minimum standards, and traceability solutions.

Various technologies and information systems have been used/experimented in the food industry. In raw food processing industry, it's rather difficult to do so. Mousavi et al. [21] proposes a practical system that traces meat processing from the individual animal to individual prime cuts in the boning hall in the framework of a modern information systems with bar code and RFID. Abad et al. [1] demonstrates an example of using RFID tags for tracking/tracing in the fresh fish cold chain. In its system, multiple sensors are utilized to capture the real-time information on temperature, humidity, and light. The information thus collected are stored and can be further analyzed. Kelepouris et al. [15] show, from a practical perspective, how RFID can be used to trace products in the food supply chain.

Cold chain traceability, transparency, and assurances (TTA) has been proved to hold value to the consumers on top of the basic food safety requirements. Dickinson and Bailey [8] shows that consumers are willing to pay for traceability in a field study of meat traceability in the United States. The findings from [28], however, suggest that consumers are more interested on information of food quality and expiration date than on the actual traceability. Therefore, the recommended labeling strategy would be to indicate the food quality and origin rather than providing consumers with detailed information of traceability. We argue that although direct information transparency of cold chain traceability might not be interesting in a marketing campaign, traceability ensures a minimum level of food safety in everyday operation, and is therefore indispensable in cold chain management.

There are very few quantitative models in existing literature that systematically describe cold chain traceability which are mostly borrowed from traditional industrial engineering and operations research on quality management and business process management. Bertolini et al. [2] attempts to use the "Failure Mode Effect and Criticality Analysis" (FMECA) model from the industrial engineering domain to detect possible critical processes in the farming and food supply chain. FMECA method helps to rank the effects of failure modes and to propose structural and operational improvements in a quantitative fashion. Jansen-Vullers et al. [14] extends gozinto graph modeling into a reference data model for the purpose of manufacturing traceability. These models nevertheless all fail to provide accurate detailed information as is deemed necessary.

We should point out that the traceability problem doesn't just exist in the food industry and cold chain management. The industry of information systems/technologies, for an example, has widely used traceability to help identify the origin of software components and to maintain product quality.

3   Framework of Supply Chain Traceability

There are various perspectives of supply chain traceability. Opara [22] finds that supply chain traceability in food industry includes product traceability, process traceability, genetic traceability, inputs traceability, disease and pest traceability and measurement traceability. Opara [22], however, fails to link these different types of traceability by a systematic model. In Fig. 1, we propose a general framework of supply chain traceability that differentiate the tracing needs in three levels: the physical flow traceability, process traceability, and service traceability.

At the physical traceability layer, original tracking information of the physical flow of a focal subject is collected regarding this subject's spatial/temporal

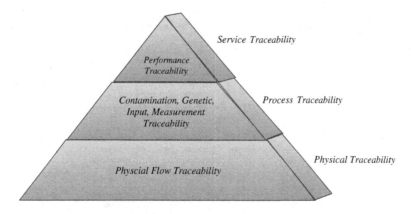

Fig. 1. The framework of cold chain traceability

information in a past time period. The raw data on physical flow and business process do not allow for drawing inference directly regarding business process traceability.

Figure 2 gives an example of food supply chain work flow. At the physical flow level, items are monitored according to their temporal/spatial information throughout the production and logistics life cycle that exist in various business processes.

At the process traceability layer, physical flow data becomes part of the causal reasoning when specific tracing objective function is raised. For example, when a food product is found to be contaminated by a certain bacteria, the question would be what's the reason of such contamination, would it be a single case, when did it happen? Normally, there's no hard 100 % evidence to answer these questions. Reasoning based on statistics and probability is normally suggested in order to find the most probable answer in everyday practice.

In process traceability, Bayesian network modeling is a natural fit to describe the reasoning process in function traceability. We consider a transitional model

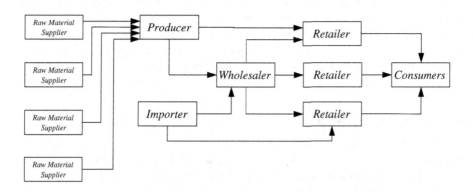

Fig. 2. An example of food supply chain work flow

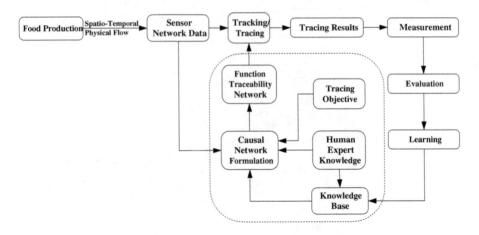

Fig. 3. Intelligent transition model of physical traceability

to map the physical flow network to a causal reasoning network. The tracking data (from a sensor network) of the physical flow of any item in the logistics and supply network consists of a series of spatio-temporal information that depicts the physical movements.

Figure 3 illustrates the proposed intelligent transition model of physical traceability into the various process tracing objective functions. In this model, first-hand food production/logistics data are collected from the sensor network system on the spatio-temporal physical flows of traceable items, components, containers, machineries, etc. This raw data is used to generate the causal network for function traceability, along with the human expert knowledge and the artificial intelligence knowledge-base, guided by the tracing objective of certain function. We call this causal network the function-based traceability network in Fig. 3, based on which, we find the most probable tracking results. Then, these results are measured and evaluated to check for validity and will be used to learn/generate the knowledge that is then stored at the local knowledge-base. This knowledge-base is then further used to improve the traceability model. The causal network formulation module combines all relevant information towards the tracking problem, including the sensor network data, both human and artificial intelligence knowledge in order to bridge all the cause-effect relationships that exist in the business processes. We now discuss the proposed Bayesian causal network based process traceability model.

3.1   Bayesian Network

Based on the classical Bayesian probability theory, Bayesian network is a statistical or dynamic data mining methodology of formal knowledge representation. Bayesian network was first introduced decades ago and its popularity has increased due to big data and various electronically communicated information. The fast development of computing machines and relevant software development has made it more possible and realistic to execute a complex statistical task generated by a Bayesian Network model [13, 23, 24]. Many scientific/engineering/social science/business research domains benefit from the Bayesian network, including biological research, health care, geographic remote sensing, computer engineering, and business research.

In a nutshell, a Bayesian Network contains a large joint probability that can be decomposed into a set of local conditional (Bayesian) probabilities. Its topology consists of information on how to integrate all the local distributions throughout the nodes and edges in the network [11]. Although Bayesian network is relatively novel to management research, such as the prior work in [3, 5, 10], we see its great potential with increased popularity of big data and Internet of Things(IoT) in the business domain.

In food production and logistics traceability literature, we are not aware of any existing discussion that utilizes Bayesian network methodology while we hold the belief that Bayesian network could be an effective model to distill the essence of function traceability in manufacturing. One of the purpose of using Bayesian network model is to assign probabilistic estimates for events that are not directly observable, and the main idea in developing Bayesian net model is to identify these events. These events are the hypothesis events that are then grouped into a set of hypothesis variables. When we have a traceability problem, such as bacteria contamination, we want to know the possible cause/origin of such contamination, any other contaminated items and their possible locations. These questions can not be directly answered from physical flow network in a straightforward way and a Bayesian causal network derived from the physical flow network seems to be the perfect tool to address these questions by linking all the possible causes and consequences together.

Because it's highly unlikely (although not 100 %) to have non-recursive (closed-loop) causal relationships in food supply chain, we only consider the recursive model when modeling traceability by path analysis. The general procedure of recursive causal modeling has two stages: the model specification and parameter estimation. At the model specification stage, a set of variables $X = \{X_1, X_2 \cdots , X_n\}$ is chosen to represent all possible cause-effect relationships. These relationships are presented in a directed acyclic graph (DAG) with each directed edge representing the conditional probabilistic dependence of a successor variable (child) on a predecessor variable (parent), as discussed in [6]. According to [23, 24], a recursive Bayesian causal network model specification has both quantitative and qualitative components. The qualitative component includes the DAG where each edge represents the statistical dependence between the two nodes; the quantitative component is a conditional distribution $p(x_i|parent(x_i))$ for each variable in $\{X_1, X_2 \cdots , X_n\}$, given its parents denoted as $parent(x_i)$.

Representing a random variable, each node in the DAG can take two or more possible values in a discrete model while it can also be continuous for certain problems. The arrows indicate the cause-effect relationship between linked variables, and the strength of these influences are presented in conditional (Bayesian) probabilities. The joint probability of the Bayesian network is:

$$P(X) = \prod_{i=1}^{n} P(x_i|parent(x_i)) \tag{1}$$

One of the main advantage of using Bayesian causal network is that probabilistic inference can be derived directly from the Bayesian probabilities $p(x_i|parent(x_i))$. Consequently, the joint probability distribution in Eq. (1) can be decomposed into a product of the proper terms of the Bayesian probability functions given the capability to estimate the probability distribution for a set of query variables, provided the set of evidence variables $p(Q, E)$. In a process traceability model, the conditional probability of any query variable Q with a state q provided with evidence e is:

$$p(Q = q|E = e) = p(q, e)/p(e) \tag{2}$$

4   Process Traceability with Bayesian Network

Traceability problem at the business process management level is directed by specific questions or objectives, similar to that discussed previously for contamination traceability, a model based on Bayesian network analysis (sometimes also called the "belief" network, knowledge maps, and probabilistic causal network) is a reasonable tool to investigate this problem (Fig. 4).

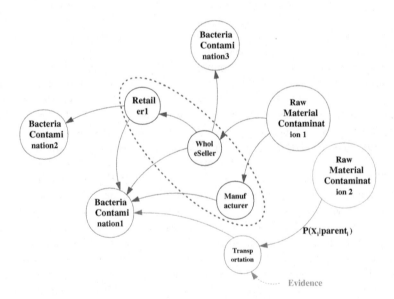

Fig. 4. Knowledge based inventory management process framework

Figure 3 shows an example of process traceability of food bacterial contamination based on causal network derived from knowledge and data at the physical flow layer. The Bayesian relationships are generated by the accumulated data collected from the sensor network and operational transactions. Once a hard evidence is collected, it generates the d-separation on the network. In this example, the evidence that there's no contamination found in transportation makes the "raw material contamination 2" independent of the "bacteria contamination 1" node. This evidence also makes the "Markov blanket" of the node "bacteria contamination 1" shrink to retailer, wholesale, and manufacturer nodes. Based on this causal network, we are able not only to analyze and estimate the possible causes of food contamination, but also to identify the possibility of contamination spread, such as in the node "bacteria contamination 2 & 3".

5 Identification Granularity in Process Traceability, Learning, and Inference

The impact of business process identification with RFID tracking/tracing tags, which can be either attached to individual items, to containers, or to pallets, can be further differentiated in the context of business process traceability. Up to now, there is still no general consensus regarding the identification level and its benefits/drawbacks in supply chain management and business process management. In fact, with RFID item-level traceability, more data tracking nodes can be collected and more evidence can be fed in to the Bayesian network-based process tracing model. Information such as the batch id, manufacturing time, location/time, transportation and storage period, temperature at different check points in the logistic chain, etc., can be the evidence to support query, as well as be a part of the network composition by becoming one of the cause-effect nodes. With container level traceability, there exists "softer" evidence because some information are lost during the grouping period. We find that if RFID item-level traceability provides additional information that doesn't exist on the "Markov Blanket" of Bayesian network, there is no need to implement RFID because these extra information are independent of the variables of interest. Otherwise, if the extra information are located on the Markov Blanket, RFID brings more valuable information to business process traceability.

We observe that given item-level traceability by using RFID, one can improve the accuracy of Bayesian probabilities on the edges of the overall network, thus increasing the overall traceability performance. Enlarging the size of traceable basket, we nevertheless make the Bayesian possibilities more vague from node to node, thus decreasing the prediction power. Eventually, we would like to find the relationship between the trackable container size and the tracing accuracy, as well as the optimal lot size to meet the minimum accuracy requirement and highest cost-benefit result.

6 Concluding Remarks

We considered the supply chain traceability problem that to our knowledge has rarely been studied. Motivated by modern tracking/tracing information & communication technology, such as IoT and RFID, we attempted to fill the gap in existing literature by investigating the various perspectives of identification and traceability. We argue that business process identification and traceability can be paramount in some domain, for example the food industry that is closely related to public safety. We define traceability at three levels: physical flow traceability, process and other function traceability, and service traceability. A Bayesian causal network based model is further developed to bridge the different layers of traceability.

We argue that the process traceability model that is presented in this study can be easily extended to address various traceability problems (other than contamination) in the cold chain and other forms of business process and supply chain. We leave it as future research to quantify the question of at which level (pallet-level, item-level, or something in the middle) should the cold chain items be tracked and traced so that the minimum requirement (such as food safety standards) can be achieved. Future research can also be directed towards finding alternative possible identification and tracking/tracing methodologies other than the Bayesian network approach that is considered in this study.

References

1. Abad, E., Palacio, F., Nuin, M., Zarate, A., Juarros, A., Gomez, J.M., Marco, S.: RFID smart tag for traceability and cold chain monitoring of foods: demonstration in an intercontinental fresh fish logistic chain. J. Food Eng. **93**(4), 394–399 (2009)
2. Bertolini, M., Bevilacqua, M., Massini, R.: FMECA approach to product traceability in the food industry. Food Control **17**(2), 137–145 (2006)
3. Blodgett, J.G., Anderson, R.D.: A Bayesian network model of the consumer complaint process. J. Serv. Res. **2**(4), 321–338 (2000)
4. Bobbit, R., Connell, J., Haas, N., Otto, C., Pankanti, S., Payne, J.: Visual item verification for fraud prevention in retail self-checkout. In: IEEE Workshop on Applications of Computer Vision (WACV), 585–590 (2011)
5. Cooper, L.G.: Strategic marketing planning for radically new products. J. Mark. **64**(1), 1–16 (2000)
6. Dawid, A.P., Lauritzen, S.L.: Hyper Markov laws in the statistical analysis of decomposable graphical models. Ann. Stat. **21**(3), 1272–1317 (1993)
7. De Kok, A.G., Van Donselaar, K.H., van Woensel, T.: A break-even analysis of RFID technology for inventory sensitive to shrinkage. Int. J. Prod. Econ. **112**(2), 521–531 (2008)
8. Dickinson, D.L., Bailey, D.: Meat traceability: are US consumers willing to pay for it? J. Agric. Resour. Econ. **27**(2), 348–364 (2002)
9. Folinas, D., Manikas, I., Manos, B.: Traceability data management for food chains. Br. Food J. **108**(8), 622–633 (2006)
10. Geng, C., Wong, M.L., Lui, H.-K.: Machine learning for direct marketing response models: Bayesian networks with evolutionary programming. Manage. Sci. **52**(4), 597–612 (2006)
11. Haddawy, P.: An overview of some recent developments in Bayesian problem-solving techniques. AI Mag. **20**(2), 11–19 (1999)
12. Hald, T., Vose, D., Wegener, H.C., Koupeev, T.: A Bayesian approach to quantify the contribution of animal-food sources to human salmonellosis. Risk Anal. **24**(1), 255–269 (2004)

13. Jensen, F.V.: An Introduction to Bayesian Networks. Springer, New York (1996)
14. Jansen-Vullers, M.H., van Dorp, C.A., Beulens, A.J.: Managing traceability information in manufacture. Int. J. Inf. Manage. **23**(5), 395–413 (2003)
15. Kelepouris, T., Pramatari, K., Doukidis, G.: RFID-enabled traceability in the food supply chain. Ind. Manage. Data Syst. **107**(2), 183–200 (2007)
16. Lee, H., Özer, O.: Unlocking the value of RFID. Prod. Oper. Manage. **16**(1), 40–64 (2007)
17. Loureiro, M.L., Umberger, W.J.: A choice experiment model for beef: what US consumer responses tell us about relative preferences for food safety, country-of-origin labeling and traceability. Food Policy **32**(4), 496–514 (2007)
18. McFarlane, D.C., Sheffi, Y.: The impact of automatic identification on supply chain operations. Int. J. Logistics Manage. **14**, 1–17 (2003)
19. Miraglia, M., Berdal, K.G., Brera, C., Corbisier, P., Holst-Jensen, A., Kok, E.J., Zagon, J.: Detection and traceability of genetically modified organisms in the food production chain. Food Chem. Toxicol. **42**(7), 1157–1180 (2004)
20. Moe, T.: Perspectives on traceability in food manufacture. Trends Food Sci. Technol. **9**(5), 211–214 (1998)
21. Mousavi, A., Sarhadi, M., Lenk, A., Fawcett, S.: Tracking and traceability in the meat processing industry: a solution. Br. Food J. **104**(1), 7–19 (2002)
22. Opara, L.U.: Traceability in agriculture and food supply chain: a review of basic concepts, technological implications, and future prospects. J. Food Agric. Environ. **1**, 101–106 (2003)
23. Pearl, J.: Probabilistic Reasoning in Intelligent Systems: Networks of Plausible Inference. Morgan Kaufmann, San Mateo (1988)
24. Pearl, J.: Causality: Models, Reasoning, and Inference. Cambridge University Press, Cambridge (2000)
25. Piramuthu, S., Farahani, P., Grunow, M.: RFID-generated traceability for contaminated product recall in perishable food supply networks. Eur. J. Oper. Res. **225**(2), 253–262 (2013)
26. Piramuthu, S., Zhou, W.: RFID and perishable inventory management with shelf-space and freshness dependent demand. Int. J. Prod. Econ. **144**, 635–640 (2013)
27. Regattieri, A., Gamberi, M., Manzini, R.: Traceability of food products: general framework and experimental evidence. J. Food Eng. **81**(2), 347–356 (2007)
28. Verbeke, W., Ward, R.W.: Consumer interest in information cues denoting quality, traceability and origin: an application of ordered probit models to beef labels. Food Qual. Prefer. **17**(6), 453–467 (2006)
29. Zhou, W.: RFID and item-level information visibility. Eur. J. Oper. Res. **198**(1), 252–258 (2009)

Secure and Reliable Power Consumption Monitoring in Untrustworthy Micro-grids

Pacome L. Ambassa[1](✉), Anne V.D.M. Kayem[1], Stephen D. Wolthusen[2,3], and Christoph Meinel[4]

[1] Department of Computer Science, University of Cape Town, Rondebosch 7701, Cape Town, South Africa
{pambassa,akayem}@cs.uct.ac.za
[2] Norwegian Information Security Laboratory, Faculty of Computer Science, Gjøvik University College, Gjøvik, Norway
[3] Department of Mathematics, Information Security Group, Royal Holloway, University of London, Egham, UK
stephen.wolthusen@hig.no
[4] Hasso Plattner Institute at University of Potsdam, Potsdam, Germany
meinel@hpi.de

Abstract. Micro-grid architectures based on renewable energy sources offer a viable solution to electricity provision in regions that are not connected to the national power grid or that are severely affected by load shedding. The limited power generated in micro-grids however makes monitoring power consumption an important consideration in guaranteeing efficient and fair energy sharing. A further caveat is that adversarial data tampering poses a major impediment to fair energy sharing on small scale energy systems, like micro-grids, and can result in a complete breakdown of the system. In this paper, we present an innovative approach to monitoring home power consumption in smart micro-grids. This is done by taking into account power consumption measurement on a per appliance and/or device basis. Our approach works by employing a distributed snapshot algorithm to asynchronously collect the power consumption data reported by the appliances and devices. In addition, we provide a characterization of noise that affects the quality of the data making it difficult to differentiate measurement errors and power fluctuations from deliberate attempts to misreport consumption.

Keywords: Micro-grid · Power consumption monitoring · Noisy data · Distributed snapshot algorithm · Wireless sensor networks

1 Introduction

A micro-grid is a small scale electricity grid based on distributed power generation and designed to supply electricity for a small community, such as a suburban locality [1]. A Micro-grid generally operates independently or as part of the main national electrical grid [2]. Typically micro-grids rely on renewable energy

© Springer International Publishing Switzerland 2015
R. Doss et al. (Eds.): FNSS 2015, CCIS 523, pp. 166–180, 2015.
DOI: 10.1007/978-3-319-19210-9_12

sources and are considered a viable solution for supplying electricity to rural and disadvantaged communities that are characterized by poor infrastructural development, low income, and a dispersed population living in remote locations [3,4]. However, the structure of the micro-grid raises issues centered on reliability and trust. Reliability in terms of guaranteeing that end users have reliable access to the power grid network to achieve their operations. Trust refers to the need to ensure that the computational system enables secure and efficient collection of consumption data in a way that ensures accuracy of the data to guide power distribution. Fair and trustworthy power distribution is essential in ensuring the stability of the micro-grid. This is because users will cease to use the grid if the service level agreements are violated resulting in a breakdown of the grid.

In this paper we propose a simple framework for a micro-grid in rural and disadvantaged areas in developing regions. The paper presents an innovative approach to monitoring home power consumption in a small smart micro-grid in a way that takes into account power consumption measurements on a per appliance and/or device basis. Our approach works by employing a distributed snapshot algorithm to asynchronously collect the power consumption data reported by the appliances and devices. This snapshot algorithm serves as a reliable and trustworthy way to report the power consumption values so that the house owner can better manage power consumption, as well as identify the sources of wastage to reduce consumption [5]. In addition, we provide a characterization of the noise that affects the quality of the power data measured. Noise distortions make it difficult to differentiate measurement errors and power fluctuations from deliberate attempts to misreport consumption.

The rest of this paper is structured as follows: Sect. 2 reviews the literature on using low power devices for monitoring the power grid as well as existing algorithms for computing the global snapshot in a distributed system. In Sect. 3, we propose a simple framework and give a description of the micro-grid system. Section 4 proposes an algorithm for the asynchronous collection of consumption data in wireless sensor networks. Section 5 describes different types of noise in energy consumption measurement. In Sect. 6, we discuss the proposed snapshot algorithms and compare it to others in the literature. Finally, Sect. 7 concludes the paper and suggests directions for future research.

2   Related Work

The modernization of electrical power grids with the integration of advanced information networking and communication technologies in the so-called smart micro-grid is a hot research topic in developed and developing countries. However, developing countries usually face major challenges where unreliable access to electricity may lead the utility provider to prioritize access and consequently, some rural and disadvantaged areas might experience load shedding. Micro-grids based on renewable energy sources, can make an important contribution to equitable access to energy. To support this idea, we consider that a micro-grid exists for power sharing in small communities, where low power devices can be used for monitoring, computation and communication. The devices currently used in such systems are not trustworthy and can be easily manipulated by end users. Mitigation mechanisms are therefore required to allow people to fairly share power.

In the field of energy monitoring and consumption feedback, solutions similar to our work consist of using sensors which are directly installed into home appliances and devices to monitor energy consumption [6–9], and wireless sensor networks (WSN) for communication. These schemes focus on individual devices and do not make assumptions about the aggregation power consumption data from multiple sensors. However, they assume that data from multiple sensors are collected precisely at the same predetermined time interval Δt and periodically aggregated at time $k\Delta t$ for $k > 0$. We consider that this assumption is unrealistic especially when are taken into consideration the nature and characteristics of wireless sensors networks.

With regard to the collection of data in distributed computing, some studies [10,11] have focused on the design of snapshot algorithms for recording global states in asynchronous distributed systems, which is considered as a fundamental paradigm of distributed computing. Global snapshot algorithms of a distributed system have been studied for applications in fault tolerance to provide a checkpoint of the system. A checkpoint involves recording the state of the process so that in case of failure, computation can restart from the last checkpoint instead of the beginning. Other applications include monitoring and detection of stable properties in distributed systems.

Chandy and Lamport [10] pioneered this field with an algorithm to record snapshots for traditional distributed systems with the following characteristics: fully connected network, static topology, reliable network and FIFO channels. Their seminal algorithm used a control message called a **marker** to coordinate the construction of snapshots among all the processes. A process initiator after taking the local snapshot of its state, sends a control message (marker), through all its outgoing channels to let the other processes take a snapshot too. From this study, a plethora of snapshot algorithms have been proposed for either FIFO or non-FIFO channels in traditional distributed systems as surveyed by Kshemkalyani et al. [12]. Most of these snapshot algorithms might not be directly applicable to home area wireless sensor networks due to the nature and limitation of sensor networks such as limited battery power, latency in message delivery, limited bandwidth, dynamic topology and reliance on unreliable communication channels.

In contrast to the algorithms proposed for static network topology, other studies have focused on designing snapshot algorithms for a network with a dynamic topology such as mobile and wireless sensor networks. In the case of mobile computing systems, Agbaria et al. [13] proposed a distributed snapshot protocol for computing the checkpoint of a mobile environment. The protocol is a modification of Chandy and Lamport's algorithm [10] to suit a mobile environment.

Research on wireless sensor networks also focuses on developing snapshot algorithms. Paula et al. [14] proposed a distributed snapshot algorithm wireless sensor networks with a flat architecture. In their work, a global state is used to build a map of the remaining energy in a sensor node at a given time. This algorithm is an adaptation of Chandy and Lamport's algorithm [10] that is supported with the "Propagation of Information with Feedback"algorithm [15]. When a node has taken its snapshot, it broadcasts a message containing its local state to all its neighbors. On reception of this message, the neighbor node forwards the message to all its neighbors as well. The algorithm terminates when all the nodes have received a snapshot from all the other nodes in the whole network. Consequently, the number of messages exchanged may lead to a high communication overhead [16]. In contrast to our proposed work, Paula et al. assume that the network is reliable and that communication channels are FIFO. Wu et al. [16] proposed the RES (Robust and Efficient Snapshot) algorithm for WSNs. RES propagates the snapshot request and the feedback via local broadcasting. Moreover, RES network topology is a tree based architecture. RES reduces the communication traffic by allowing each parent node to do a local aggregation of the messages received from its children and its own measurement before sending it to its parent node instead of sending individual messages. However, the energy and communication bandwidth in this aggregation is generally expensive in terms of energy and communication bandwidth. We adopt a different network architecture, namely flat where the relationship between all the sensor nodes are the same. Gamze et al. [17] proposed DS^+, a robust distributed snapshot algorithm that captures the global state of a WSN. The communication network relies on a tree based network architecture. In order to capture the snapshot, the Gamze et al. assumed that the wireless sensor network is synchronized. However, this assumption is unrealistic in practice because each individual node has its own clock and there is no shared clock in a distributed system that is further characterized by latency in communication. Moreover, Gamze et al. assumed that the topology of the WSN is static and the sink knows the number and the identity (ID) of all the nodes present in the network during the snapshot process.

Previous work on recording a global state mainly focuses on snapshot algorithms for reliable and trustworthy distributed systems. In our paper we design a snapshot algorithm to support a reliable collection of home energy consumption based on the assumption that the low power devices used to measure the consumption are inaccurate, and that the consumption data measured are also flawed. The network used to communicate consumption is unreliable and has security concerns which may lead to network attacks.

3 System Description

3.1 System Design

In this section, we consider a simple micro-grid framework for supplying power to communities in rural areas where supply from the national power grid is either not available or frequently disrupted [1]. The community is composed of a number of household in the neighborhood sharing electricity, such as a small village. The electricity shared within the community is generated locally from a variety of renewable sources of energy (wind turbine, solar PV). The network models are divided into power networks (power line) and communication networks. We assume that house owners cannot afford to buy individual meters and utility providers do not want to provide a single meter per household in the micro-grid because they consider that there is no economic benefit. The problem is then, how to allow the end users to control and manage their power consumption. We propose to use both efficient and low cost information technology for that purpose. A meter is allocated to a group with a few number of houses connected to that meter. The group could be formed, for instance by putting together all neighborhood consumers. Inside a house, the energy is consumed by a set of appliances and devices connected to the power network and consumption of such appliances is communicated via the communication network.

This framework is represented in the model depicted in Fig. 1 below.

To implement the proposed framework, we consider that the power grid is built in a low income or rural area in a developing region. To resolve the problem of monitoring and collecting data on energy consumed by appliances and devices found in homes, we propose to use devices present in every household such as hand-held mobile devices (smart phones, laptops and smart phones). Therefore, we hypothesized that cheap and low quality sensors are deployed and attached to each individual electrical appliance and device to monitor power consumption. The consumption data measured by the sensors are sent to an aggregation point which is a hand-held mobile device, also called a sink, connected wirelessly to measuring device within the home. The homeowner can access the power

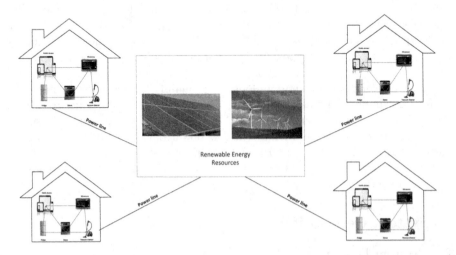

Fig. 1. Micro-grid network: example

consumption on the hand-held mobile device. The communication media in this system are wireless (bluetooth, Zigbee, WiFi).

The home network meter, or network between households in the same neighborhood, allows one to monitor and control the equipment consumption both locally as well as aggregated [7].

In this work, we shall focus on the household level and model the behavior of the network inside the household.

4 Asynchronous Collection of Home Power Consumption Data

4.1 Notation

Notations used in this section are similar to notation from Backes and Meiser [18] and models communication between home appliances using a wireless sensor network. Let us consider a household with its appliances and devices. We define $\mathcal{A}$ the set of all possible appliances within the household, $n = |\mathcal{A}|$. We assume for the sake of simplicity that the home devices can be either activated (consuming power) or inactivated (not consuming power). We describe the set of active devices between two snapshot as A_j, with $A_j \subseteq \mathcal{A}$ and $j \in [1,p]$ and $|A_j| = p$. We also assume that a set of nodes denoted $s_1, s_2, \ldots, s_n$ represents sensors embedded into each individual home appliances to monitor its power consumption. The readings of the sensors s_j corresponds to the power consumed by the appliances A_j. To obtain the consumption of the whole house, each individual measured value from the sensor associate to a device is then communicated to the sink denoted M for aggregation.

The appliances' energy consumption fluctuates over time. This leads to the so called time series data which is a sequence of measurements over the time that consist of the pairs of consumption values x_j and time t_j. We represent the jth measurement by the pair (x_j, t_j) where $j \in \mathbb{N}$. The overall household's power consumption is estimated by a mobile devices M and represents the aggregation of the amount of energy measured by each of $s_1, s_2, \ldots, s_n$ and transmitted to M at different times due to the problem of synchronization.

4.2 Network Model

The network within the home consist of sensors installed into each individual home appliance to acquire energy consumption and communicate it via Wireless Sensor Networks (WSN). The WSN can be represented as a undirected graph denoted $G = (S, E)$, where S is a set of all the sensors nodes in the networks (each sensor nodes correspond to a vertex in a graph) and E is a set of all communication links among the nodes in S. G is called the communication graph of this WSN. Two sensor nodes s_i and s_j are said to be connected if and only if s_i communicates directly with s_j (in such a case s_i and s_j are neighbors). The neighbor set $N(s_i)$ of the vertex s_i is the set of vertices adjacent to s_i. The number of adjacent node is denoted $|N(s_i)|$. Let $|S| = n$ and $|E| = m$.

Such a network is modeled as an asynchronous distributed system with unreliable communication channel, and the nodes are untrustworthy.

The main challenge is to compute the household power usage under the following conditions: (1) the absence of a shared clock between different sensors and between sensors and the sink point (synchronization problems); (2) the latency in the network traffic, (3) the sensor nodes are highly susceptible to physical damage and failure and (4) the presence of adversaries which may lead to network attacks such as jamming, eavesdropping, data modification, and denial of service attacks. As a result, it is difficult or even impossible to communicate the sensing data at precisely the same predetermined time in such environment. The main problem that arises therefore is how to collect energy consumption of electrical appliances which cannot be recorded precisely at the same time because of synchronization problem. This, in fact, is similar to a fundamental problem in distributed computation, namely recording the global state in an asynchronous network. The global state in a distributed system is defined in [10] as the collection of the local states and state of message in transit. One possible solution is to use the distributed snapshot algorithm which aims to provide a consistent view of the system at some specific time instance [12].

A snapshot of a distributed system represents a consistent global state of the system. It is modeled as $\left\{ \bigcup_i LS_i, \bigcup_{i,j} SC_{i,j} \right\}$, where LS_i is the local state of the processor P_i and $SC_{i,j}$ is the state of the channel $C_{i,j}$ which is the communication channel from process P_i to process P_j. The state of the process P_i is defined by the content of processor registers, stacks, and local memory. The state of the channel is characterized by the set of message in transit in the channel. In this work, the global state corresponds to the picture of energy consumption of the home appliances which is communicated to the sink point to compute the household's energy consumption.

A global snapshot algorithm for distributed system with FIFO communication channel was proposed by Chandy and Lamport [10]. Basically, this algorithm works as follows: after recording its local state, a process sends the marker message through all its outgoing channels. When receiving the marker message for the first time, it allows the process that has not yet recorded its local state to record its state and the state of the channel on which the marker is received as empty. Otherwise, the state of the incoming channel on which the marker is received is recorded as a set of messages received on that channel after recording the local state, but before receiving the marker on that channel. The algorithm terminates when each process has received a marker on all its incoming channels. Furthermore, Chandy and Lamport's algorithm allows more than one process to initiate the snapshot at the same time.

The Chandy and Lamport's algorithm for global state recording allows each process to record its state and the channel state. However, in our micro-grid system, we used a distributed snapshot algorithm to independently and coordinately record consumption of each individual appliance and collect the recorded values in such a way that allows us to communicate such data from the node to the aggregating mobile devices. We assumed that the snapshot can only be initiated by the sink node. So there is a need for an algorithm which will cope with the different characteristics of such an environment.

Before presenting our proposed algorithm, let us briefly introduce the message structure, variables and notation:

- **Marker:** the control message that informs the sensor node to record the value(s) measured (local state). It contains the following information: $s_i d$, the ID of the sender node; and *snapnumb*, an integer which indicates the snapshot number.
- **Feedback:** the message sent by a sensor to the sink node. It contains the following information: s_{id}, identifier of the sender node; $Nsnd$, the new measurement recorded; *snapnumb* an integer which indicates the snapshot; and M_{id}, the ID of the sink node.
- *lmd:* a real number which is the reading of the sensor at a given point in time.
- *Osnd:* the old value collected in the previous snapshot and stored in the sensor memory.
- *flag:* A Boolean value that indicates if a sensor node has received the marker and recorded its local snapshot.

We assume that each node has a unique ID and it knows the IDs of $N(s_i)$, its adjacent neighbors. Each node can obtain this information by periodically sending a "HELLO" message.

4.3   Proposed Algorithms

When designing a snapshot algorithm for collecting home appliance and device power consumption in the smart micro-grid, there are a number of important factors to be considered: the nodes are highly susceptible to failure; they are constrained in terms of computation power, energy, bandwidth and memory; dynamic changes can occur in the network topology and the communication channel is unreliable and non FIFO.

To design the snapshot algorithm, we first compare the distributed snapshot algorithms proposed in the literature for traditional distributed systems [10] with to other snapshot algorithms for WSN that have been proposed in [14,16,17].

Our solution presented in Algorithm 1, like the algorithm from [10], uses the marker message to coordinate the collection of a snapshot, but the main difference is that our solution is for unreliable networks. Both the algorithm proposed in [14] and ours consider a flat network topology. However, Paula et al. in [14], assume that the communication channel is FIFO and reliable which means that the messages are never lost.

RES [16], DS^+ [17] and our approach allow the sink to initiate the snapshot and messages are transmitted through the network by propagation, but there are some differences between these algorithms. Firstly, RES and DS^+ operate on a tree network topology architecture which is not the case in ours where the flat topology is assumed. Secondly, RES reduces the communication traffic by allowing each parent node in the tree to aggregate the feedback messages received from its child nodes in a single message instead of sending them individually. Such aggregation is generally expensive in terms of energy and communication bandwidth in a node that is dependent on battery power. Moreover, the failure of the parent node may lead to a loss of important data. In our case, the aggregation is done once in the sink node. Finally, as mentioned by Gamze et al. [17], RES defines only how a single global snapshot is taken where ours defines how consecutive global snapshots can be taken to monitor the continuous energy consumption in the household. Our solution differs from DS^+ [17] in three ways: first, it considered a WSN as an asynchronous distributed system which means that there are no bounds on the processing times and communication delays. Second, it assumes that the topology of the WSN is dynamic due to node and link failures. Third, the wireless sensor network topology is flat.

The uniqueness of our proposed algorithm presented in Algorithm 1 is that after taking the snapshot on each node in the system, only n node will send a feedback message that represents the number of appliances which have been activated in between two collections.

We describe below our proposed algorithm presented in Algorithm 1 for recording and collection of electricity consumption data in an unreliable, untrustworthy and flat WSNs.

At the initiation of the snapshot, the control message (marker) is broadcasted to all the nodes p in the network. Such a broadcast operation may lead to a large number in messages retransmissions and duplications. This as a consequence, leads to a huge amount of energy wastage if each sensor node forwards the broadcast messages [19]. To avoid this, a two phase approach is used: (1) Find a spanning tree in G using for example the algorithm proposed by Li et al. [20]. (2) Use the spanning tree to perform communication in Algorithm 1.

Our solution presented in Algorithm 1 works as follows: to record a global state or take a distributed snapshot, the sink node (mobile device) initiates the snapshot collection (Initiation procedure). It sends a snapshot query to the sensor node by broadcasting a control message called marker to all the nodes $s_i, i \in [1, p]$ in the network. Upon receiving the marker message, Marker $(s_{id}, \text{snapnumb})$, the receiver (an adjacent neighbor s_j with $s_j \in N(s_i)$ first check the flag value. If the value of flag is false, it means that this sensor node s_j has not yet received the marker (receive marker for the first time) then it will record the value of its current readings lmd. After recording its sensing value, s_i also broadcast the control message Marker $(s_i, \text{snapnumb})$ to its adjacent neighbor. Otherwise if s_j receives the marker from a different node s_i, it checks the value of the flag, if this is true, s_j does nothing.

As noted before, when the sensor node receives the control message (marker) for the first time it records its current measured values lmd corresponding to the sensors reading x_j. Such value is assigned to $Nsnd$. After that the value of the variable $Nsnd$ is compared with the value of the previous snapshot $Osnd$ stored in the sensor memory. This is achieved so that if they match ($Nsnd = Osnd$) it means that between two collections, the energy consumed by that appliance did not change, implying that the appliance has not been used during that period of

Algorithm 1. Distributed Snapshot algorithm for collection home energy consumption

---

1: initialization $flag = false$, $snapnumb = 1$;
2: **procedure** SNAPSHOT INITIATION
3:     **for** each node $i = 1 \rightarrow n$ **do**
4:         M broadcast Marker message to all the node $s_i, i \in [1, n]$
5:     **end for**
6: **end procedure**
7: **procedure** MARKER RECEPTION(s_{id}, snapnumb)   ▷ for each sensor node s_i
8:     on receipt of marker packet at s_i
9:     **if** $flag = false$ **then**   ▷ s_i has not yet record its state
10:         Take snapshot lmd;
11:         $Nsnd \leftarrow lmd$;
12:         $flag \leftarrow true$;
13:         Send the Marker message to $N(s_i)$ ▷ $N(s_i)$ set of adjacent neighbor
14:     **end if**
15: **end procedure**
16: **procedure** FEEDBACK $(s_{id}, Nsnd, snapnumb, M_{id})$
17:     **for** each sensor s_j $j = 1 \rightarrow p$ **do**
18:         **if** $Nsnd \neq Osnd$ **then**
19:             Send($s_{id}, Nsnd$, snapnumb, M_{id});
20:             $Osnd \leftarrow Nsnd$;
21:         **end if**
22:     **end for**
23: **end procedure**
24: $snapnumb \leftarrow snapnumb + 1$.

---

time and the Feedback message will not be sent. Otherwise if they do not match ($Nsnd \neq Osnd$) it means that the appliance has been activated and the energy usage has changed. In such a case, the Feedback message with the new value of $Nsnd$ is sent to the sink using a multi-hop communication via other sensor nodes that acts as relays when there is no direct link between the sensor sender and the sink node. The value in $Osnd$ which is the measured value collected in the previous snapshot is then overridden by the new value of $Nsnd$.

At the termination of the algorithm, the sink (mobile device M) obtains the global state of the system. The global state is the "picture" of energy consumed by all active appliances in the time period between two successive snapshots. M may now compute the whole home consumption, for example by summing $T = \sum_{j=1}^{n} x_j$, where T is the sum of the measurements collected.

As mentioned earlier, the device used to measure home power consumption consists of a number of low cost and low quality sensors. So data recorded from the readings of such sensors may be noisy and by extension the aggregation results may be inaccurate. In order to improve the data quality and effectively use such data, we modeled the errors associated with the consumption measurements in such a way to identify how to correct measurement errors in the power data.

5   Noise Modeling in Energy Consumption Data

Since the consumption of home appliances is recorded by an untrustworthy device, such data may be associated with noise. Such noise comes from multiple sources such as errors from the physical measurements and adversary actions. The errors account for the difference between the measured value and the true value; while the adversarial manipulated readings are ones that an adversary may provoke by controlling the sensor and injecting some signals which may cause fluctuations that corrupt the measured values. Generally, there are many sources of errors from physical measurements also called measurement errors such as measurement methods, measuring devices, environmental conditions, human beings, etc.

5.1   Measurement Errors

Measurement errors is the difference between the measured value and the true value (value to obtain if the measurement was perfect). Let u be the true value, x be the measured value, and β be the measurement error. Then, $\beta = x - u$ or $u = x - \beta$. According to [21], we distinguish three different types of measurement errors: systematic errors, random errors and negligent errors from the power consumption measured.

Systematic Errors. Systematic errors of measurement (also called bias) are the component of errors that in repeated measurement, remains constant or varies in a predictable manner. Systematic errors result from imperfections of the sensing device, inexact adjustment and pre-settings. For example, appliances power consumption measured by sensors s_i are consistently smaller or greater than the true value. When the shift between measured and true consumption values is small, the measurement is described as correct. There is no standard statistical techniques for quantifying systematic errors [22]. Systematic errors can be reduced by estimating their possible sizes based on the known properties or specifications of the sensor being used and observational procedures.

Random Errors. By contrast, random errors of the measured value (or uncertainties) are the components of errors that vary in sign and magnitude. It means that considering N measurements $x_i = u + \beta_i$, $i = 1, \ldots, N$ from s_i where u is the true value and β_i the measurement error. The numerical values $x_1, \ldots, x_N$ are randomly different. For example, the appliance i is activated, the reading of s_i taken at the $snapnumb = 1$ will differ from the one taken at $snapnumb = 2$. Random errors are caused by many uncontrolled and variable factors.

As mentioned before, multiple power measurements of one sensor s_i may have numerical fluctuation due to tiny random perturbations. The combination of such tiny perturbations is the overall random error which can be represented by a random variable X. Therefore, it is assumed that random errors follow Gaussian distributions. This results from the central limit theorems of statistics which states that the combination of many similar random perturbations tends to a Gaussian distribution.

The Gaussian probability distribution function $f(x; \mu, \sigma)$ is defined in (1)

$$f(x; \mu, \sigma) = \frac{1}{\sigma\sqrt{2\pi}} \exp\left[-\frac{(x-\mu)^2}{2\sigma^2}\right]. \tag{1}$$

Where the function has x as a variable, and two parameters μ the mean and standard deviation σ.

In practice the consumption value measured is discrete and the mean $\mu = \frac{1}{N}(x_1 + x_2 + \cdots + x_N) = \frac{1}{N}\sum_{i=1}^{N} x_i = u + \frac{1}{N}\sum_{i=1}^{N} \beta_i$ is an arithmetic average of energy measured values. While standard deviation σ is defined by:

$$\sigma = \sqrt{\frac{1}{N-1}\sum_{i=1}^{N}(x_i - \mu)^2}. \tag{2}$$

The mean μ and standard deviation σ based on all the available energy consumption measured with s_i, will help to predict that the following consumption will lie in the interval $x - \sigma \leq x \leq x + \sigma$.

Negligent Errors. Negligent errors, also known as gross errors, may be due to accidents, mistakes or a malfunction of the measuring device (sensor). As a consequence, the inherent consumption values measured are largely different when compared to the other available data. For example, considering N consumption measurements $x_1, \ldots, x_N$ from s_i there is a value x_j that is significantly less (respectively greater) than all the others. Negligent errors in power data can also be called outliers.

When we do not consider negligent errors, accuracy of power consumption data, is considered the combination of correctness and precision [21]. Correctness is the magnitude of systematic errors and precision when the spread of the measured is small relative to the average measurements or in absolute magnitude. This accuracy indicates by which extent the measurement is wrong and gives an idea of how close the power consumption measured value is compared to the true value.

Adversary manipulation of the power grid system would affect the stability of the system. An attack that is more difficult to detect, and which can be accomplished by an adversary with the appropriate knowledge, is malicious data injection.

5.2   Malicious Data Injection Attack

Unlike the case of a conventional meter, the devices used for monitoring the consumption of home appliances are totally controlled by users who could manipulate the power consumption measured by the sensors. Such modifications can be attempts by the attacker to maliciously inject false data into the data stream in order to misreport energy consumption values. For example, an individual inside his home and without any control can compromise sensor nodes so that they create slight variations in single data readings that on their own can be similar to random measurement errors, but when accumulated on an aggregated scales, these actions allow for power cheating. According to [23], there are two types of false data injection attacks: random false data injection attacks and targeted false data injection attacks. In the former, the attacker aims to cause wrong estimation of energy usage. Whereas, in the latter, the attackers want not only to inject erroneous data, but also want to inject the erroneous signal precisely at a chosen time in such a way that it is difficult to differentiate it from normal consumption data. For example in the morning when the inhabitants have their breakfast and the energy usage of the fridge varies due to multiple openings of the fridge door. The targeted false data injection attacks can cause more damage to the system because it is not easy to detect.

6   Performance Analysis

In this section, we analyze the performance of our proposed algorithm and compare it with Chandy and Lamport's algorithm, the snapshot algorithm for WSN proposed by Paula et al. [14], the RES algorithm [16] and the DS^+ algorithm [17]. All the algorithms are analyzed in terms of the message complexity, which is defined as the number of message exchanged by all the nodes in the network when considering the worst case scenario.

Chandy and Lamport's algorithm in a system with n processes and m channels requires that each process after recording its local state, sends m marker messages. At the termination of the algorithm the total number of message exchanged between nodes is m^2. Consequently, the message complexity is $\mathcal{O}(m^2)$. The WSN snapshot algorithm by Paula et al. [14] considered two scenarios. The first scenario uses the broadcast algorithm to collect the local state: the number of messages sent by each node in the algorithms considering a system with n sensors is equal to $n + 2$ for n node is $n(n + 2)$ and the complexity is $\mathcal{O}(n^2)$. In the second scenario the architecture of the network is a tree and uses the PIF. In this case the number of messages sent is constant and equal to 3, so the total number of messages involved in the algorithm for a system with n node is $3n$ [14] and hence a complexity of $\mathcal{O}(n)$. The RES algorithm to record global snapshot, requires that each node only sends two messages, so the total number of messages involved in the algorithm is $2n$ leading to a message complexity of $\mathcal{O}(n)$. DS^+ requires that each single node sends a constant number of messages which can slightly vary in the case of retransmission. The number of messages exchanged at the termination of the algorithm for a system with n nodes, is close to $3n$, hence, a complexity of $\mathcal{O}(n)$. Our proposed algorithm collects consumption measurements of appliances distributed in a household. It first assumed the availability of the spanning tree for communication. The spanning tree reduces redundancy so that the maximum number of messages each node can send is two (the marker message and the feedback). The complexity of such algorithm in a network with n nodes is equal to $\mathcal{O}(n)$.

7   Conclusion

Reliable access to energy and trust in the power sharing system are major problems to fair energy sharing on micro-grids in rural and disadvantaged environments. This paper proposes a simple framework for power sharing systems that use untrustworthy low power devices for computation and communication. Furthermore, we enhanced the design with a distributed snapshot algorithm that collects the energy consumption of appliances and devices found in homes. The distributed snapshot algorithm proposed, is a reliable solution for collecting energy data in an asynchronous and unreliable distributed network. Additionally, we take advantage of the inaccuracy of the measuring devices to build a mathematical model for various measurement errors that may appear in such a system. This would help to differentiate the energy consumption fluctuation due to measurement errors from false data injection that may misreport energy consumption.

In our proposed future work, we shall firstly, based on the characteristics of device's power consumption, establish an accurate mathematical model of different home appliances' power consumption in a micro-grid. This will allow us to characterize the power usage of a single appliance as well as a class of devices or appliances. Secondly, we will use the mathematical model to generate realistic data with a simulation platform. Such data will be used to predict the average power consumption of each individual household and of the whole micro-grid. Finally, we will take advantage of the data generated to implement the proposed snapshot algorithm and simulate it. We will then compare the results obtained from the theoretical analysis with the results of the simulation.

References

1. Chowdhury, S., Crossley, P.: Microgrids and Active Distribution Networks. IET Renewable Energy Series. Institution of Engineering and Technology, UK (2009)
2. Considine, T., Cox, W., Cazalet, E.G.: Understanding microgrids as the essential architecture of smart energy. Grid Inerop Forum, December 2012
3. Erbato, T.T., Hartkopf, T.: Smarter micro grid for energy solution to rural Ethiopia. In: Innovative Smart Grid Technologies (ISGT), pp. 1–7. IEEE (2012)
4. Mariam, L., Basu, M., Conlon, M.: Community microgrid based on micro-wind generation system. In: 2013 48th International Universities' Power Engineering Conference (UPEC), pp. 1–6, Sept 2013
5. Darby, S.: The effectiveness of feedback on energy consumption: a review for defra of the literature on metering, billing and direct displays. Technical report, Environmental Change Institute, University of Oxford (2006)
6. Erol-Kantarci, M., Mouftah, H.T.: Wireless sensor networks for smart grid applications. In: 2011 Saudi International Electronics, Communications and Photonics Conference (SIECPC), pp. 1–6, April 2011
7. Porcarelli, D., Balsamo, D., Brunelli, D., Paci, G.: Perpetual and low-cost power meter for monitoring residential and industrial appliances. In: Design, Automation Test in Europe Conference Exhibition (DATE), 2013, pp. 1155–1160, March 2013

8. Yerra, R.V.P., Bharathi, A.K., Rajalakshmi, P., Desai, U.: WSN based power monitoring in smart grids. In: 2011 Seventh International Conference on Intelligent Sensors, Sensor Networks and Information Processing (ISSNIP), pp. 401–406, Dec 2011

9. Han, P., Wang, J., Han, Y., Zhao, Q.: Novel WSN-based residential energy management scheme in smart grid. In: 2012 International Conference on Information Science and Technology (ICIST), pp. 393–396, March 2012

10. Chandy, K.M., Lamport, L.: Distributed snapshots: determining global states of distributed systems. ACM Trans. Comput. Syst. **3**(1), 63–75 (1985)

11. Lai, T.H., Yang, T.H.: On distributed snapshots. Inf. Process. Lett. **25**(3), 153–158 (1987)

12. Kshemkalyani, A.D., Raynal, M., Singhal, M.: An introduction to snapshot algorithms in distributed computing. Distrib. Syst. Eng. **2**(4), 224–233 (1995)

13. Agbaria, A., Sanders, W.H.: Distributed snapshots for mobile computing systems. In: Proceedings of the Second IEEE Annual Conference on Pervasive Computing and Communications, 2004, PerCom 2004, pp. 177–186, March 2004

14. da Silva, A.P.R., Teixeira, F.A., Lage, R.K.V., Ruiz, L.B., Loureiro, A.A.F., Nogueira, J.M.S.: Using a distributed snapshot algorithm in wireless sensor networks. In: Proceedings, The Ninth IEEE Workshop on Future Trends of Distributed Computing Systems, 2003, FTDCS 2003, pp. 31–37, May 2003

15. Segall, A.: Distributed network protocols. IEEE Trans. Inf. Theory **29**(1), 23–35 (1983)

16. Wu, W., Liu, H., Wu, H.: Res: a robust and efficient snapshot algorithm for wireless sensor networks. In: 2012 32nd International Conference on Distributed Computing Systems Workshops (ICDCSW), pp. 231–236, June 2012

17. Gamze, U., Kemal Cagri, S., Sebnem, B.: DS+: reliable distributed snapshot algorithm for wireless sensor networks. J. Comput. Netw. Commun. **2013**, 9 (2013)

18. Backes, M., Meiser, S.: Differentially private smart metering with battery recharging. In: Garcia-Alfaro, J., Lioudakis, G., Cuppens-Boulahia, N., Foley, S., Fitzgerald, W.M. (eds.) DPM 2013 and SETOP 2013. LNCS, vol. 8247, pp. 194–212. Springer, Heidelberg (2014)

19. Liang, O., Sekercioglu, Y.A., Mani, N.: A low-cost flooding algorithm for wireless sensor networks. In: Wireless Communications and Networking Conference, WCNC 2007, pp. 3495–3500. IEEE, March 2007

20. Li, N., Hou, J.C., Sha, L.: Design and analysis of an MST-based topology control algorithm. IEEE Trans. Wirel. Commun. **4**(3), 1195–1206 (2005)

21. Wang, Z., Yi, D., Duan, X., Yao, J., Gu, D.: Measurement Data Modeling and Parameter Estimation. CRC Press, Boca Raton (2011)

22. Hughes, I.G., Hase, T.P.A.: Measurements and Their Uncertainties: A Practical Guide to Modern Error Analysis. Oxford University Press, New York (2010)

23. Liu, Y., Ning, P., Reiter, M.K.: False data injection attacks against state estimation in electric power grids. ACM Trans. Inf. Syst. Secur. **14**(1), 13:1–13:33 (2011)

cl-CIDPS: A Cloud Computing Based Cooperative Intrusion Detection and Prevention System Framework

Zahraa Al-Mousa and Qassim Nasir[(✉)]

Department of Computer and Electrical Engineering,
University of Sharjah, Sharjah, UAE
{u00028486, nasir}@sharjah.ac.ae

Abstract. Cloud Computing is one of today's most promising technologies due to its cost-efficiency, flexibility and scalability for computing processes. However, the complex architecture of cloud infrastructure and the different levels of users lead to special requirements especially in security area. The Cloud provider is responsible for providing secure, reliable and trustful services to its consumers. Network intrusion detection system and network intrusion prevention system (IDPS), is a pioneer active security-defensive mechanism that is ideal to be used in cloud computing. Collaborative or cooperative IDS had been a hot topic for the last few years. However, there were some limitations in previous techniques indicating that they are not sufficient to cover all security threats in clouds. The main objective is to propose a cloud based cooperative intrusion detection and prevention system (cl-CIDPS). The system adds several contributions to the area of IDPS in clouds by proposing an integrated design that considers detection, prevention and logging capabilities applying both signature and anomaly detection mechanisms. cl-CIDPS was evaluated using a powerful network security simulator tool (Nessi2) that is capable of testing detection units and communication schemas. NeSSi2 was extended for a cloud-based IDPS presenting a valuable simulation background that can be used by future researches to evaluate similar proposed techniques for cloud computing infrastructure.

Keywords: IDS · IDPS · Cloud computing · Intrusion detection and prevention system

1 Introduction

The IT industry is a rapid growing environment that requires always innovative technologies to emulate exiting solutions adding more capabilities and features. Cloud computing is a special one that offers substantial features to the marked attracting intruders to improve their skills and exploit vulnerabilities. Due to its complex architecture and different levels of users, security of cloud services is the key issues to be looked upon among several design constrains [1]. Cloud computing can be considered an Internet-based environment that focuses on sharing resources or computations. Its main intention is to provide services for target users in a cost-efficient and flexible way.

© Springer International Publishing Switzerland 2015
R. Doss et al. (Eds.): FNSS 2015, CCIS 523, pp. 181–194, 2015.
DOI: 10.1007/978-3-319-19210-9_13

Cloud providers deploy virtualization to a physical infrastructure base to provide resources to users in an economical way. There are three main types of service that can be provided in a cloud environment: Software as a service (SaaS), Platform as a service (PaaS), and Infrastructure as a service (IaaS). Each of these services defines a certain level of resources to be delivered. Talking about cloud computing refers to both the applications level services in the lower level up to the hardware in the datacenters that provide those services in the upper level. The special about such an environment is that costumers or end users pay only for what they need regardless of the underlying storage or infrastructure.

Within this attention-grabbing environment, security issues arise with its entire constrains: privacy, confidentiality, integrity, authentication and availability. Similar types of attacks to those in regular computing networks can target a cloud computing infrastructure but with new vulnerabilities and weaknesses to exploit. Intrusion detection system (IDS) is a pioneer active security-defensive mechanism that is ideal to be used in cloud computing. IDS is a real-time monitoring system that is essential to detect or prevent intrusions before they actually take place [2]. Network intrusion detection system and network intrusion prevention system (IDS/IPS) are sometimes combined in one term IDPS that defines IDS that afford the required prevention capabilities. Nevertheless, a single IDPS deployed independently in cloud regions, without any cooperation and communication, can easily suffer from problems such as single point of failure and low detection capabilities [3].

The cloud provider is responsible of providing secure, reliable and trustful services to consumers. Initially and most importantly cloud providers need to recognize attacks targeting virtualized components as well as direct attacks on the underlying infra-structure. Correlating and sharing detected packets along with generated alerts can increase the detection rate significantly. The Intrusion Detection Message Exchange Format (IDMEF) has been proposed as a standard to enable interoperability among different IDS approaches [4]. Collaborative or cooperative IDS had been a hot topic for the last few years [5, 6]. However, few only consider cooperative IDS in cloud based infrastructures [3, 4, 7]. There were some limitations in such techniques indicating that they are not sufficient to cover all security threats in cloud [8]. The main limitations were related to detection capabilities, prevention techniques and evaluation results. Our main objective is to propose a cloud based cooperative intrusion detection and pre-vention system (cl-CIDPS) that complements existing solutions. The proposed system is leveling the cloud infrastructure by the supervision of the cloud provider and with the deployment of two different detection modes. The framework will be practically evaluated using a powerful network security simulator tool (NeSSi2) that is capable of simulating detection units and communication schemas.

The rest of the paper is organized as follows: Sect. 2 will provide a background study of the problem discussing some existing solutions. Section 3 will provide an overview cl-CIDPS architecture and some design constrains, followed by system implementation and evaluation results in Sects. 4 and 5. Finally, conclusion and future plans will be demonstrated.

2 Study Background

Security issues are becoming the greatest challenge in cloud computing models. These issues can eventually reduce the growth of cloud computing market effecting enterprises businesses and industries [9]. The exponential increase of security threat in clouds indicates that intrusion detection and prevention techniques are one of the major concerns that should be considered by providers. Since cloud computing is a distributed environment, it requires monitoring tools at different nodes especially if the cloud spreads across multiple geographical regions. Correlating data and alerts between different sensors are mandatory to increase the detection rate and prevent single point of failure. Cooperative IDPS has been a hot security issue for cloud computing researches and several studies were intended to propose new models in this area.

Collaborative or cooperative IDPS is a hot topic that had been discussed previously in several researches [2, 5, 6, 10]. However, those studies targeted distributive environments in general and did not consider cloud computing requirements and challenges. Several challenges emerged as a result of the cloud infrastructure and level of services among which security issues [11]. Cloud computing environment are exposed to same security risks as traditional network but with new opportunities and additional vulnerabilities. Since this study concentrates on cooperative communication between stand-alone IDPS agents, the focus of this section will be on cooperative IDPS framework in cloud-based environment. In the discussed frameworks, an IDPS agent can work independently with full detection and/or prevention capabilities. Cooperative mechanisms between those stand-alone agents are proposed to enhance the detection rate and performance.

Roschke et al. proposed an extensible IDS management architecture which consists of several sensors for each VM (virtual machine) with a central management unit per user [4, 12]. The main claim was that in cloud computing the user need to be allowed to fully control the IDS to adopt it to his/her own requirements. Furthermore, if the user (consumer) is running more than one VM it would be valuable to have separate sensors for each VM directed to a centralized management unit to identify attacked hosts and backup in case of DDOS attacks. The IDMEF standard is used to represent and exchange the alarm information between different sensors and the management unit. A standardized interface is designed to provide a unified view of result reports for users. The cloud provider needs to secure the IDS and optimize its efficiency; hence, the Cloud provider is in charge to enable different IDS and enable them to be attached to a specific VM. The provider can recognize attacks on the user VMs by using the IDS management system. The study proposed a clear and simple architecture to be deployed in the cloud without increasing the complexity of the IDS itself. However, the paper didn't discuss any of the IDS limitations and provide no evaluation results for the proposed framework.

Vieira et al. in [13] proposed a framework for Intrusion Detection System with both knowledge and behavior analysis to detect intrusions in Grid and Cloud Computing. In such environments, IDS must be distributed to monitor each node and alert other nodes when an attack occurs. Additionally, some attacks can be invisible for network-based IDSs or to host-based IDSs deployed distinctly. In the proposed method, each IDS node recognizes events that could be attacks and alerts them the other nodes. The implementation was done through Grid-M, three types of data where simulated: legitimate actions, behavior anomalies and policy violation data. The results show low processing cost while still providing a satisfactory performance for real-time implementation. However, exchanging data between nodes was not efficient. The proposed method didn't add any benefits to detection rate from the communication schema addition. The study didn't also discuss the implementation cost of deploying individual IDS each with management system and a distinct storage.

DCDIDP, A Distributed, Collaborative, and Data-driven Intrusion Detection and Prevention Framework for Cloud Computing were another alternative proposed by Zargar et al. [1]. DCDIDP framework covers Infrastructure, Platform and Software levels. The infrastructure level is comprised of three logical layers: network, host, and global. Based on certain metrics, several collaborative clusters of physical routers and hosts are created within the infrastructure layers for each cloud provider. The shared database is divided into types stored at the global infrastructure layer where the collaboration among different cloud providers occurs. On the platform layer, each cloud customer is permitted to configure her/his own IDPS according to the requirements. In the overall, the framework deploys IDPS services at each layer such that all have access to both network-based and host-based sensors at the infrastructure level. Although number of IDPS deployed is large enough to cover wide range of threats; this may add a significant performance overhead. Moreover, the study may be considered cooperative framework sharing alerts and data more than a collaborative work. The study didn't provide any implementations to support the concept.

A cooperative intrusion detection system for clouding computing network was proposed by Lo in [3]. The main purpose was to reduce the impact of DoS attack and distributed DoS attacks (DDOS). IDS is deployed in each cloud computing region in a way that each will send alerts when they recognize a severe attack defined in a block table. Each IDS contain intrusion detection, alert clustering and threshold computation and comparison, intrusion response and blocking, and cooperative operation. After operations and threshold comparing, cooperative IDS sends alert message to each other, if one of the cloud computing regions suffers from DoS attack. The proposed system was implemented by adding three modules into Snort: block, communication and cooperation modules. Compared to pure Snort based IDS, the computation time and the detection rate in the proposed system was almost the same; leading to the fact that the new system adds nothing but preventing the system from single point of failure attack.

3   cl-CIDPS Overview

The study goal is to provide a complete framework of a cloud based cooperative IDPS (cl-CIDPS) that is intelligent enough to cope with cloud computing circumstances and threats. cl-CIDPS is proposed to help complementing presented cloud IDPS solutions. In addition, it provides a novel simulation environment to evaluate present and future frameworks without disturbing cloud users. cl-CIDPS is designed to be integrated in a cloud computing environment, supporting the infrastructure layer within the same cloud provider. The scheme follows peer-to-peer communication principles in order to avoid a single point of failure and increase the robustness of the system. Both behavioral and signature based analysis will be used in a network based IDPS, distributed in different cloud regions. Moreover, Correlated data will be logged for further forensics investigations. NeSSi2 will be extended for the first time tool for cloud computing and will evaluate cl-CIDPS according to the Detection rate and the system performance. The goal of this chapter is to give a conceptual overview of the proposed framework: functionality, block diagram, level of integration, administrative value and security practices.

3.1   cl-CIDPS System Features and Architecture

A structured architecture for cl-CIDPS components is presented in Fig. 1. This architecture integrates all major blocks that functions in each cl-CIDPS agents. The packet sniffing block is responsible of analyzing each received packets. These packets will be analyzed by both signature and anomaly based system. Several storages exist to facilitate the detection process: Signature List, IP-block List and Authentic List. Signature list enclose list of known and detected signatures. The IP block list contain list of malicious IP addresses. List of authentic IDPS agents' addresses and keys are stored in the authentic list. Upon the detection, The Prevention block will decide the proper action. Moreover, the malicious packets are sent to the logging and alert system blocks.

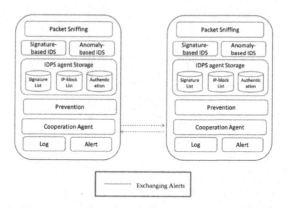

Fig. 1. cl-CIDPS main blocks and components

Level of Integration. Cloud providers are responsible to ensure that users get the right security services and should insure that those services are not affecting the cloud benefits. For each deployed model (e.g. SaaS, PaaS, or IaaS), there exist trade-offs in integrated features, such as complexity vs. extensibility and security. Moreover, if the service provider controls the security at the virtual machine lower part of the cloud architecture, the consumers will be exposed to different threats and will be in-charge for deploying and handling the security capabilities [9].

Cloud providers hold several obligations in term of arranging and coordinating computing resources. Figure 2 shows the Service Orchestration, modeled by NIST [14]. It refers to the composition of cloud system components that require provider's management. The model represents three-layered types of system components. The service layer is on the top, where providers define level of services for users to access. The graph shows optional dependency relationships between the main types of services. Resource abstraction and control layer are placed in the middle and are responsible to manage hardware resources. Virtual machines, hypervisors and virtual data storage are examples of resource abstractions components. The lower physical resources include all the physical computing resources such as processors, storage components and network devices. The cloud provider needs to ensure reliable, efficient and secure practice of the fundamental physical resources. Our main target is in securing the cloud infrastructure level since it can affect all the top layers and eventually the whole cloud computing environment.

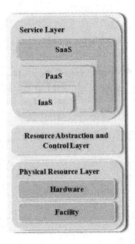

Fig. 2. Service orchestration, modeled by NIST [14]

Peer-to-Peer Communication Model. The pure definition of peer-to-peer communication (P2P) refer to completely distributed agents where all nodes have equalized functionality and performance. However, in the practice there exist degrees of centralization that are still considered P2P networks. There are three main types stated by [15]. Purely Decentralized Architecture indicates that all nodes are exactly the same in activities with no central coordination. Partially Centralized Architecture differ from the later one that some nodes deploy some major tasks in addition to the rest such as being a central agent for file sharing. Hybrid Decentralized Architecture deploys a central server assisting the intra-connection between nodes to maintain directories of some related metadata.

The P2P infrastructure considered in cl-CIDPS is based on a purely decentralized architecture. All nodes can act as both sender and receiver to exchange alerts and detect attacks. However, nodes may differ in their signatures and IP-addresses logged lists until updated by all agents.

3.2   cl-CIDPS Main Blocks Methodology and Workflow

Within cl-CIDPS framework, IDPS agents are integrated in each edge node in every cloud region. When getting targeted by an intrusion message, the agent will send out the alert to other IDSs defined in its authentic list. All agents are required to exchanges alerts and have the ability to drop the message or prevent it from attacking other nodes in the network. After undertaking the correct action, the new signatures and IP-addresses is added into the block table if the messages or the attacker are regarded as a new intrusions. Signature-based and anomaly-based detection modes are developed separately in cl-CIDPS framework. Each of the two detection modes has its own detection mechanism but similar communication procedure.

cl-CIDPS Signature-Based Detection Mode. Signature-based detection mechanism is based on content inspection. It is considered more precise and accurate than anomaly-based detection and has no false positive rate. However, it has its own limitation that makes it cover limited types of attacks since the attack patterns have to be known in advance [16]. Several worms can be detected by pattern-matching algorithms such as code red attack.

Each individual signature-based cl-CIDPS agent is identical to the other and is communicating in a pure P2P fashion. Figure 3 shows the work flow of each signature based agent. Packets are analyzed through the packet sniffer and sent through various level of comparison. The first level of comparison is to check if the received packet is an alert. This is done by extracting the digital signature and validating the sender through the authentic list. The authentic list is the list of valid addresses of all peer agents and associated authentication keys. If it is an alert, the message is decrypted and the new signature and malicious IP-address are sent to the log and added to the associated IP-block list and signature list. If the message was not an alert, it is passed through the detection block to be compared in with lists malicious of signatures. Upon a positive detection, the agent will send an alert that enclose the new signature and IP-address to the remote agent after encryption. The detected signature and IP-address will be logged also for further investigations. If the packet was not detected as a worm packet it will be processed and sent to the designated destination.

cl-CIDPS Anomaly-Based Detection Mode. Anomaly-based detection mode is a wide definition that can contribute different level of methodologies and techniques. It is a general term that indicates detecting abnormal behaviors of the designated network. In cl-CIDPS framework, an anomaly-based IDPS agent can detects DoS attacks based on a pre-determined threshold. The threshold is computed based on the regular byte rate or bytes received per unit of time. This rate is computed for each received source IP-address. If the rate exceeded a normal value, the agent should drop the packet and log information. Several studies consider calculating byte rate as an indicator of a

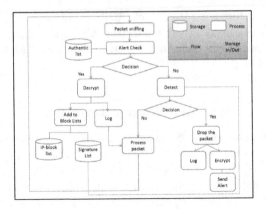

Fig. 3. Workflow of cl-CIDPS signature-based detection agent

targeted DoS attack [17, 18]. This threshold is valid to detect DoS floods coming from a certain source address and needs several improvements to detect DDoS attacks coming from different sources.

Figure 4 shows the work flow of the anomaly-based detection agent. Very similar to the signature-based IDPS, it checks first if the message was an alert. The difference is that it computes the byte rate and compares it to the threshold. If it exceeded the threshold value, it will drop the packet, log and send and alert to the remote agents.

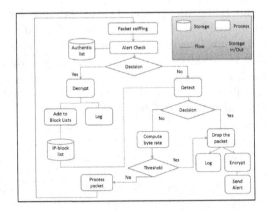

Fig. 4. Workflow of cl-CIDPS anomaly-based detection agent

4   System Implementation

Cloud Computing infrastructure and services oppose several limitations for researchers to develop a real workspace experiments. There is always a need for simulations in cloud environment. Moreover, there exist additional challenges in collaborative IDS evaluation. It may results in high risk of interfering with authentic users by infecting them or overloading the bandwidth. In addition, establishing a dedicated large-scale test bed for collaborative IDS can be expensive especially before the solution is fully implemented [5]. Due to these motivations, this research went toward simulation tools looking for the most optimal solution. For cloud computing as a new emerged area, few simulators exist to serve researchers needs. CloudSim is one of the interesting cloud computing simulators that focus on providing a generalized and extensible framework that enables modeling emerging cloud computing infrastructures and application services. However, the concentration in CloudSim is on specific system design issues such as power and performance rather than security concerns [19].

NeSSi2 is a novel network security simulator. It is an open source project developed at the DAI-Labor and sponsored by Deutsche Telekom Laboratories [20]. The DAI-Labor, referring to Distributive Artificial Intelligent Laboratory, is a well-known institute in Berlin-Germany that performs researches and solution development in order to serve new generation of systems and technologies. NeSSi2 is designed by DAI-Labor as a network simulation tool with extendable features to support detailed examination and testing chances of network security algorithms, detection units and frameworks.

cl-CIDPS was implemented in different phases to allow wide range of evaluation scenarios. Each of the two detection modes was implemented independently as a separated application in both cooperative and non-cooperative schemas. The applications were coded by java using Eclipse. They were then installed using maven tool and integrated in NeSSi2 software. The main applications added are: signature-based detection application, anomaly-based detection application and dual mode detection application. All of them where tested in cooperative and non-cooperative styles. Each of the proposed detection, prevention and logging capabilities where integrated in the code. The cooperative model was also integrated in the same detection unit making use of all these security capabilities. The applications also create logs for network forensics investigation. These log files include the malicious IP-Address followed by the associated signatures and recorded date and time at which the attack took place.

To evaluate cl-CIDPS framework two types of attacks were considered. The main attacks chosen are worm profile that can simulate code red attack and DoS attack. Each of these attacks can be detected by a different detection mode. The attacks are already integrated in NeSSi2 but slight modifications were added to adapt them to cl-CIDPS evaluation requirements.

5 System Evaluation

A typical cloud computing infrastructure environment consists of several connected distributive networks. Each network contains storages, servers or client machines according to the cloud requirements and each of these is referred to a cloud region [3]. To evaluate cl-CIDPS frame work, we built a network topology that consists of two cloud regions. In each region we placed several nodes with different functionality profiles. Cl-CIDPS applications were assigned to the two edge nodes connecting cloud-1 and cloud-2. Initially each cloud consists of two servers and two clients' machines connected by a 1-Gbit IP-link. The profiles simulated are: UDP client and server, Echo client and server applications. UDP client application sends packets to a special version server and receives replays accordingly. The Echo client application sends requests within uniform time interval while the Echo server replay to these request. These two profiles were already integrated in NeSSi2. Router forwards the packet to the desired destination according to an automatic generated routing table. Two worm nodes were activated in both regions generating random IP-addresses trying to find a connection and distribute worms. The packets counts and needed time to process them increased accordingly.

In NeSSi2, The duration of executing a simulation is determined by two bounds: replications and ticks. Ticks are the time units to measure all runs. Replications specify number of times the simulation is executed. In cl-CIDPS evaluation, all running simulations are repeated once for duration of 2000 ticks. This number was chosen according to the research scope and feasibility. Thought this duration, all nodes are running a simulated application. For evaluating the performance, the first measured value is number of packet processed in this network without counting duplicated packets. This number affects the performance of the system and is increased according to time and performed of attacks. Calculating number of packets was based in the statistics provided for each profile and link. The second performance measure is the estimated time to process these packets, and this was calculated by a manual stopwatch. The performance can be evaluated by number of packets processed per second. Finally, the detection rate was calculated considering detected incidents divided by total number of incidents. We developed two separated schemas to evaluate cl-CIDPS signature and anomaly detection application. In each, the performance measures and the detection rate were calculated.

5.1   Evaluating cl-CIDPS Signature-Based Detection Framework

Two scenarios were considered in cl-CIDPS signature-based detection mode evaluation. Table 1 presents the calculated results for both cooperative and non-cooperative schemas. The second column represents the results after adding the cooperation mechanism to exchange alerts between the two agents with different number of signatures in each agent. Upon the detection of attacks, the agent sends alert message to his neighbor including the IP-address of the malicious machine and the generated signatures. After authenticating the sender, the recipient agent adds the new signatures and IP-address to their associated storage and keeps detecting the coming packets. Observations show that larger numbers of packets were detected while the performance has closer results to the non-cooperative one. The detection rate in the second scenario was estimated to be 100 % while this value can range according to the probability of sending signature alerts before the other agent receives the attack. Moreover, a 100 % detection rate is obtainable in a simulation schema if generated signature worm attacks within a specific period of time are included within the agent storage list. If the worm attack and cl-CIDPS signatures are expanded and differentiated we may get less detection rate value.

Table 1. Evaluating cl-CIDPS signature-based detection application

Scenario	Non-cooperative signature detection agents	Cooperative signature detection agents
Number of packets processed (per 2000 ticks)	990 packets	1,010 packets
Estimated duration (sec)	22.72 packets	20.07 s
Performance (packets/sec)	43.57	50.32
Detection rate	70.1 %	100 %

5.2   Evaluating cl-CIDPS Anomaly-Based Detection Framework

cl-CIDPS anomaly based detection application was implemented separately to evaluate the detection rate and the performance of the system. The detection unit allows the user to choose a certain parameters in each of the anomaly sender receiver and the DoS attack.

In NeSSi2 DoS application, the users are permitted to enter the packet size, starting tick, the victim IP-address and the delay between sending packets. In the scope of evaluating the implemented anomaly-based detection unit, two scenarios were conducted similar to those of the signature-based detection system. The calculated results are shown in Table 2. Starting from a normal scenario, two bot machines where targeting one web server. The amount of packets sent reached 2,422 packets that were processed within 15.60 s. The observation shows similar statistics in both cooperative and non-cooperative schemas but with less processing time.

Table 2. Evaluating cl-CIDPS anomaly-based detection application

Scenario	Non-cooperative anomaly detection agents	Cooperative anomaly detection agents
Number of packets processed (per 2000 ticks)	975 packets	977 packets
Duration (sec)	32.19 s	24.48 s
Performance (packets/sec)	30.29	39.91
Detection rate	95.37 %	96.4 %

5.3   Evaluating cl-CIDPS Dual-Mode Detection Framework

To evaluate simulated cl-CIDPS, the two detection modes were integrated in one application. All scenarios were running within the same simulated cloud environment. Table 3 presents the calculated results based on the defined parameters. Initially, the normal clouds performance was evaluated placing four passive bots machine. No detection agents were placed. The packets sent to and out of each node are calculated through the statistics user interface facility. Estimated packets processed within 5000 ticks were 4,504 packets within 39 s. After that, two worm nodes and two DoS nodes were activated. The packets counts and needed time to process them increased accordingly. Within the same simulation interval, packets processed were 6,924 within 60.2 s. After adding independent dual-mode detection agents in both routers, number of packets decreased and accordingly the performance. Figure 5 shows example of the recorded events in Nessi2 user interface for one of the detection agents. Users can observe number of detected anomalies, signatures and received alerts.

Table 3. Evaluating cl-CIDPS dual-mode detection application

Scenario	Non-cooperative dual-mode detection agents	Cooperative dual-mode detection agents
Number of packets processed (per 2000 ticks)	4,625 packets	4,513 packets
Duration (sec)	181.16 s	105.0 s
Performance (packets/sec)	25.52	42.98
Detection rate	94.93 %	99.61 %

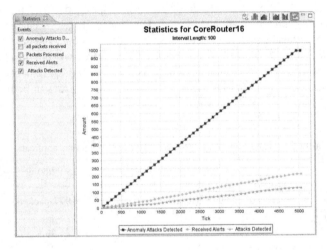

Fig. 5. Example of recorded events for one of cl-CIDPS detection agents

6 Conclusion and Future Work

Designing intrusion detection and prevention system for cloud environment require advance knowledge in network management, security aspects and communication protocols. This work attempts to encapsulates all these trades and propose a system that can be integrated in the cloud infrastructure level. cl-CIDPS was evaluated within a simulated cloud environment and proved its efficiency in detecting attacks and exchanging alerts. cl-CIDPS is built on the cloud infrastructure level deploying a pure peer-to-peer communication protocols. The proposed framework adds several new contributions to the area of IDPS in clouds by proposing an innovative complete design that is the first to deploy two detection modes considering detection, prevention and logging capabilities. The proposed schema used NeSSi2, a novel network security simulator tool, to evaluate the system performance and detection rate. Neesi2 was extended for the first time to evaluate cooperative IDPS in cloud-based environment. The two applications developed were: signature and anomaly based detection applications in both cooperative and non-cooperative. Evaluations approached to examine the efficiency of the communication schema on the detection rate and network performance. The results show significant improves in the performance for both detection modes. It was also proved that exchanging signatures between different cl-CIDPS agents can improve the detection rate considerably. Several extensions can be added to cl-CIDPS that will be considered in our future work plans. Cloud regions can be extended to incorporate more than two regions and observe the effect of that on the system performance and detection rate. More logging capabilities can be added and evaluated according to cloud forensics investigation parameters. Moreover, data collected from cl-CIDPS can be correlated with data collected from other security tools such as honeypots and firewalls.

References

1. Zargar, S.T., Takabi, H., Joshi, J.B.: DCDIDP: a distributed, collaborative, and data-driven intrusion detection and prevention framework for cloud computing environments. In: IEEE 7th International Conference on Collaborative Computing: Networking, Applications and Worksharing, pp. 332–341 (2011)
2. Qu, X., Liu, Z., Xie, X.: Research on distributed intrusion detection system based on protocol analysis. In: IEEE ASID 3rd International Conference on Anti-counterfeiting, Security, and Identification in Communication, Hong Kong, pp. 421–424 (2009)
3. Lo, C.C., Huang, C.C., Ku, J.: A cooperative intrusion detection system framework for cloud computing networks. In: IEEE 39th International Conference on Parallel Processing Workshops (ICPPW), San Diego, pp. 280–284, September 2010
4. Roschke, S., Cheng, F., Meinel, C.: Intrusion detection in the cloud. In: DASC2009 Eighth IEEE International Conference on Dependable, Autonomic and Secure Computing, Chengdu, pp. 729–734 (2009)
5. Bye, R., Camtepe, S.A., Albayrak, S.: Collaborative intrusion detection framework: characteristics, adversarial opportunities and countermeasures. In: Usenix Workshop on Collaborative Methods for Security and Privacy, CollSec, USENIX Association, August 2010
6. Luther, K., Bye, R., Alpcan, T., Muller, A., Albayrak, S.: A cooperative AIS framework for intrusion detection. In: ICC2007 IEEE International Conference on Communications, pp. 1409–1416. IEEE, Glasgow (2007)
7. Gul, I., Hussain, M.: Distributed cloud intrusion detection model. Int. J. Adv. Sci. Technol. **34**, 71–82 (2011)
8. Modi, C., Patel, D., Borisaniya, B., Patel, H., Patel, A., Rajarajan, M.: A survey of intrusion detection techniques in cloud. J. Netw. Comput. Appl. **36**, 42–57 (2013)
9. Subashini, S., Kavitha, V.: A survey on security issues in service delivery models of cloud computing. J. Netw. Comput. Appl. **34**(1), 1–11 (2011)

10. Rainer, B.: Group-based IDS collaboration framework-a case study of the artificial immune system. Ph.D. dissertation, Dept. Elect. Eng., University of Berlin (2013)
11. Patel, A., Taghavi, M., Bakhtiyari, K., Júnior, J.C.: An intrusion detection and prevention system in cloud computing: a systematic review. J. Netw. Comput. Appl. **36**(1), 25–41 (2013)
12. Roschke, S., Cheng, F., Meinel, C.: An advanced IDS management architecture. J. Inform. Assur. Secur. **5**, 246–255 (2010). USA
13. Vieira, K., Schulter, A., Westphall, C., Westphall, C.: Intrusion detection for grid and cloud computing. IT Prof. **4**, 38–43 (2009)
14. Mell, P. and Grance, T.: The NIST definition of cloud computing. NIST Special Publication 800–145, National Institute of Standards and Technology, Gaithersburg, MD, United States (2011)
15. Androutsellis-Theotokis, S., Spinellis, D.: A survey of peer-to-peer content distribution technologies. ACM Comput. Surv. (CSUR) **36**, 335–371 (2004)
16. Pao, D., Or, N.L., Cheung, R.C.: A memory-based NFA regular expression match engine for signature-based intrusion detection. Comput. Commun. **36**, 1255–1267 (2013)
17. Mirkovic, J., Prier, G., Reiher. P.: Attacking DDoS at the source. In: IEEE 10th International Conference on Network Protocols, IEEE Proceedings (2002)
18. Shevtekar, A., Ansari, N. A.: Proactive test based differentiation technique to mitigate low rate DoS attacks. In: IEEE 16th International Conference on Computer Communications and Networks (ICCCN), pp. 639–644 (2007)
19. CloudSim: A Framework for Modeling and Simulation of Cloud Computing Infrastructures and Services, The CLOUDS Lab: Flagship Projects (2006). http://www.cloudbus.org/cloudsim/
20. NeSSi[2] (2013). http://www.NeSSi2.de/

Author Index

Adibi, Sasan   61
Ahmad, Asma'a   84
Alajeely, Majeed   84
Alins, Juanjo   16
Al-Mousa, Zahraa   181
Amadou Kountché, Djibrilla   31
Ambassa, Pacome L.   166
Andersson, Karl   1

Batten, Lynn M.   47
Booth, Todd G.   1

Covaci, Stefan   101

Doss, Robin   47, 84

Ertl, Benjamin   101
Esparza, Oscar   16

Fukuda, Yutaka   129

Gombault, Sylvain   31
González, David   16

Hidaka, Takeo   129

Ikenaga, Takeshi   129

Kang, James   61
Kayem, Anne V.D.M.   166
Khan, Bilal   139

Li, Gang   47
Lo Iacono, Luigi   113

Mak-Hau, Vicky   84
Mata, Jorge   16
Meinel, Christoph   166
Muñoz, Jose L.   16

Nasir, Qassim   181
Nguyen, Hoai Viet   113
Nobayashi, Daiki   129

Piramuthu, Selwyn   156

Seideman, Jeremy D.   139

Thanh, Tran Quang   101
Tissera, Menik   47
Tsukamoto, Kazuya   129

Vargas, Antonio Cesar   139

Wolthusen, Stephen D.   166

Zampognano, Paolo   101
Zhou, Wei   156